Student Success

Foundations of Self-Management

Gian Paolo Roma

SUNY
PRESS

Published by State University of New York Press, Albany

© 2023 State University of New York

All rights reserved

Printed in the United States of America

No part of this book may be used or reproduced in any manner whatsoever
without written permission. No part of this book may be stored in a retrieval system
or transmitted in any form or by any means including electronic, electrostatic,
magnetic tape, mechanical, photocopying, recording, or otherwise without the prior
permission in writing of the publisher.

For information, contact State University of New York Press, Albany, NY
www.sunypress.edu

Library of Congress Cataloging-in-Publication Data

Name: Roma, Gian Paolo, 1962– author.
Title: Student success : foundations of self-management / Gian Paolo Roma.
Description: Albany, NY : State University of New York Press, [2023] |
    Includes bibliographical references and index.
Identifiers: LCCN 2023002651 | ISBN 9781438494890 (pbk. : alk. paper) | ISBN
    9781438494906 (ebook)
Subjects: LCSH: Vocational guidance. | Behavioral assessment.
Classification: LCC HF5381 .R753 2023 | DDC 650.1—dc23/eng/20230510
LC record available at https://lccn.loc.gov/2023002651

10   9   8   7   6   5   4   3   2   1

To my greatest teachers:
Arlene, Alli, and Cori.

You are rewarding a teacher poorly if you remain always a pupil.

—Friedrich Nietzsche

CONTENTS

Section III: Choice

Section IV: Commitment

Section V: Coping

Section VI: Caring

ILLUSTRATIONS

Figures

Photos

Tables

ACKNOWLEDGMENTS

I am indebted to the team at SUNY Press. I especially want to thank my editors Richard Carlin, Susan Geraghty, Dana Foote, and Sue Morreale for their encouragement, wisdom, and professionalism. I also want to express my appreciation to the following people who have been so generous with their support, time, advice, input, expertise, and experience.

Katherine Collette, MSW
Binghamton University
School of Management

Jack Duffy, PhD
Dalhousie University
Rowe School of Business

Jessica Esperon-Meneilly, MST
Susquehanna Valley High School
Teacher and Academic Advisor

Michele Forte, PhD
SUNY Systems
State University of New York

Erin Frye, MBA, MS
SUNY Broome Community College
Business Department

Brenda Gainer, PhD
York University
Schulich School of Business

D. Lee Heron, PhD
SUNY Broome Community College
Business Department

Robert Hurley, PhD
Fordham University
Gabelli School of Business

Deborah Moeckel, PhD
SUNY Systems
State University of New York

INTRODUCTION

If my mind can conceive it, if my heart can believe it, then I can achieve it.

—Muhammad Ali

You can learn the behavioral concepts in this book and successfully apply them to your life. Whether you are a young student or an experienced working adult, the five elements of behavior that demonstrate behavioral understanding are all the same:

- Communication, which conveys appropriateness

- Choice, which conveys judgment

- Caring, which conveys concern for others

- Commitment, which conveys duty

- Coping, which conveys fortitude

These are the **5C Elements of self-management**. We all convey these five behavioral elements to one extent or another. This book introduces you to communication, choice, caring, commitment, and coping: what they are, why they are important to you, and how to assess them in yourself and others.

Have you ever been in situations at school or at work and felt like you were not sure of what to do, or thought about why you behave the way that you do, or wondered what is the best way to handle a certain situation? *Student Success: Foundations of Self-Management* will guide you on your self-management journey and help you understand why thinking about and adjusting your own behavior are a necessary part of success. The 5C Elements are the building blocks of personal and social achievement. Commit to understanding and continuously improving them, and your results in school and beyond will improve.

As you learn about the importance of the 5C Elements on success, you'll find yourself reflecting on your own behavior and also on the behavior of others. You will start to see things that you may not have noticed or thought about before, because you will have a comprehensive framework through which to view the 5C Elements that is clear and understandable. You'll start to feel more comfortable with your decision-making and be confident in your behavior. You'll be better equipped

5Cs Elements of Self-Management or SM: The five behavioral elements that every person must manage that cannot be delegated to others: communication, choice, caring, commitment, and coping.

1

to trust your own judgment and successfully adapt to almost any situation. This book will change the way you think about behavior and help you better navigate situations in your private and public lives.

Rather than assiduously following what you learn about communication, choice, coping, commitment, and caring, you will use the 5C Elements to inform your approach to how you manage your own behavior and for general guidance as you go about your daily life. The main reason that you should study the 5C Elements is to establish your own personal policies about how you will conduct yourself so that you can anticipate and avoid much of the needless pain and personal anguish that's associated with blindly walking through life. **Personal policies** are defined as *self-created rules that govern your behavioral conduct*.

No child wakes up in the morning and thinks, "When I grow up I want to feel guilty and have **regrets** about my own behavioral conduct." Yet, according to research, 90 percent of us have big regrets about how we've conducted ourselves.[1] These types of "regret-related"[2] feelings can profoundly impact the way that you think about yourself and the quality of your life.

Have you ever reflected on your own behavior? Have you ever thought to yourself or even said to yourself: I think that my behavior is good, but

- How good is my behavior?

- How good is my behavior compared with others?

- How good should my behavior be?

- How do I know that my behavior is good?

If you have asked yourself these questions, what have you done about trying to obtain analytical and objective answers? Before I wrote this book, on so many occasions my only action was to answer these types of questions with, "Yes, of course my actions and motives are good." But I wasn't sure why I was so convinced of my own correctness; I just assumed (sometimes incorrectly), even though I was unable to say how or why I reached this conclusion.

This book gives you the tools that you need to examine and assess your own behavior in a much more objective, precise, and valuable way to you. The book is intended to help you improve the **quality** of your behavioral decision-making and answer such questions as

- What is effective behavior?

- What is effective decision-making?

Personal Policies: Self-created small-scale rules that govern your conduct.

Regret: Sadness associated with some wrong done or some disappointment.

Quality: The degree or grade of excellence associated with behavioral decision-making.

- What is behavioral assessment?

- What can I do to improve my own behavior?

These types of **self-reflection** questions will help you to develop and continuously improve your own behavior. Importantly, these types of questions will also help you predict and steer clear of many of the avoidable struggles that are associated with interacting with other people in an uninformed manner.

People experience behavior. What do others experience when they interact with you? The people that interact with you will have these same types of questions about you, because your behavior can impact them. They will want to know if they can trust you and if it's in their best interest to be involved with you. They will be looking for answers to questions like

Self-Reflection: Examination, contemplation, and analysis of one's thoughts, feelings, and behaviors.

- Are you respectful of others?

- Are you easy to work with?

- Are you reliable?

- Are you appropriate?

- Are you nice?

- Are you reasonable?

- Do you use good judgment?

The threefold purpose of this text is to provide (1) broad understanding and comprehension of the five behavioral elements; (2) to develop an understanding of how the 5C Elements relate to you; and (3) to help you answer these types of questions for yourself, so that you can objectively understand how your own conduct may be impacting you. With these objectives in mind, the book incorporates these key features:

1. **Content deals with a subject of value to you . . . yourself.** The main reason that you should study these 5C Elements is to get your thinking in order about how you will conduct yourself so that you can anticipate and avoid many of the problems that are associated with behavioral complacency. The content has been designed to meet your individual needs. You will be able to objectively assess your own behavior and create a self-management plan that includes your own personal policies that will inform how you will approach communication, choice, caring, commitment, and coping.

In dealing with these subjects, however, the main aim of the text is to ensure fundamental understanding of the five elements of self-management. Upon completing each chapter, you should have a basic understanding of what the relevant behavioral element is, why it's important generally, and how it specifically relates to you.

2. Competence in fundamental behavioral skills is emphasized. Each behavioral element is retaught, reviewed, and its underlying ideas reemphasized. Upon completing the book, you should have real competence in the use of the 5C Elements as they relate to your life. You should also have a thorough working knowledge of how behavior is assessed. You should also be able to use these skills to solve many of the more practical problems associated with living with yourself and others, because you will have a vocabulary to discuss many of the intangible aspects of behavior. Although it is essential that you thoroughly understand behavior generally, it is more important that you understand how the 5C Elements impact you, and why you behave the way that you do.

3. Numerous self-reflection activities are provided. The book has many self-reflection activities to complete. Each chapter has important terms and discussion of meaning questions to help you apply the subject matter to your own life. You should complete all of these activities to understand the nature and quality of your own behavior. In addition to these types of self-reflection activities, the book also offers other activities that will help you understand how to measure and manage your own behavior, including:

- **Behavioral observation scales** and mapping tables to assess and record your level of behavioral proficiency for each the 5C Elements.

- **Employability profile** into which you will log the results of all of your 5C assessments.

- **Personal policy contracts** so that you can write down your personal obligations to yourself for each behavioral element.

- **Behavioral adjustment model** that you can use to improve your level of proficiency in each behavioral element.

These activities are for your use alone. After you assess yourself on the different behavioral elements, you will be able to make candid comments, write down notes to yourself, and record any insights you might have gained along the way.

How to Use This Book

As you have probably figured out, this book is different because the subject of this book is you.

Behavioral Adjustment Model: Behavioral approaches that focus on changing behaviors in behavioral decisions.

Communication, choice, caring, commitment, and coping are all important for you to know and understand now, but the material cannot be presented all at once. So, the book is broken down into six sections. Following this overview, each section provides clear and concise definitions of each behavioral element. In addition, the definitions for all of the component parts of each element are also presented. Throughout the volume, key terms appear in bold and their definitions are italicized. You can also find complete definitions of key terms in the glossary at the end of this book. I recommend that you start at the beginning and work your way through each chapter, one by one. You will quickly catch on to the style and format, as each chapter is organized by its behavioral element, guiding you through both the hows and whys of each element.

Throughout each chapter, research will be presented that underpins each element, and examples will be provided that help reinforce the major concepts. You will also get a chance to put the 5C Elements into practice.

I would encourage you to pay particular attention to the definitions, the research that is cited, and the examples, but please don't worry too much about trying to commit all of this to memory. Hopefully, these will become as engrained in you as the multiplication tables are in arithmetic. This book is about self-understanding and self-improvement, not memorization.

You will notice that there are self-reflection exercises that will help you think about why you think, feel, and act the way that you do. When you come to these "What do you think?" or "Think about it" exercises, you will have an opportunity to consciously look inward to gain perspective on your own inner thinking and gain some understanding about what really matters to you. Here are some guiding questions that you can ponder as you think about the different self-reflection exercises in the book:

1. Who am I?

2. Who do I want to be?

3. What do I really want in life?

4. How do I really feel about myself?

5. How do I want to feel about myself?

6. What are my values?

7. What matters most to me?

8. What is the right next step for me?

These types of questions are how you define yourself to yourself. When you are asking yourself these questions, pay close attention to what thoughts come to mind. You can jot down your thoughts in the spaces provided to better understand your own thinking. Any of your answers that are contrary to what is important to you may require closer scrutiny, because they may contribute to regret later on.

Self-management is a real-time skill. Like driving, there is no way to educate you on how to effectively deal with every situation. That's the challenge of self-management: to build and use communication, choice, caring, commitment, and coping in the right combination so that you can respond effectively to both the expected and unexpected situations you encounter.

I wrote this book because self-management is a requirement for successful living. You are responsible for directing the course of your life. Without luck or inherited wealth, behavioral skill is a precondition for realizing individual and societal potential. Although there are many opinions about the purpose of education, it is not unreasonable to argue that it is twofold: (1) to help all people (individually and collectively) fulfill their unrealized potential; and (2) to give all people the tools that they need to leave the world a better place than they found it. If you demonstrate that you manage your own behavioral affairs in a manner that aligns with both of these aims, you will achieve something of great value. You will achieve contentment with yourself, which Socrates describes as "natural wealth." As the great philosopher said, "Contentment is natural wealth, luxury is artificial poverty."

You will learn how to develop your own self-management style and, importantly, build effective relationships with others. The book is organized so that you should be able to achieve mastery of the behavioral fundamentals needed for a fulfilling life. My hope is that this book will help you more effectively deal with your daily challenges so that you can be the person that you hope to be.

Gian Paolo Roma
Professor and Chair
Business Programs Department
SUNY Broome Community College
State University of New York

Key Terms

- 5Cs of Self-Management
- Behavioral Adjustment Model
- Personal Policies
- Quality
- Regret
- Self-Reflection

Section I

OVERVIEW

A summary of a comprehensive, rational,
and applied self-management methodology

1

GETTING STARTED

Section I

OVERVIEW

A summary of a comprehensive, rational,
and applied self-management methodology

After reading this chapter, you should be able to:

- Describe what reason is and list the elements of the reason-based behavior cycle.

- Discuss how impulse control differentiates adult behavior from infant behavior.

- Describe how cause and effect (our actions and their impact) creates specific behavioral consequences.

- Explain why rules of conduct are so important to individual success and social cohesion.

- Define behavioral competency and self-management.

- Understand the 5Cs of self-management.

> I went down to the river,
> I set down on the bank.
> I tried to think but couldn't,
> So I jumped in and sank.
>
> —Langston Hughes

The Reason-Based Behavior Cycle

Ideally, human behavior that is governed by reason follows a predictable order of related actions: desires beget feelings, feelings beget thoughts, thoughts beget choices, choices beget character, character begets relationships, and relationships beget results (see figure 1.1). In a reason-based

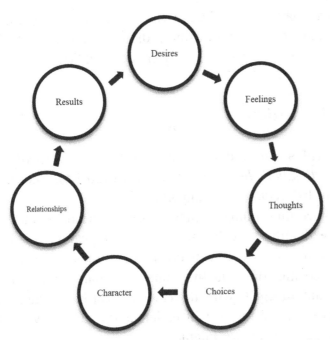

Figure 1.1. The Reason-Based Behavior Cycle. *Source:* Author-created.

world, thoughts are organized before choices involving actions are made or words are spoken.

But when our choices are not governed by reason, we may bypass thinking altogether and make impulsive choices based primarily on our desires and feelings. For example, infants are all impulse. They act and react based on the feelings in their bodies without considering consequences. Infants "coo" when they are happy and cry when they are uncomfortable. Infants do not think about where and when it is appropriate to relieve themselves because their feelings control their choices.

As we mature, we hopefully become more aware of how our desires and feelings influence our choices. We begin to understand the concept of **behavioral cause and effect**. At its most basic, behavioral cause and effect *describes a process where "if A does this, B happens."* For example, if you stick a pin in a balloon, the balloon will pop. Of course, life is more complicated than this model might suggest, but the point is that everything we do (our actions) inspires a reaction. If I ignore you when you ask me for a favor, you're likely to become annoyed or angry with me.

Behavioral Cause and Effect: Describes a process where "if A does this, B happens."

Over time, as we mature we create rules for ourselves that govern our conduct because we begin to understand the notion that our behaviors have good and bad behavioral consequences not only for ourselves but also for others. **Behavioral consequences** are defined as *the result of our behavioral choices.* We may even begin to realize that if we go about

Behavioral Consequences: The result of our behavioral choices.

our daily lives without a system of rules to guide our own thinking and conduct, it may become increasingly difficult to enjoy interacting with others because unmanaged behavior creates conflict.

Behavioral Rules

Behavioral Rules:
Unambiguous personal policies that govern an individual's behavior within particular contexts involving others.

Behavioral rules can be defined as *unambiguous personal policies that govern an individual's behavior within particular contexts involving others.* Why are behavioral rules important?

Rules governing human behavior are important because we inhabit this world with others. Although this may appear to be obvious, it is precisely because we exist with others that rules governing individual conduct are so important. In the same way that traffic signals help us understand and anticipate what drivers will do at intersections, behavioral rules are necessary so that we all understand and "know what to expect from each other"[1] when we interact.

Behavioral rules are the structure within which we interact with each other in society. Like traffic signals, behavioral rules help us understand what we are all responsible for as we navigate the challenges on the road of life. Our hard-won freedoms require that we all understand and willingly follow behavioral rules so that everyone knows what to expect

What Do You Think?

Imagine for a moment that you are driving in New York City and suddenly all the traffic signals stopped working. How would this change how you interact with other drivers? Would it make it harder for you to cross a busy intersection? What other problems would this cause?

_____

_____

_____

_____

_____

_____

_____

from everyone else when we encounter each other on our collective journey. This is true regardless of situation or context. In the same way that drivers cannot freely ignore stop signs, we cannot ignore behavioral rules without severe consequences to ourselves and society. If everyone easily wove together their competing desires in a fair and just way when they interacted, then there would be no need for behavioral rules. It is precisely because some people do not conduct themselves well when they interact with others that rules are necessary.

All rules that govern human interactions must be fair, understood, and most importantly willingly followed by everyone. Rules help communities of people (i.e., families, schools, neighborhoods, workplaces, cities, and countries) manage individual desires within contexts involving others. In a larger sense, all **rules of conduct** are *human-made social constructs or norms that help groups of people balance the competing desires of individuals so that everyone can interact socially without creating too much conflict*. Rules of conduct between people create social cohesion.

Behavioral rules create the framework within which society manages individual desires in the game of life. If individuals genuinely do not want to fail in the game of life (in school, work, or with family and friends), they should understand and then organize their own life so that both their own desires and the desires of others can be successfully woven together.

Rules of Conduct: Human-made social constructs or norms that help groups of people balance the competing desires of individuals so that everyone can interact without creating too much conflict.

What Do You Think?

What would human existence be like without rules of conduct? Suppose at the opening of a baseball game the umpire announced, "We're suspending all rules of play during this game." What would happen? How do rules of conduct affect schools, families, debates, and other group events?

_____

_____

_____

_____

_____

_____

To understand and organize your own desires, you need to be able to comprehend and accept the notion that multiple desires exist simultaneously and compete for dominance within everyone. For instance, it's possible for you to simultaneously want to have good dental hygiene, but also not want to floss your teeth every morning. Although these two desires are antithetical to each other and cannot both be fulfilled, they can coexist within your head. It will become obvious that these two desires cannot both be successfully fulfilled when you go to the dentist and you learn that not flossing has created a painful cavity. It is the pain that will help you learn that good dental hygiene is not possible without flossing. I had a dentist who once described the pain that you feel when the cavity is filled as "the ignorance leaving your body." You've learned your lesson; to avoid future pain, you'd better practice good dental hygiene.

You must also understand that your own choice of which desire to follow can simultaneously impact reality for yourself and others. For example, people might simultaneously want to smoke cigarettes but, at the very same time, also desire good health for themselves and others. The idea that smoking cigarettes is related to good health is removed from reality by something more than a respectful distance. Yet, the United States Department of Health and Human Services reports that "since 1964 approximately 2,500,000 nonsmokers have died from health problems caused by exposure to secondhand smoke."[2] Each time smokers choose to light up around others, they simultaneously increase the risk of serious health problems or death, not only for themselves but also for those around them.

The degree of concern you have for yourself is always in relation to others. Although it can be rightly argued that an individual must have the right to pursue one's own life, liberty, and happiness, doing so without understanding and following rules is irresponsible for the individual and society. So, if individuals and societies can accept the notions that desires compete for dominance within all people and that organizing and prioritizing our desires is a good idea for individuals and society as a whole, then it makes sense to organize a system of thinking around these things.

Rules governing human behavior would not be necessary if only we each lived our lives without social contact with others. The only person that could be harmed by the choices of a person existing in complete isolation is that individual. Although obvious, it is precisely because of others that rules governing individual conduct are so necessary. Behavioral rules are necessary because of our unending struggle to fulfill our own desires within contexts involving others. Others include not only people who think, act, believe, and look like you but also people who do not. A partial list of others may include your teachers, classmates, coworkers, bosses; members of different political parties; followers of different religions; different ethnic groups; LGBTQ+ individuals or heterosexuals; or even people whose group status is based on a particular circumstance, such as motorists versus pedestrians. As of the printing of this book, more than eight billion others inhabit this world with you.

How can we better prepare ourselves to be more resilient, prepared, and effective at reaching our goals in this increasingly diverse, demanding, changing, and competitive world involving so many others? One way is to learn and practice the basic behaviors that are necessary to achieve goals. We can define **behavior** as *how an individual or group acts or conducts themselves when interacting with another individual, group, or event.*[3]

Your success and achievement, be it academic, social, career, financial, or otherwise, will primarily be a function of your own behavior. You will have a greater impact on your future than your parents, siblings, friends, schools, religion, government, and employers. That's because you are responsible for directing the course of your life.

Behavioral Competency: You Are Responsible for You

True self-confidence and genuine competence are outcomes of sustained efforts made over long periods to achieve goals and cannot be inherited or acquired by those unwilling to endure the rigors of life. Although others can help you plan on how best to achieve your goals, ultimately you are the only person that can turn your plans into reality.

Behavioral competency can be characterized as *a basic understanding and consistent practice of a set of skills that nurtures trust.* **Trust** is having *confident reliance in others in situations involving vulnerability or risk.*[4] Behaviorally competent people understand how their own behavior affects trust. They have an emotional and intellectual appreciation of the role trust plays in goal achievement and a willingness to consider how their own actions and words affect trust. Trust is the outcome of responsible behavior. A simple definition of **self-management (SM)** is *the ability to achieve one's own goals in a trustworthy manner.*

We can think in the abstract of individual behavior as either strengthening or weakening trust—or as being healthy or unhealthy, respectively. **Healthy behaviors** are defined as *behaviors that are responsible, strengthen trust connections, and create goodwill among people.* Examples of healthy behaviors are showing up on time, working hard, appre-

Behavior: How an individual or group acts or conducts themselves when interacting with another individual, group, or event.

Behavioral Competency: A basic understanding and consistent practice of a set of skills that nurtures trust.

Trust: Confident reliance in others in situations involving vulnerability or risk.

Self-Management (SM): The ability to achieve one's own goals in a trustworthy manner.

Healthy Behaviors: Behaviors that are responsible, strengthen trust connections, and create goodwill among people.

Unhealthy Behavior:
Conduct that is harmful to
you or others.

ciating others, and effectively adapting to difficult or changing situations. **Unhealthy behavior** is *conduct that is harmful to you or others*, such as lack of effort, being unreliable, disrespecting others, using poor judgment, and making reckless decisions. These actions can cause others to feel upset, frustrated, scared, and angry, which can destroy goodwill and cooperation among people.

Unhealthy behaviors may require other people (e.g., supervisors, professors, parents, advisors, family members, police) to intervene to prevent negative outcomes from occurring. In the United States our founders created an entire branch of government to manage unlawful behavior. People that are convicted of legal wrongdoing can be forced to live behind bars for years (even their entire lives), unable to interact with the outside world because they cannot be trusted to manage their own affairs without hurting themselves or others. The most extreme examples of behavioral intervention are jail and the death penalty, but lesser degrees of unhealthy behavior also erode trust among law-abiding citizens.

What Do You Think?

Label these behaviors as either healthy or unhealthy.

	Eating an entire container of ice cream in one sitting.
	Exercising on a daily basis.
	Staying up all night when you have an exam at 8:00 the next morning.
	Flying an airplane blindfolded.
	Reading instructions carefully before using a dangerous piece of equipment.
	Using hand sanitizer when entering a busy indoor space during a pandemic.
	Smoking.

Relationships: Types of
interpersonal connections
between yourself and
others.

Ultimately, **relationships**—or how we interact with each other—are what bind us together. The same is true for organizations in which people interact, such as schools, hospitals, partnerships, corporations, not-for-profits, small businesses, and government entities. Relationships between people and within organizations can be good or bad and depend on the way people interact with each other. Without trust it is difficult to build healthy relations with others because people do not willingly interact with people they do not trust. Because trust is the cornerstone of all healthy relationships, it is necessary and appropriate to study and understand what trust is and how it is built. Behaviors make visible what is trustworthy and untrustworthy about a person's character. SM requires that people organize and control their own behavioral reactions through self-imposed, trustworthy rules of conduct or personal policies. Self-management's main aim is on understanding and then continuously improving your emotional, intellectual, and physical reactions to life's events.

The 5C Elements of Self-Management

The behaviors discussed in this book are called the 5C Elements of SM: (1) communication, (2) choice, (3) commitment, (4) coping, and (5) caring (see figure 1.2). These 5C Elements can be self-cultivated, self-assessed, and self-managed by almost anyone. They are the individual responsibilities that every person must manage within themselves and cannot be delegated to others. Simply put, everyone is responsible for how they communicate, how they make choices, how caring they are to

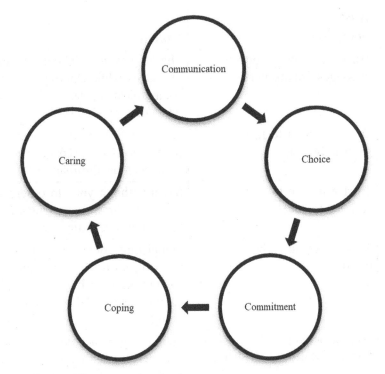

Figure 1.2. The 5C Elements of Self-Management. *Source:* Author-created.

others, how committed they are to the activities they are involved with, and how well they cope with the challenges in their lives. These behavioral responsibilities cannot be outsourced to others.

This book's core mission is to explain how the 5C Elements build trust and how you can apply them to your life to build a better world for yourself and others. The 5C Elements are multifaceted and transmit different character traits that are linked to specific types of trust. Simply put, a person can be trustworthy in one of the 5C Elements but not another. For example, it is entirely possible for you to be committed to a job or college but not care about the people that you work or go to school with. Likewise, it is also possible for you to commit to one activity (but not another), cope with one situation (but stress out over another), care about one person (but no one else), make a good choice in one situation (but react poorly in another), or communicate appropriately to some people (but not others).

Most importantly, the 5C Elements can be used to identify, diagnose, and evaluate trustworthiness and behavioral performance. Each of the 5C Elements has a specific trust dimension and a clearly defined trust definition that describes the standard of behavior that is expected for each of the 5Cs (see table 1.1).

Table 1.1. Trust Dimension and Definition of the 5C Elements

5C Elements of SM	Trust Dimension	Trust Definition	Example
Communication	Communication-based	Trust a person to convey messages appropriately.	Checking your cellphone for text messages while chatting with friends communicates a lack of interest in what they're saying.
Choices	Judgment-based	Trust a person to use good judgment.	Texting while driving shows poor judgment as opposed to keeping your eyes on the road.
Caring	Relationship-based	Trust a person to show concern for others.	Saying "thank you" to others who help you shows more consideration than simply walking away.
Commitment	Activity-based	Trust a person to be dutiful.	Completing your homework or showing up to class on time communicates a higher level of commitment to school than never doing so.
Coping	Situation-based	Trust a person to demonstrate fortitude during difficult times.	Completing a race despite experiencing leg pains shows a higher level of fortitude than dropping out.

Source: Author-created.

Behavioral conduct that is contrary to these standards would, by definition, be self-defeating and undermine one's self-interest. Behaviors like communicating inappropriately, prioritizing unimportant matters ahead of important matters, failing to meet obligations to others, handling difficult situations poorly, or disrespecting others are problematic because they are antithetical to the 5C trust definitions. They create **credibility gaps** that can damage relationships and, therefore, reduce your own chances of getting ahead in life because they create mistrust.

Credibility Gaps: The difference between what we say and what we do.

What Do You Think?

You're interviewing a possible new employee for a job as an accountant with your firm. When you call her references, you discover that she has lied on her resume; she didn't attend college, and she never worked for any of the companies that she lists under her job experience. You also discover that she was charged with embezzling funds from her last employer. How would this affect your feelings of trust toward this person? Would you hire her? Why or why not?

_____

_____

_____

_____

_____

_____

According to a report published in 2022, only 64 percent of first-time undergraduates who matriculated in the fall of 2014 finished a degree within six years.[5] This means that 36 percent of students who attempted college failed to graduate after six years. Although there are many factors affecting college graduation rates—such as tuition and other costs; inability to balance school, jobs, and family; and academic preparedness—many students don't graduate due to poor behavioral choices. They may not communicate appropriately, use good judgment, follow through and meet their obligations in their classes, or cope well with the difficulties they encounter in college. In short, they may not graduate because they fail to understand or have a palpable sense of duty about their own behavioral obligations; they may not be engaging in trustworthy and responsible behavior.

Key Terms

The following terms will help you, particularly if you learn how to explain them and use them in the right places and situations.

- Behavior
- Behavioral Cause and Effect
- Behavioral Competency
- Behavioral Consequences
- Behavioral Rules
- Credibility Gaps

- Healthy Behaviors
- Relationships
- Rules of Conduct
- Self-Management
- Trust
- Unhealthy Behavior

Discussion Questions

1. What is the basic idea of self-management?

2. What is the difference between a trust definition and a trust dimension?

3. Explain why behavioral rules are important.

4. What are the seven variables in the reason-based behavior cycle? Explain each in your own words.

5. What are the 5C Elements and how do they relate to you?

6. What are the five trust dimensions and which 5C Element is each of the trust dimensions associated with?

7. What does the author mean when he says that trust is multi-faceted?

To Sum Up

- In a reason-based world, thoughts are organized before choices involving actions are made or words are spoken.

- Infants do not think about where and when it is appropriate to relieve themselves because their feelings control their choices.

- As we mature we create rules for ourselves that govern our conduct because we begin to understand the notion that our behaviors have good and bad behavioral consequences not only for ourselves but also for others.

- Behavioral competency is a basic understanding and consistent practice of a set of skills that nurtures trust.

- Rules of conduct are human-made social constructs or norms that help groups of people, large and small, weave together the competing desires of individuals so that everyone can enjoy interacting socially with everyone else without creating too much conflict.

- The 5C Elements of SM—communication, choice, commitment, coping, and caring—can be self-cultivated, self-assessed, and self-managed by almost anyone.

2

CONTINUOUS BEHAVIORAL IMPROVEMENT

After reading this chapter, you should be able to:

- Explain the difference between behavioral occurrences and behavioral patterns.

- List all of the elements of the continuous behavioral improvement process.

- Describe behavioral evaluation and the five levels of the behavioral observation scale.

- Explain the three variables of the Fogg Behavioral Model (FBM).

Understanding Behavioral Occurrences and Behavioral Patterns

Before we continue, let us stop and define two key terms that are essential to understanding behavior: behavioral occurrences and behavioral patterns. What is the difference between these two terms:

Behavioral Occurrence:
One-time event or a single behavioral incident that happens.

Behavioral Pattern:
Conduct that is repeated, predictable, and self-created.

- A **behavioral occurrence** is *a one-time event or a single behavioral incident that happens*. For example, a person might be absent or late or not do their homework once for reasons that are usually not self-created.

- A **behavioral pattern** is *conduct that is repeated, predictable, and self-created*. Behavioral patterns reveal themselves after a number of behavioral occurrences have happened.

For instance, frequent occurrences of rude and disrespect-ful behavior toward others would be indicative of an uncar-ing (more specifically uncivil and inconsiderate) behavioral pattern.

When assessing and diagnosing behavioral performance (in yourself or others), there are two reasons why it is important to determine if the behavior in question is an isolated behavioral occurrence or a behavioral pattern: First, life happens. From time to time unforeseen circumstances occur (bad weather, car problems, illness, and personal issues). When situations occur that are the result of chance, bad luck, or events beyond your control, it is entirely reasonable not to conform to what is behav-iorally expected because the motivation to act in a contrary manner is not self-created. For example, it is entirely reasonable for a person to be late or absent if he or she has a flat tire or a car accident or is stuck in the middle of a snowstorm.

Second, human beings are not perfect; we make mistakes. Because humans are human, it's unreasonable to expect that they can operate at peak performance all the time.[1] People make mistakes because they can be inattentive, preoccupied, bored, tired, irritable, upset, sad, hurt, depressed, worried, overly enthusiastic, scared, or overwhelmed. Emotions, feelings, and states of mind can cause people to be careless and act before they think. When normally trustworthy individuals are thoughtless and act in ways (intentionally or otherwise) that do not conform to their established or accepted pattern of behavior, the conduct is said to be **out-of-character**.

Both chance and out-of-character occurrences are discrete events that should not happen repeatedly. When either one becomes the norm, behavioral patterns come into view.

How Behavioral Occurrences Become Patterns

Behavioral occurrences become behavioral patterns when conduct is repeated, frequent, predictable, and self-created. While some behavioral patterns are healthy, some are not. Some are responsible and strengthen trust, while others are irresponsible and weaken trust. For example, over the course of a semester, repeated occurrences of absenteeism would be indicative of possible commitment-related problems; always attending class and atten-tively taking notes would give a more positive message to your professor.

Sometimes behavioral patterns are difficult to see or take time to reveal themselves. The important thing to remember is that trustworthy and untrustworthy behavioral patterns exist and reveal character traits (good and bad) about each of us. Just knowing the distinction between behavioral occurrences and behavioral patterns is an important first step in understanding how to assess and improve behavioral performance.

Out-of-Character: Behavior that normally trustworthy individuals do that is thoughtless (intentionally or otherwise) and does not conform to their established or accepted pattern of behavior.

What could be more important than understanding your own behavioral patterns? One of the main goals of this book is to provide a framework to identify, assess, and diagnose your own behavioral performance.

What Do You Think?

Which of the following describes a behavioral occurrence versus a behavioral pattern?

	Felisha exercises every morning before work.
	Henry is always five minutes late to class, and also walks out of class to talk on his cell phone.
	Bonifacio always waits until the night before a test to study.
	Antonia misses class because she had an interview.
	Sydney always waits until the last minute to register.

How Our Behavior Influences Trust

Why are behavioral patterns important? Behavioral patterns communicate how trustworthy we are to others.

A recent study published in the *Harvard Business Review* found that "98% of workers polled reported experiencing uncivil behavior" in the workplace.[2] Behaviors like incivility that undermine the dignity, confidence, and self-worth of others can weaken or possibly even sever the trust connections that bind people together. Once trust is broken, unhappiness, conflict, and polarization often result, any of which can compromise or destroy goodwill among people. Many of the biggest problems we face in society can be traced back to untrustworthy behavior that has destroyed people's willingness to cooperate with one another.

This study suggests that most people (young and old) go through life without giving any serious thought to their own behavior and how it can affect their lives individually and our society as a whole. If 98 percent of people surveyed experience relationship mistrust at work, everyone's goodwill and willingness to cooperate has been compromised. How can we move forward collectively when no one trusts each other? How can this be good for us individually or the world as a whole?

Continuous Behavioral Improvement Process Model (CBIP)

How can we improve our behavior over time? The **Continuous Behavioral Improvement Process** (CBIP; figure 2.1) is defined as *a method*

Continuous Behavioral Improvement Process: A method for improving the 5Cs through incremental and informed thinking about one's own behavior.

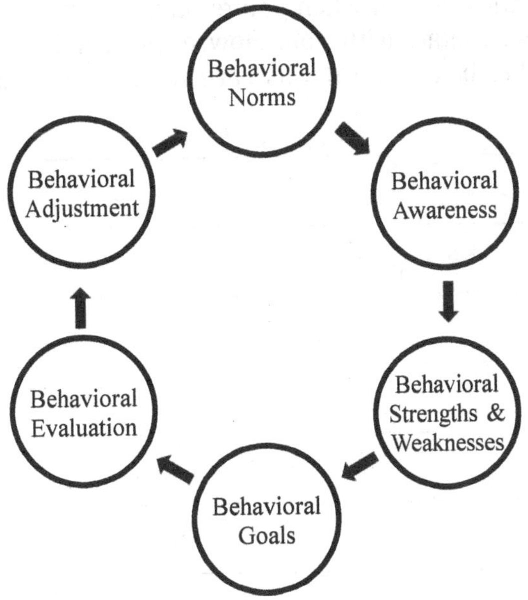

Figure 2.1. The Continuous Behavioral Improvement Process. *Source:* Author-created.

for improving the 5Cs through incremental and informed thinking about one's own behavior. CBIP relies on the individual to identify areas of behavioral improvement within themselves; individuals know themselves better than others do and are therefore uniquely qualified to identify and solve their own behavior-related problems. Because you are required to come up with ideas for improving your behavior, you are more invested in the behavioral outcome, which increases the chance of successful and sustainable improvement.

Behavioral Norms

Behavioral Norms:
Generally accepted social qualities or characteristics that are deemed essential for successfully living together in society.

For CBIP to work, you must first be willing to accept the notion that societies must have ground rules to function properly. **Behavioral norms** are *generally accepted social qualities or characteristics that are deemed essential for successfully living together in society.*

Behavioral norms are the foundation upon which our communities and social order are built and that allow individuals to interact with one another without too much conflict. In the United States, we believe that individuals have the absolute right to pursue life, liberty, and happiness. But it can be persuasively argued that how we pursue our rights to life, liberty, and happiness is as important as the rights themselves.

What Do You Think?

Maria never says hello when she greets her fellow students each morning, while Scott just mumbles a few words when he walks into class. Juan often turns his back on you when you're having a discussion, while Alice never makes eye contact with you. How does their behavior affect you? Are these or other behavioral norms particularly important to you? Why?

_____

_____

_____

_____

_____

_____

_____

_____

Behavioral Talent

It takes **behavioral talent** to *achieve your goals without hurting others and yourself.* How individuals interact with each other is just as important, if not more important, than what people actually do together. We may damage the community in which we all live if we as individuals pursue our own life, liberty, and happiness without following any ground rules, or without regard for others and the behavioral norms that others expect. Being nice, working hard, or communicating appropriately are not about being politically correct; on the contrary, it is that doing otherwise hurts everyone. If we all drink from the same polluted water, we all suffer. How can societies function or move forward in a healthy manner if individuals poison the society that we all live in?

Individuals who are unaware of or unwilling to adopt these generally accepted behavioral norms hurt themselves because their behavior is contrary to the common interests of the people and groups that they interact with. This is not to say that people cannot think or believe differently. It is simply an assertion that behavioral norms exist and that they are the boundaries within which we create understanding between others and ourselves. Without behavioral norms to guide our collective interactions with each other, our actions and words may create an incorrect understanding of our intentions.

Behavioral Talent:
Achieving your goals without hurting others and yourself.

Behavioral Awareness

After you have identified the behavioral norms that you deem important for pursuing life, liberty, and happiness, the next step in CBIP is **behavioral awareness**. Behavioral awareness is defined here as *the degree to which you have knowledge of or are concerned about your own behavior relative to behavioral norms.*

Although our behavior is observable and in plain view for everyone to see and interpret, some people may not be aware of their own behavior in relation to behavioral norms. To become behaviorally aware, you must become conscious of yourself in real time during the situation.

Behavioral awareness happens when conscious decision-making starts and acting on impulse (without thinking) stops. When we consciously consider (think about) something and then make a choice among different behavioral alternatives, we become aware of and therefore responsible for our behavioral actions. In addition, it is infinitely wiser to think about what we do before we do it. For example, imagine you are in difficult driving conditions and another driver recklessly cuts you off in traffic. Do you get upset and fly into a rage without thinking, or

Behavioral Awareness:
The degree to which you have knowledge of or are concerned about your own behavior relative to behavioral norms.

do you get upset but pause and think about the best way to respond? If you fly into a rage, your emotions are controlling your reactions. If you pause and think about the best way to respond and then respond in a way that is best for the situation, you're controlling your reactions.

The development of the capacity to think before acting is what differentiates adulthood from adolescence and, for that matter, distinguishes humans from all other life forms on the planet. Legally, adulthood starts at the age of eighteen years. At eighteen, we are legally responsible for our behavioral decision-making. Acting on impulse is not a legal defense, nor is it appropriate behaviorally.

What Do You Think?

Do you get upset when other people drive poorly? If so, why do you react that way and what does getting upset accomplish?

_____

_____

_____

_____

_____

_____

Individuals who are over the age of eighteen years and repeatedly demonstrate patterns of impulsive conduct are not behaviorally aware. They are adolescents disguised as adults. Without behavioral awareness we cannot fully understand the impact of our decision-making on others or on the trajectory of our lives. Without behavioral awareness we cannot comprehend our own behavioral strengths, weaknesses, and behavioral tendencies.

Behavioral Strengths and Weaknesses

Behavioral Strengths and Weaknesses: Aspects of behavioral conduct that are either helpful or not in your relations with others.

After you become behaviorally aware, you are capable of objectively and accurately identifying your own **behavioral strengths and weaknesses**. That does not mean that you will do so; it just means that you have become conscious of your own behavior. Behavioral strengths and weaknesses are defined here *as aspects of behavioral conduct that are either helpful or not in your relations with others*. Whether you develop a sophisticated understanding of your behavior is a function of your willingness *to objectively examine your own thoughts, feelings, and actions*. This is called **self-reflection**.

In his seminal article entitled "Managing Oneself," Peter Drucker wrote that "success in the knowledge economy comes to those who know themselves—their strengths, their values, and how they perform best."[3] Drucker believed that one of the most important things people should figure out about themselves is what they do best so that they can make their greatest contribution. In his view, people can perform best only from strength, but they must be aware of their own unproductive habits (weaknesses) that prevent them from achieving the outcomes that they desire.

Self-Reflection: Examination, contemplation, and analysis of your own thoughts, feelings, and behaviors.

What Do You Think?

"What are your strengths?" is an easy question to answer. "What are your weaknesses?" is a more challenging one. No one is perfect. Being honest with yourself demonstrates self-awareness. Explain an aspect of your behavior that is challenging for you and an example from your life that demonstrates some of the challenges that this has created for you (i.e., procrastination, sleeping in, difficulty to work with).

_____

_____

_____

_____

_____

_____

_____

Only after you understand your unique combination of behavioral strengths and weaknesses can you create an informed long-term plan for behavioral success. Although identifying information about yourself is a lifelong process, you will begin the process of defining your own behavioral strengths and weaknesses throughout this book. By understanding behavioral norms, developing behavioral awareness, and clarifying your behavioral strengths and weaknesses, you will be in a better position to create informed and meaningful behavioral goals for yourself.

Behavioral Goal

Behavioral Goals: The values and character traits that you aspire to achieve.

A goal is an end state that you strive to attain. There are many types of goals, including professional, personal, spiritual, financial, and behavioral. **Behavioral goals** are *the values and character traits that you aspire to achieve*. For example, you might take an "alcohol-free January" pledge to celebrate the New Year, a plan that has become popular over the past few years. Your goal is to eliminate all alcoholic beverages from your diet for one month. If you can keep to your plan, you will ultimately achieve your goal.

Why is it important to figure out the type of person that you aspire to be and what you want to stand for? Your behavioral choices transmit information about your values, ethics, judgment, manner, emotions, friendliness, interest, desire, motivation, attitude, aptitude, dependability, and work ethic. In short, your behavioral choices reveal your values and character.

How other people perceive us, and how we perceive ourselves, is largely a consequence of our own behavioral decision-making. Like a compass, behavioral goals point us in the right direction when we make choices. But unlike a compass that only points us in a particular direction, behavioral goals help us deal with all the difficult obstacles and struggles that we encounter along our journey.

Returning to our alcohol-free pledge, imagine the many obstacles that might interfere with you achieving your goal:

- You go to a party where everyone else is drinking and your friends encourage you to join in.

- Your partner likes to have a glass of wine with dinner and is distressed when you forgo one.

- You're the best man at a wedding and must lead a toast to the bride and groom.

These all pose potential obstacles to you achieving your goal or sidelining you on your way to reaching your destination. Each involves making a conscious choice: Should you stick to your plan or make an exception based on the changing circumstances? Without behavioral goals, how would we know if our choices were moving us in the right direction? All journeys end at destinations; behavioral goals are destinations.

What Do You Think?

What character traits (social, emotional, physical, and intellectual) do you want people to think of when they think of you? Please make a list of one-word adjectives that you would like other people to use to describe you.

_____

_____

_____

_____

_____

_____

Behavioral Evaluation

Our choices about what we say and do, how reliable we are, how hard we work, how nice we are to others, and how we communicate are all in plain view for others to see. As such, our behavior provides information about our nature and character that can be collected, measured, and evaluated to help people understand each other. Our behavior demonstrates our values and our willingness to adhere to behavioral norms.

Our behavior in school, work, relationships, and in everyday life reveals traits to the world; traits about our maturity level, nature, and character (good and bad). It also shows others that we know how to successfully navigate (or not) the world.

To see how one might objectively evaluate behavior, consider the following scenario.

Three brothers are sitting on a couch after dinner, and there is a big pile of dishes sitting in the sink waiting to be washed. One of the brothers is responsible, one is somewhat responsible, and one is irresponsible. How can you tell which brother is which?

The responsible brother gets up and willingly does the dishes without needing to be asked. The somewhat responsible brother does the dishes but only after being asked. The irresponsible brother doesn't do the dishes, even after being asked.[4] The experience of dealing with each of these brothers is completely different. The brother that does the dishes without being asked is a self-manager. The other two brothers are not yet able to get the job done without prompting. And even when prompted, one of the brothers still did not get the dishes washed. This simple example demonstrates the three primary levels of self-management. This example demonstrates the degree to which each of these brothers has developed the ability to regulate themselves.

If you need to be asked or told to do basic things such as showing concern for others, exhibiting commitment, making good choices, or communicating appropriately, you are unknowingly demonstrating that these basic behavioral traits are not yet woven through the fabric of who you are. You demonstrate that you have either not yet developed the ability to self-regulate or that you are unwilling to do so. Either way, the experience of dealing with you requires behavioral guidance (or adult supervision) and is completely different from interacting with people who do not require outside intervention. People who need to be told to be nice, show up on time, and work hard are very different from people who don't need to be told to do these basic things. The key to understanding and evaluating your behavior is the degree to which you willingly do that which is your responsibility.

Self-Management 101: if you need to be prompted by others to do a behavior, regardless of the behavior, you are not self-managing.

Responsible People Are Accountable for Their Own Behavior

Responsibility: A palpable sense of duty about one's obligations to others.

Behavioral Guidance: The degree to which you require others to help manage your own behavior.

Responsible people self-manage. They have *a palpable sense of duty about their obligations to themselves and others.* Conversely, people who do not willingly act in a responsible manner require **behavioral guidance**; they cannot be confidently relied on to fulfill their obligations unless others supervise them. Even with supervision, some people don't fulfill their obligations. Behavioral guidance is defined here as *the degree to which you require others to help manage your own behavior.*

There is an inverse relationship between trust and guidance; the more behavioral guidance required to fulfill our basic behavioral obligations, the less we can be entrusted with responsibility (figure 2.2). Students who need to be told to do their homework or to go to class require behavioral guidance. The experience of dealing with students that need to be told what to do is completely different from dealing with students who don't need this guidance. The opposite is also true of course: the less behavioral guidance people require, the more they demonstrate that they can be entrusted with responsibility. Self-managed behavior does not require behavioral guidance from others.

Figure 2.2. Trust versus Behavior Relationship. *Source:* Author-created.

Behavior That Requires Guidance from Others Is Not Self-Managed Behavior

Self-management skills are particularly important for students because they are self-employed. Students work for themselves; they are their own bosses. It is a self-evident truth that students who choose to work hard by putting in long hours of studying, attending all their classes, rewriting their class notes, completing all their assignments, and attending tutoring sessions understand their academic subject matter much better and outperform students who do not do so. However, many other students still do not work hard.

Many students have a tough time making the connection between their own behavioral performance and their academic performance. If they don't do well in school, they may even mistakenly assume that they are not academically inclined when, in fact, they may never have taken the time required (by everyone) to actually learn the material. They may never have behaved like students.

What Do You Think?

Three sisters (triplets) recently graduated from high school together, and they live at home with their parents. All three sisters are enrolled in college. They all have identical schedules and have enrolled in these courses:

Self-Management	3 credits
College Writing	3 credits
Chemistry 1 with Lab	4 credits
Microeconomics	3 credits
College Algebra for Business	3 credits
	16 credits

They arrive home after the first day of the semester and have a lot of homework. One of the sisters is committed to college, one is not committed to college, and one is somewhere in between. How could you tell which is which?

- The sister who independently (without guidance from others) follows through and does all her work, including going to class, without having to be asked to do so is the most committed to college. This sister communicates that she can be entrusted with the responsibility of going to college because she willingly manages her own affairs. This sister does not require guidance to be successful.

- The sister who needs to be asked or told to do her schoolwork and go to class, but eventually does so, is somewhat committed to college. This sister requires guidance from others to be successful.

- The sister who fails to follow through and meet her obligations, even with guidance from others, communicates that she cannot be entrusted with the responsibilities of college.

Behavioral Observation Scale (BOS)

Because each of the 5C Elements is defined in terms of specific behavioral standards, they accurately describe what reflects effective behavioral performance. The 5C Elements are core behavioral standards that can apply to everyone, regardless of societal rank or station in life, not just to students or children. They provide the lens through which behavior can be objectively viewed and evaluated.

The major advantages of defining each of the behavioral competencies are:

1. To help people set their own expectations of themselves.

2. To help people decide for themselves what they should expect from others.

3. To provide a common standard to evaluate the experience of interacting with others, thereby improving consistency, situational judgment, and decision-making.

Table 2.1 outlines the 5C Element **behavioral observation scale (BOS)**[5] performance model.[6] A BOS is *a measure of your behavioral performance of the 5C Elements.*

The three performance standards set forth three different behavioral effectiveness levels (Role Model, Meets Expectations, and Below Expectations).[7] Each of these levels will be discussed in more detail in later sections.

Notice that the key differentiating factors between the different effectiveness levels are willingness and the degree to which a person requires behavioral guidance. In self-management, **willingness** is defined as *behavior that is done by choice and without reluctance.* The more independently and willingly a person demonstrates the 5C Elements with-

Behavioral Observation Scale: A measure of your behavioral performance of the 5C Elements.

Willingness: Behavior that is done by choice and without reluctance.

Table 2.1. The 5C Self-Management Behavioral Observation Scale Performance Model

5	4	3	2	1
Role Model		**Meets Expectations**		**Below Expectations**
Independently and willingly provides evidence of behavioral understanding of the 5C Elements and can be trusted with responsibility.		With guidance from others, provides evidence of behavioral understanding of the 5C Elements and can be trusted with responsibility.		Even with guidance from others, fails to provide evidence of behavioral understanding of the 5C Elements and to be trusted with responsibility, and is unwilling to work on the responsibility of self-management.

Source: Author-created.

out guidance, the more effective they will be at managing their own behavior:

- The Role Model level willingly behaves as expected.

- The Meets Expectations level does what is expected but not without behavioral guidance.

- The Below Expectations level does not do what is expected even with guidance.

It is important to remember that a person can be deemed a "Role Model" at one 5C Element but be below expectations at another. For example, a person might be evaluated as being a role model regarding commitment to school, but be below expectations when it comes to showing concern for other students or faculty. The behaviorally competent individual is aware of and working on all the 5C Elements, not just one or two.

These three different performance levels (Role Model, Meets Expectations, and Below Expectations) can be further broken down into a five-point behavioral observation scale (BOS). The BOS measures how consistently a person demonstrates or models the 5C Elements (see table 2.2).[8]

Table 2.2. The Five-Point Behavioral Observation Scale (BOS)

5 = Almost always performs as described by the Role Model standards.
4 = Sometimes performs as described by the Role Model standards and sometimes performs as described by the Meets Expectations standards.
3 = Almost always performs as described by the Meets Expectations standards.
2 = Sometimes performs as described by the Meets Expectations standards and sometimes performs as described by the Below Expectations standards.
1 = Almost always performs as described by the Below Expectations standards.

Source: Author-created.

What Do You Think?

Using the behavioral observation scale in the following table, write in the right-hand margin the number (1, 2, 3, 4, or 5) corresponding to the degree to which you consistently exhibit the behavior described in the statement. Note that there are no right or wrong answers. All that is important is that you indicate how consistently you exhibit the behavior described in the action statement.

	Trust Category	Rating (1–5)
Communication	I communicate appropriately.	
Choice	I prioritize important matters ahead of unimportant matters when I make decisions.	
Commitment	I follow through and meet obligations.	
Coping	I adapt effectively to difficult, changing, and complex circumstances.	
Caring	I show thoughtful concern for others.	
AVERAGE		

This quick assessment shows how the behavioral observation scale works and how the 5C Elements relate to you. What was your average? Explain your answer.

_____

_____

_____

_____

_____

_____

_____

Behavioral observation scales and your individual assessment results for each of the 5C Elements are used throughout this book and will be logged into your employability profile at the end of each section. An **employability profile** is *a manual or electronic form that is used to*

Employability Profile: A log or scorecard of all the behavioral observation skills assessments.

compile your own behavioral self-assessments on each of the 5C Elements. Once logged, a simple arithmetic mean or average can be used to calculate a behavioral competency rating. An additional blank copy of the employability profile can be found in the appendix at the back of the book.

Tracking your behavioral performance will help you compare and assess your actual behavior against your own defined behavioral standards and against the 5C standards established in this book. This comparison will help you understand the extent to which your performance deviates from what you expect from yourself and what others expect from you. After you understand how your behavior deviates from the standards you set for yourself, you can take the necessary actions to improve it. However, it is important to keep in mind that some minor deviations in performance can be expected. You are not a machine. So, try concentrating your attention on big deviations in your behavioral performance instead of trying to control each and every deviation.

1	2	3	4	5
Below Expectations		**Meets Expectations**		**Role Model**
Even with guidance from others, fails to provide evidence of behavioral understanding of the 5C Elements and cannot be trusted with responsibility, and is unwilling to work on the responsibility of self-management.		With guidance, provides evidence of behavioral understanding of the 5C Elements and can be trusted with responsibility.		Independently and willingly provides evidence of behavioral understanding of the 5C Elements and can be trusted with responsibility.

Where:

5 =	Almost always performs as described by the "Role Model" standard.
4 =	Sometimes performs as described by the "Role Model" standard and sometimes performs as described by the "Meets Expectations" standard.
3 =	Almost always performs as described by the "Meets Expectations" standard.
2 =	Sometimes performs as described by the "Meets Expectations" standard and sometimes performs as described by the "Below Expectations" standard.
1 =	Almost always performs as described by the "Below Expectations" standard.

Communication
Trust a person to convey messages appropriately.

	Audience
	Involvement
	Message
	Evidence
	COMMUNICATION MEAN

	BEHAVIORAL COMPETENCY RATING (MEAN OF MEANS)

Choices
Trust a person to use good judgment.

	Communication
	Commitment
	Coping
	Caring
	Choice
	CHOICE MEAN

Commitment
Trust a person to be dutiful.

	Dependability Attendance
	Dependability Accountability
	Dependability Contribution
	Hard Work Time Deliberate Practice
	Hard Work Delayed Gratification
	Hard Work Effort Energy
	Hard Work Effort Determination
	Hard Work Effort Stamina
	Quality Measure of Excellence
	Quality Continuous Improvement
	COMMITMENT MEAN

Coping
Trust a person to demonstrate fortitude during difficult times.

	Coping Change Demonstration
	Coping Adversity Self-Awareness
	Coping Adversity Self-Restraint
	Coping Adversity Self-Improvement
	Coping Complexity Capacity
	Coping Complexity Capability
	Coping Complexity Activities
	COPING MEAN

Caring
Trust a person to show concern for others.

	Caring Civility Listening
	Caring Civility Courtesy
	Caring Civility Consideration
	Caring Helpfulness Concern
	Caring Helpfulness Cooperation
	Caring Helpfulness Compromise
	Caring Conscientious Thoughtfulness
	Caring Conscientious Carefulness
	Caring Conscientious Fairness
	Caring Common Good Respect
	Caring Common Good Equity
	Caring Common Good Goodwill
	CARING MEAN

Behavioral Adjustment

> When you know how to create tiny habits, you can change your life forever.
>
> —B. J. Fogg, "Tiny Surprises for Happiness and Health"

Knowing what we should do and doing what we should do are two different things. We know what we should be doing; the hard part is actually doing it. For instance, all students know that they should go to class and study. For thirteen years before college from K through 12, teachers drill into their students the importance of showing up to class on time and doing homework. Yet, each year hundreds of thousands of students are academically dismissed from colleges because they miss class and/or do not do their homework.

If you have struggled with doing what you are supposed to do, you may want to consider the work of Stanford University researcher Dr. B. J. Fogg that focuses on changing behaviors in positive ways.[9] According to Dr. **Fogg's Behavior Model (FBM) Equation** (figure 2.3), *three variables must converge at the same moment for any behavior to occur: motivation, ability, and trigger.* If any of these three variables change, it's not the same behavior.[10]

When a behavior does not occur (such as studying, doing homework, or going to class), at least one of these three elements is missing. Either the person is

- Not motivated to perform the desired behavior

- Doesn't have the ability to perform the desired behavior

- Doesn't have a prompt that reminds them to do the desired behavior

Fogg's Behavior Model (FBM): Behavioral model that asserts that three variables must happen at the same time for any behavior to occur: motivation, ability, and trigger.

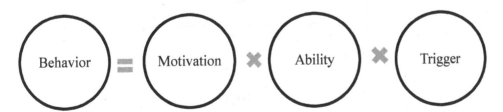

Figure 2.3. Fogg's Behavior Model (FBM) Equation. *Source:* Author-created.

For instance, if a student is continually late to class, they are either not motivated to get to class, don't have the ability to get to class, or don't have a trigger that reminds them to go to class. If a student is motivated and has the ability to get to class (we can call this will and skill), then the trigger may be to set an alarm one hour before class to remind them they need to get to class. Although this seems simple enough, many students don't have triggers to remind them about things that they need to do. If triggers are set and you still do not perform the desired behavior, then the cause of the behavioral issue is either motivation (will) or ability (skill).

According to FBM, we will perform a desired behavior when our motivation and ability are above the action line (figure 2.4), and we get a trigger to do the behavior. Looking at figure 2.4, if we make the desired behavior too hard, we will not do it.[11]

The key to FBM is to create new, **tiny habits**, *repeated behaviors that are easy to do and require little motivation*, and to also figure out a trigger to activate them. Doing things that are hard to do requires a lot of motivation.

How do we trigger these new, tiny habits? According to Dr. Fogg, rather than trying to change our existing behaviors, "we make our existing behavior the event that triggers the desired behavior." For example,

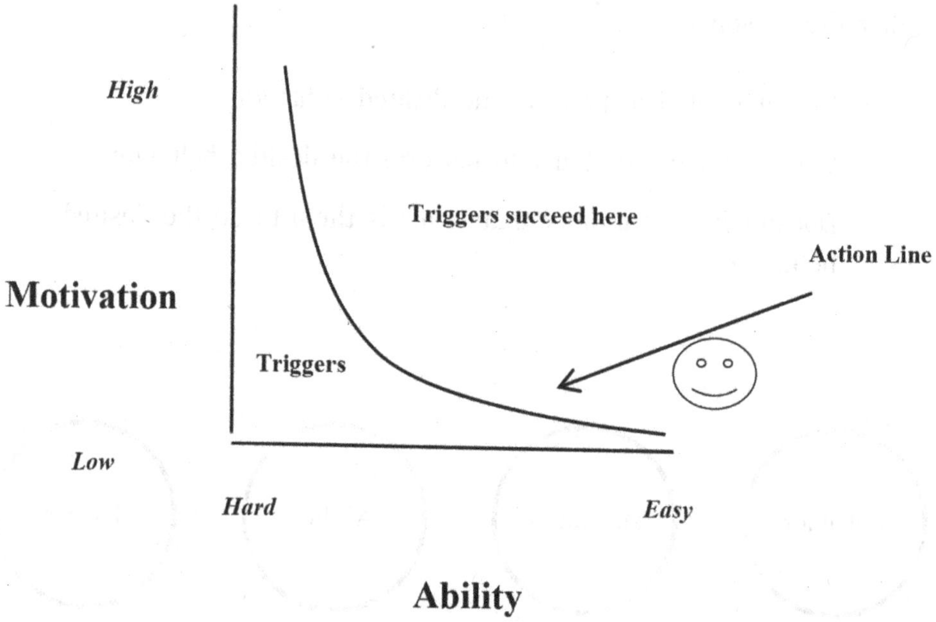

Tiny Habits: Repeated behaviors that are easy to do and require little motivation.

Figure 2.4. Fogg's Behavior Model (FBM) Graph. *Source:* Author-created.

suppose that you want to start exercising more, you might use your existing morning routine to trigger it. You already make yourself a cup of coffee every morning. You could make that the trigger that initiates a new, brief exercise routine like walking up and down a flight of stairs in your house once. On the second day, you could walk up and down the steps twice, and so on until you can walk up and down the steps for the entire time the coffee is brewing. If a coffee pot takes five minutes to brew, you might be able to walk up and down the steps twenty times within a few weeks. If you make the exercise routine too strenuous and difficult on the first day, you may not want to continue, because big behavior changes require too much internal motivation (coaxing) to do. According to Dr. Fogg, "If we keep repeating the tiny habits, over time they will become the new habit because of repetition."

Habits are about repeating behaviors. We will be using this tiny habit technique at the end of each unit to help coax and nurture the behaviors covered in this course.

Changing Habits

How do you employ tiny habits in your life? As you think about changing your habits, Dr. Fogg suggests thinking about framing the tiny habit like this:

Format for a tiny habit:

After I (insert existing behavior),
I will (insert new tiny behavior).

Example:

"After I am awakened by my alarm, I will put one foot on the ground."

Please take a few moments and try to come up with one tiny habit that you can use to help you improve your behavioral performance. Remember to use the format "After I (insert existing behavior), I will (insert new tiny behavior)."

After I _____ ,

I will _____ .

Personal Policy Contract

One of the greatest challenges you will have in college and life is managing your own behavior. As we have noted, you probably know what you should be doing; the hard part is actually doing it. If you really want to change your own behavior and achieve your goals, whatever they may be, research shows that people who write down specific goals are far more likely to be successful than those who do not write down their goals or have no goals at all.[12]

To help you achieve your behavioral goals, you will be writing them down and creating **personal policy contracts** (see table 2.3). By signing and dating the personal policy contract, it becomes an obligation to yourself that cannot be broken.

Personal Policy Contracts: Commitments that you make to yourself about how you will apply your personal policies.

Table 2.3. Personal Policy Contract

Behavioral Goal: _____	
Goals	Example: I will work on the following behavioral goals in college. [These may include: improving your dependability; completing homework; studying better; improving work ethic; acting appropriately; reducing school stress; improving time management and judgment.]
Personal Policies	Example: Personal policies I will commit to so that I can achieve my goal. [These may include that you will: never miss class or be late to class; study at least two hours every day; stop and think about your audience before you communicate; actively listen; never miss an assignment; ask questions in class if you don't understand the material.]
Public Commitments	Example: Public commitments that I will make to regularly measure how I am doing relative to my goals and personal policies. I will send my goals, personal policies, and quick weekly progress reports to a supportive friend and the professor. [These may include: "I didn't miss any classes this week"; "I studied three hours on Monday, four hours on Tuesday, and I turned my phone off before every class."]
Signature: _____ Date: _____	

Source: Author-created.

Key Terms

The following terms will help you, particularly if you learn how to explain them and use them in the right places and situations.

- Behavioral Awareness
- Behavioral Goals
- Behavioral Guidance
- Behavioral Norms
- Behavioral Observation Scale
- Behavioral Occurrences
- Behavioral Patterns
- Behavioral Strengths and Weaknesses
- Behavioral Talent

- Continuous Behavioral Improvement Process
- Employability Profile
- Fogg Behavioral Model
- Out-of-Character
- Personal Policy Contracts
- Responsibility
- Self-Reflection
- Tiny Habits
- Willingness

Discussion Questions

1. What is a behavioral pattern and how does that differ from a behavioral occurrence?

2. Explain each of the variables in the continuous behavioral improvement process.

3. What is the difference between a skill-related versus will-related behavioral problem?

4. What was the main point of the "three sisters and homework" exercise?

5. There are three behavioral effectiveness performance standards (Role Model, Meets Expectations, and Below Expectations). Explain the different levels and give examples to illustrate your points.

6. What are the three variables in Fogg's Behavioral Model (FBM)? Explain each with an example.

7. According to FBM, when will a person make sure that he or she does a desired behavior?

To Sum Up

- Behavioral occurrences become behavioral patterns when conduct is repeated, frequent, predictable, and self-created. While some behavioral patterns are healthy, some are not. Some may be responsible and strengthen trust, while others are irresponsible and weaken trust.

- Many of the biggest problems we face in society can be traced back to untrustworthy behavior that has destroyed people's willingness to cooperate with one another.

- Continuous Behavioral Improvement Process relies on the individual to identify areas of behavioral improvement within themselves; individuals know themselves better than others do and are therefore uniquely qualified to identify and solve their own behavior-related problems.

- Because certain behaviors lead to better performance than others, it is appropriate and necessary for you to study, understand, and evaluate the relationship between your behavior and your performance.

- The key differentiating factors between the different behavioral effectiveness levels are willingness and the degree to which a person requires behavioral guidance. The more independently and willingly a person demonstrates the 5C Elements without guidance, the more effective they will be at managing their own behavior.

- You are responsible for how you communicate, how you make choices, how considerate you are of others, how committed you are to the activities you are involved with, and how well you cope with difficulty in your life.

- Use this book to help you develop your own strategies for improving your behavioral performance. Understanding and controlling your own behavior will affect not only your academic future but also your life after graduation.

Section II

COMMUNICATION

How to understand and assess
communication-based trust regarding
message appropriateness and effectiveness,
and an introduction to the
AIME communication methodology

3

COMMUNICATION BASICS

After reading this chapter, you should be able to:

- Understand the terms *verbal*, *nonverbal*, and *written communication*.

- Discuss the theorists Watzlawick, Bavelas, and Jackson's statement: "One cannot *not* communicate."

- Describe the 7/93 rule developed by psychologists Mehrabian and Wiener, and how communicating effectively is affected by their research.

- Explain the distinction between effective and ineffective communications.

- Explain why you should be more careful when communicating via email or other electronic means.

Understanding Communication

The most important thing in communication is hearing what isn't said.

—Peter F. Drucker

Communication is the most fundamental of the 5C Elements because it is the mechanism through which you reveal yourself to others. Based on the way you communicate with others, they can determine how motivated (or unmotivated) you are, how much you care (or do not care) about them, how reliable (or unreliable) you are, how likeable (or unlikable) you are, how articulate (or inarticulate) you are, how sensible (or foolish) you are, how reasonable (or unreasonable) you are, how stable (or unstable) you are, and how trustworthy (or untrustworthy) you are. In other words, it is with your own nonverbal, verbal, and written communications that you reveal your true nature and character to others. Others, in turn, interpret all that information to determine if they want to be associated with you (or not).

To put it another way, because your own communication defines the type of person that you are to others, it shapes your **public persona** and has the power to alter your destiny. Communication is so fundamental to academic, professional, and personal success that it is arguably the most important 5C Element. For that reason, communication is the first of the 5Cs to be presented.

What Is Communication?

Communication can be defined as *the process that creates a shared understanding of meaning between people.* You do this by using three different communication forms: (1) **nonverbal communication**, which *conveys understanding and meaning through your behavior and choices;* (2) **verbal communication**, which *conveys understanding and meaning through your speaking and listening;* and (3) **written communication**, which *conveys understanding and meaning through your reading and writing.* Let us begin with the least understood of these communication forms, nonverbal communication.

Nonverbal Communication

In 1967, three communication theorists named Donald deAvila Jackson, Janet Beavin Bavelas, and Paul Watzlawick coined the communications axiom: "One cannot *not* communicate."[1] Everything that you do communicates some kind of message about you. They continued: "Activity or inactivity, words or silence all have message value: they influence others and these others, in turn, cannot not respond to these communications and are thus themselves communicating."[2] So, everything that you say and do communicates facts and information about yourself that influences how others see you. Your actions and words profoundly affect others' beliefs about and behavior toward you. What and how you communicate helps others determine your underlying nature and whether they want to associate with you. It is through your own communications that people figure out whether you understand how to be **appropriate**. People decide to like you, trust you, hire you, or even to marry you based on *the*

Public Persona: Your public reputation.

Communication: The process that creates a shared understanding of meaning between people.

Nonverbal Communication: Conveys understanding and meaning through your behavior and choices.

Verbal Communication: Conveys understanding and meaning through your speaking and listening.

Written Communication: Conveys understanding and meaning through your reading and writing.

Appropriate: The extent to which all of your communications are perceived as suitable for a particular audience or situation.

extent to which all of your communications are perceived as suitable for a particular audience or situation.

Another profound aspect of communication that very few people know about is that much of what you communicate every moment of every day is done nonverbally. One of the earliest pioneers and most influential researchers in the area of nonverbal communications was behavioral psychologist Dr. Albert Mehrabian. Mehrabian studied the effectiveness of the spoken word. His research resulted in the **7/93 rule**. When interacting with others in person, only about 7 percent of the meaning of our feelings and attitudes is communicated through words.[3] A whopping 93 percent of the meaning of our feelings and attitudes is communicated nonverbally. Why is the 7/93 rule important?

It helps us understand the overall impact of our nonverbal communications in creating understanding with others. Although our words are extremely important to creating understanding—in documents such as contracts, laws, and academic writing—when the meaning of our words is not clearly understood, people will take notice and pay special attention to nonverbal communication.

For example, if you say "I love you" to someone, and that person is not sure if you are sincere, that person will have a heightened awareness of your nonverbal cues. They will notice if you look away, or are not looking them in the eyes, or cross your legs away from them, or start shuffling papers. If your verbal and nonverbal communications are not in sync, people will interpret the true meaning of your communications from your nonverbal cues.

The feelings and emotions associated with love are the same around the world, but love has a different word in each language. In Kenya, the word for love is *upendo*; in the Ukraine, the word for love is любов; in Arabic, the word for love is الحب; and in Hebrew, the word for love is אהבה. The word for love is not the feeling or emotion associated with being in love. So, if two people grew up in different parts of the world and spoke two completely different languages, would they still be able to fall in love? Sure they would, because feelings, moods, emotions, and actions all speak for themselves. They all communicate a great deal nonverbally. When the words that we use to say I love you conflict with the nonverbal "language of love," the nonverbal cues will rule the day. Let us take a look at nonverbal communication more closely.

Nonverbal communication is a form of communication that "conveys information about emotions, needs, intentions, attitudes, and thoughts without the use of verbal language."[4] How do we communicate nonverbally? We communicate nonverbally with our tone and volume of voice, silence, eye contact, facial expressions, gestures, posture, and body language. Your nonverbal communications convey a great deal of information

7/93 rule: When interacting with others in person, only about 7 percent of the meaning of our feelings and attitudes is communicated through words.

to others about your feelings and attitude, and the kind of person you are. Most importantly, as you learned, you are not credible when your verbal and written communication are not backed up by your nonverbal communication. To that extent, your nonverbal communication is what is real about you and therefore defines who you are to others. You continually inform others nonverbally about your values, ethics, judgment, manner, emotions, friendliness, interest, desire, motivation, attitude, aptitude, dependability, and work ethic. Although verbal and written forms of communication are extremely important, your nonverbal communication reveals a great deal about your true feelings and attitudes.

Think about It

Nonverbal communication is a part of our daily interactions with each other. Looking at these images, what do you think each person is trying to communicate?

Effective Communication: Produces an accurate understanding of your intentions.

Ineffective Communication: Creates an inaccurate understanding of your intentions, which can lead to communication problems.

People who communicate effectively accurately convey what they intend to convey, not something else. If **effective communication** *produces an accurate understanding of your intentions*, then **ineffective communication** *creates an inaccurate understanding of your intentions, which can lead to communication problems* and misunderstandings between people. In other words, ineffective communication creates disconnects between what people think that they are communicating and what they are actually communicating.

For example, let's assume that you regard yourself as a courteous person toward others, yet you do not use your turn signals when you drive. You constantly cut in and out of lanes, honk your horn at other cars, and tailgate those who you think are driving too slowly. These behaviors are what other drivers experience when they interact with you on the road. As such, they will become your defining characteristics to other drivers. Your behavior defines you to other drivers as inconsiderate because you do not even take the time to respectfully acknowledge the presence of other drivers who share the road with you.

Behaviors like courtesy, politeness, and concern for others matter because human reality includes others. Why is it important to realize that human reality includes others? Although obvious, if you were supposed to drive alone on the road of life, nobody else would be on the road with you. Similarly, if human reality only included you, no one else would be here. But that is not the case. It is precisely because of other drivers that courteous behavior while driving matters. If you drive in a manner that does not respectfully acknowledge the existence of other drivers, your behavior does not comport with the reality that everyone else can clearly see.

How would you feel if you made an appointment to talk with your professor outside of class for extra help on an assignment and they didn't show up at all? There may be reasons why they didn't show up; something came up at the last minute, perhaps, or they forgot about the appointment. But if this happened more than once, how would it make you feel? The professor's inability to keep this appointment will indicate to you that they don't care about you or your needs. If your professor's actions make visible to you that they lack behavioral understanding and skills that dependable and hard-working people demonstrate, they are communicating messages that may be the exact opposite of their intentions. You will not have the same level of respect for them if they had met with you at the scheduled time.

Because "one cannot *not* communicate,"[5] people are either effective or ineffective at communicating with others, or fall somewhere in between.

Effective communication produces results that you desire or intend, while ineffective communication can create an incorrect understanding of your intentions, which can lead to the opposite result.

Although other people's willingness to cooperate with you is affected by many factors other than the messages that you communicate (e.g., culture, workload, and past experience), what and how you communicate should not be a barrier to what you seek. By understanding how you convey information nonverbally, you will be in a better position to avoid communication problems that result from your behavior and decisions in the future. Next, we take a look at how to effectively communicate meaning and understanding through your reading and writing, and speaking and listening—written and verbal communication.

Written and Verbal Communication

Although nonverbal communication is the primary way that we communicate, formal writing and public speaking skills always top the list of skills needed to succeed in college and at work.[6] Training in these skills is also the most common and required part of higher levels of education.[7] For example, college students are required not only to prepare, organize, and write persuasive essays and research papers, they are also required to prepare, organize, and give oral presentations in front of groups.

But, with the rise of electronic forms of communications like smartphones, email, texting, Zoom and Microsoft Teams meetings and chats, academic discussion boards, and social media sites (i.e., YouTube, Facetime, TikTok, Facebook, Twitter, LinkedIn, WhatsApp, Instagram, Reddit), written and verbal communications have become much less academic and more casual and hurried. This is true even in academic or professional settings where formal ways of communicating are still more appropriate. For example, when communicating with people like family and friends, it may be okay to use all lower case, no punctuation, emojis, slang, acronyms, and informal language. But it is definitely not okay to send overly familiar, informal, and unprofessional communications to professors, current or future employers, or others who don't know you personally. For example, you should never write or say "heyyyy," "i," "eye'm," "u," "lol," "thats," "ty," "omg," "hi" or any other such language to more formal academic or professional people because it is not appropriate. Appropriateness should be the priority whenever you communicate, regardless of person, topic, or circumstance.

Integrity: When our words and behaviors are in alignment.

Think about It

Sometimes it's difficult to see when our nonverbal, verbal, and written communication forms don't align. We may inadvertently send out messages that are contradictory and in doing so damage the bonds of **integrity** and trust.

To illustrate, take a look at the following emails. They are actual emails from students to professors. What messages are the students communicating about themselves in these messages? Please use one-word adjectives to describe the messages the students are sending about themselves to their professors.

	Message(s)
"heyyyy, i know i havent been there for a while but things have just bee crazy i went to va then go sick but il be back thur can you give me any work is missed/??"	
"hey i was wondering if you could send me the homework and everything else that we did in class and again i am sorry that i could not be there but if you would send me the homework for monday and last monday and wednesday please so that i can get what we did in class and so i can study the things and know what we did thank you that would be great thankyou see you on monday and sorry that i could not e there"	
"I know u have been absent and made you upset. I know when u looked at me you saw potential this going away college was just difficult for me I just hope you have in your heart to pass me I probably did let you down and you didn't want see that from me because I had you before I was trying pass all my other classes just so I won't be kicked out of school you may say I'm begging and I am you might say it won't be fare for others but I always at your class just late and just didn't sign in those 6 times I saw the videos u put up I was there when u helped people with the schedule I couldn't do my schedule because I owe the school money and they had me on hold"	
"eye will find out, eye'm gonna have to call the library. 9-noon, thats three hours That is enough time for me to take both, right? Yeah i'm good with that."	

Were these student emails appropriate to send to a professor? If not, why not? Did you write down adjectives like responsible, hardworking, competent, caring, resilient, fair, dependable, appropriate, or honest to describe these emails, or something else? Please explain your overall impression of these emails.

_____

_____

_____

_____

_____

_____

Moreover, because electronic communications are easy to share, permanent, and not private, informally communicating via any electronic form is a much more high-stakes communication than using other communication formats, that is, talking, meetings, and paper memorandums and letters. That being said, even these formats are not free of risk. Anyone can forward a text message to someone else or post it on another website; your words may travel much further than you expect. Your spur-of-the-moment communication with another may come to haunt you as it is repeated in other contexts.

Key Terms

- 7/93 Rule
- Appropriate
- Communication
- Effective Communication
- Ineffective Communication
- Integrity

- Nonverbal Communication
- Public Persona
- Trust
- Verbal Communication
- Written Communication

Discussion Questions

1. Explain what effective communication is. Please provide examples.

2. Why is our behavior more credible than our words?

3. What is the primary communication problem that damages integrity and trust? Please provide examples to illustrate your point.

4. Why is appropriateness important when you communicate? What are some ways that students communicate inappropriately to professors?

5. Explain the 7/93 rule that Mehrabian and Wiener discovered in their research.

6. Explain what Watzlawick, Bavelas, and Jackson meant with the communication axiom: "One cannot *not* communicate."

7. List as many things as you can think of that you communicate nonverbally.

To Sum Up

- Nonverbal communications are 93 percent of what we communicate. Our actions speak much louder than our words.

- Good communication creates understanding between people and that effective communication involves conveying messages appropriately to others.

- There are three types of communication:

  o Nonverbal: What you communicate to others without using spoken or written words

  o Verbal: Spoken communication between you and other people

  o Written: Words that are written down on paper or electronically and shared with others

- Electronic forms of communications are high stakes because they easy to share, permanent, and not private.

4

DEVELOPING A PERSONAL COMMUNICATION STRATEGY AND POLICY

After reading this chapter, you should be able to:

- Explain what a personal communication strategy (PCS) is and list the five questions that a well-written PCS should answer.

- Define the AIME Model and explain the terms *audience, involvement, message,* and *evidence.*

- Explain what a personal communication policy (PCP) and the five PCPs are for:

  o Law, ethics, and professionalism

  o Clarity of meaning and conciseness of style

  o Grammar, spelling, punctuation, and capitalization

  o Listening and understanding

  o Formality in written and oral communications

Personal Communication Strategy

Because everything that you do has message value and everything you communicate has some degree of risk, it makes sense to create a **Personal Communication Strategy (PCS)** that clarifies the messages you should be

Personal Communication Strategy (PCS): A plan for how you will communicate.

communicating about yourself whenever you communicate, regardless of the communication form (nonverbal, verbal, or written). More importantly, your PCS should also clarify the messages that you should never communicate, because doing so can cause long-lasting damage to your reputation.

A personal communication strategy (PCS) is simply *a plan for how you will communicate*. It includes answers to questions like:

- Whom am I communicating with?

- Why am I communicating with them?

- How should I communicate with them (nonverbal, verbal, written)?

- When should I communicate with them?

- What should I communicate about myself?

These are the most basic questions of all communications. Ask yourself these five questions every time that you communicate and you will increase your communication effectiveness and reduce the chances of communication mishap. Their answers will provide a clear roadmap for communicating with or without preparation.

Audience, Involvement, Message, Evidence: The AIME Model

To help you answer these five basic questions of communication, you will learn how to AIME when you communicate. AIME stands for: Audience, Involvement, Message, and Evidence.

The AIME Model (table 4.1) is a communication tool that can help you clarify, organize, and answer the five basic questions of communication. The AIME Model requires that you gather information on audience characteristics, level of audience involvement, key **messages**,

AIME (Audience, Involvement, Message, and Evidence) Model: A communication tool that can help you clarify, organize, and answer the five basic questions of communication.

Messages: The substance and meaning of communications to audiences.

Table 4.1. Audience, Involvement, Message, Evidence (AIME)

Audience	A person or group of people that are influenced by the content of your communications.
Involvement	The connection (strong/weak) that you have with each audience type.
Message	The substance and meaning of communications to audiences.
Evidence	Plainly visible criteria that audiences will react to and use in forming conclusions or judgments about you.

Source: Author-created.

and **evidence** to substantiate message claims prior to communicating so the content of your communications do not go in the wrong direction. "Ready, AIME, fire" is a helpful memory technique to remember that you should always ready yourself to communicate by aiming your communications before pulling your communication trigger. Remember, that the quote is "ready, AIME, fire" not "ready, fire, AIME."

Once you understand the basics of the AIME Model, you will see more clearly what effective communication is and what it is not. You will be able to adjust your messaging in more thoughtful ways because you will understand that some content may not be appropriate for some audiences or circumstances. You will also be able to use audience, involvement, message, and evidence when communicating with people that you've interacted with thousands of times, and also use them when you are meeting people for the very first time.

Audience

Audience is one of the most important concepts in effective communications. You may think of the term *audience* as a person or group of people that attend a performance of some kind, like a Broadway play, live professional sporting event, movie, or college course. Audiences experience and react to performances. If they dislike a performance, they may react by booing and refusing to go to future performances. If an audience likes a performance, they may react by cheering and clapping. For example, Spike Lee is an avid New York Knicks basketball fan. He has court-level season tickets and is a fixture at almost all Knicks home games. You can see him pacing the sidelines cheering on the Knicks and trying to get into the heads of opposing players. How would Mr. Lee react if he went to a game seven playoff elimination game at Madison Square Garden against the Boston Celtics and his Knicks got blown out by twenty-five points? Now try to imagine how he would react if his Knicks came from behind and beat the Celtics with a last-second buzzer beater. Can you predict how Mr. Lee would react?

All audiences have expectations, and if their expectations are not met, the audience will react in some way. The tricky part is that sometimes audience reactions are not as visible as Spike Lee's antics at Knicks games. In fact, sometimes people do not say anything when their expectations are not met. Their only reaction may be to never return for another performance.

You too also react to the "behavioral performances" of other people. For example, imagine that you went with a friend to a restaurant on a Saturday at 7:30 a.m. for breakfast and you ordered scrambled eggs, juice, wheat toast, and coffee and the waitstaff was slow, unhelpful, rude, and disinterested. How would you react? Would you say nothing? Would you give the waitstaff a tip? How would this experience make you feel?

Evidence: Plainly visible criteria that audiences will react to and use in forming conclusions or judgments about you.

Think about It

Because you "cannot *not* communicate," you are ceaselessly conveying messages to different audience types that experience and react to the substance and meaning of your behavioral performances. What messages are you communicating about yourself? More importantly, what messages should you be communicating about yourself?

_____

_____

_____

_____

_____

Audience: A person or group of people that are influenced by the content of your communication.

Audience Types: An audience's unique combination of identifying characteristics, including different priorities and expectations of you.

Audience Profile: A representation of the identifying qualities of each audience type.

Audience is defined as *a person or group of people that are influenced by the content of your communication*. Audiences are different and can be categorized into segments called **audience types**. Each audience type that experiences you has a *unique combination of identifying characteristics including different priorities and expectations of you*. These characteristics can be compiled into an **audience profile**, which is *a representation of the identifying qualities of each audience type*.

Let us look at another audience example. Suppose that a mathematics professor was teaching a class and all of the students were either absent, late, on their phones, or did not do their homework. The professor is an audience type experiencing the students' behavioral performances. Can you predict how the professor would react?

Think about It

Students and professors are different audience types. What are some of the characteristics that are typical and unique to the average student audience and the average professor audience? What are your professors' priorities and expectation of you as a student? The aim of this exercise is to use the information that you gather to create audience profiles of yourself and your professors to keep on hand whenever you're trying to judge the appropriateness of your communications and your intentions with your professors.

Professors' Profile	Students' Profile
1.	1.
2.	2.
3.	3.
4.	4.

Professors are just one audience type. Another example, politicians interact with several different audience types. As examples, a politician may interact with several different types of audiences: potential voters, professional colleagues, their staff, the press that reports the news. The head of a corporation also has specific audiences, including stockholders, suppliers, workers, lawmakers who regulate the business, and so on. Understanding the unique audience profiles of each audience type will help you to better predict how each audience type will react to the content and meaning of your communications. Before we go any further, take a few minutes to jot down some other audience types with whom you regularly interact. Also, please create an audience profile for each audience type. Please list their priorities and expectations of you. Try to make the list as comprehensive as possible.

Audience Type	Audience Profile
1.	1.
	2.
	3.
	4.
2.	1.
	2.
	3.
	4.
3.	1.
	2.
	3.
	4.
4.	1.
	2.
	3.
	4.
5.	1.
	2.
	3.
	4.

Involvement

Now that you have identified the different audience types that you interact with and their respective characteristics are profiled, let's define their drives, goals, and opinions regarding their expectations of you.

Involvement: A measure of the degree to which an audience type cares about the outcomes of your behavioral choices.

Involvement is *a measure of the degree to which an audience type cares about the outcomes of your behavioral choices.* An audience type's involvement measure can range on a scale from high involvement to no involvement and everything in between. That's because some audience types will care a great deal about the outcomes of your behavioral decision-making, and other audience types will not care.

In general, audience types with a big stake in your behavior, which are those audiences whose success and or reason for being relies on your behavior, will have high degrees of concern about your behavioral choices. They will have emotional reactions to your "behavioral performances." For example, parents are an audience type that can be generally profiled as being highly involved with their children. The typical parent has high degrees of love and concern about their children's well-being. They experience genuine feelings of happiness when their children do well. When children are happy, parents feel happy. But when the children of highly involved parents struggle in life, these parents typically experience genuine feelings of sadness and worry about their children. Highly involved parents seem to experience the same emotional highs and lows that their children experience.

On the other end of the involvement scale are audience types with low levels of involvement with you. These audience types are not impacted much by your behavior and will therefore have lower degrees of concern about your behavior. To illustrate the difference between high-involvement and low-involvement audience types, imagine that that you have just failed the very first test that you ever took in college. You failed because you really didn't study that much for the test and you were out the night before partying with friends. Now, suppose that the class average for the test was an 82 percent. How would you feel about your performance? How would your parents react? How would your classmates react? How would your friends react?

Most parents would be very concerned and worried about a child's low score because of the loving connection that bonds parents and children together. Parents and children share feelings and both are concerned about each other's long-term well-being. When their children are happy parents are happy. On the other hand, your test score probably would not impact your classmates in the least. That is because classmates are not personally impacted by your test score. In fact, they might even feel a sense of reassurance about themselves at your low performance because they might even be competing with you. Think about it, when your classmates score poorly on exams, do you feel anxious and concerned for them?

Here's another example. Suppose that at the very beginning of a semester you were assigned to write a group paper with five of your classmates in a world history class about World War II. The syllabus's grading rubric stipulated that 50 percent of your grade would be based on the quality of your paper, class attendance, participation, and online posts. But, the other 50 percent of your grade would be based on the quality of the group's compiled submission of all five papers. Each group member had thirteen weeks to research, write, and submit their part to the group. On week thirteen, the group met to pull everything together, but one of the group members hadn't done their part. How would you react to the team member that didn't do their part? This example shows that your involvement with audiences is fluid and can dramatically change depending on the circumstances. The thing to remember is that your audiences have varying expectations of you and will react to your behavioral performances depending on circumstances and the degree to which your behavior impacts them.

Think about It

You are involved with many other audiences. Understanding what motivates and is important to each of them will help you judge the appropriateness of the messages that you communicate and anticipate the reactions of audiences to your behavioral performances. How involved are the following audience types in your academic performance in college? Are they impacted by your academic performance? If so, in what ways are they impacted? Please jot down your thoughts.

	Audience Type	Involvement (Describe the degree to which each of these audiences is impacted by your academic performance.)
1	Professors	
2	Friends	
3	Transfer or graduate schools	
4	Future Employers	

Message

Let us return to the idea that talking and writing are not the main ways you communicate. As you will recall, only 7 percent of the substance and meaning of what you communicate is conveyed using words.[1] Yet many people try to explain away their own behavioral performance with words. This can be problematic because communicating with words through writing and speaking is actually quite a difficult thing to do well. To give you an idea of how difficult it is to communicate effectively using words, try to describe with words these two figures (see figure 4.1). Suppose that you were asked to describe with words the shapes of Shape A and Shape B, and then explain how both shapes are positioned in the drawing. How many words would you need to clearly describe what you are seeing?

Although the drawing is difficult to describe with words, the images are easy to understand visually. They are discernable without words. In the same way that this image speaks for itself, so too does your behavior. Your behavior reveals your feelings, moods, emotions, intentions, nature, and character. And because behavior speaks for itself, words that contradict behavior can reveal integrity-related issues, which can affect your relations with others. In fact, integrity is revealed *when our words and behaviors are in alignment.*

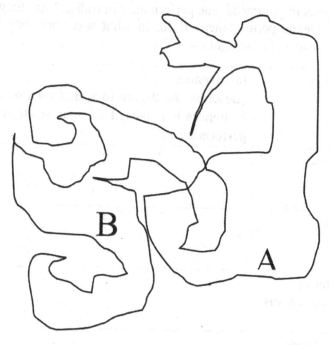

Figure 4.1. Communication Figure.

Everything that you do has message value. By making sure that your nonverbal, verbal, and written communications are conveying the same messages, you will be in a better position to communicate with integrity, a fundamental building block of trust. Creating understanding and meaning between people is a very difficult thing to accomplish without trust. We need look no further than the United States of America's current political climate to see how hard living and working in harmony with each other can be without trust. Without trust, meaningful and healthy long-term relations between individuals, regardless of context, (i.e., state and local governments, countries, religions, sexual orientations, races, and genders) are difficult because feelings of safety, belonging, forgiveness, openness, and goodwill cannot take root. Trust is the fertilizer that enriches the soil of human relationships. As the late author and leadership authority Stephen Covey noted, "Trust is the glue of life. It's the most essential ingredient in effective communication. It's the foundational principle that holds all relationships."[2] If audiences trust you, they will feel safe around you and be more willing to associate and be involved with you. The opposite is also true. If audiences don't trust you, they may not willingly want to interact or associate with you. They may not come right out and say anything to you, they just will not let you into their lives.

Think about It

Whom do you trust? Write down a person's name and the reasons why you selected that person. Specifically, what are the behaviors that inspire you to trust them? For example, "I trust my mom because she works very hard and has always been there for me." Please be as descriptive as possible by using as many adjectives as you can think of like "hardworking" and "dependable" to describe what makes this person trustworthy in your eyes.

Trustworthy Person	Reasons Why You Trust This Person (Please use adjectives to describe what makes this person trustworthy.)
	1
	2
	3

The one constant that either inspires or erodes trust is behavior. What adjectives did you use to describe the person's behavior that inspires you to trust them? Did you use adjectives like responsible, hardworking, competent, caring, resilient, fair, dependable, appropriate, or honest to describe this person? These adjectives represent how you think trustworthy people should be conducting themselves. In order for you to trust someone, they need to communicate certain traits. What's important to realize is that these adjectives are the building blocks of trust, not just for you, but for everyone. These are the exact same expectations that will inspire your audiences to trust you. Audiences will be looking for these behavioral traits when they interact with you.

What adjectives would audiences use to describe you? If you can honestly answer that they would describe you as being responsible, hardworking, competent, caring, resilient, fair, dependable, appropriate, and honest, you're on the right track. Audiences will forgive your flaws as long as you don't break the bonds of trust with them. But, if your behavior reveals that you are not these things, the foundation upon which trust is built can crumble. And audience forgiveness for trust-related shortcomings can disappear.

When the integrity and trust connections that bind you to your audiences break, audiences will react. They may immediately withdraw their involvement and support from you altogether, gradually become less sympathetic to your plight, or (the most pernicious of all) they may even outwardly pretend to be involved with you but inwardly walk away from you. And when people walk away from you, they probably will not even let you know, so you may not even realize that their support has been withdrawn until it is obvious that it has dried up.

Although there are ways to try to repair trust-related relationship problems, people are generally not eager to reengage with people that they do not trust. A better approach is to ceaselessly monitor and build trusting relationships with your audiences so that they don't become damaged in the first place. To do that, it is helpful to think about trust as the byproduct of the 5C Elements discussed in this book. Trust grows as a natural consequence of consistently communicating the following 5C Elements:

- Communication, appropriateness

- Choice, good judgment

- Caring, concern for others

- Commitment, duty regarding obligations

- Coping, fortitude

Whether you realize it or not, you are always communicating your understanding of the 5C Elements. The 5C Elements build trust, and the absence of these will diminish trust. In the same way that the students revealed what is true about themselves in their emails, your manner, tone of voice, emails, level of interest, motivation, dependability, judgment, nonverbal cues, appropriateness, and respectfulness reveal what is real and true about you. Remember that you cannot *not* communicate. What does your nonverbal, verbal, and written communication reveal about you?

Evidence

People sift through all of your written, verbal, and nonverbal communication looking for behavioral evidence of integrity and trust in all of the aspects of life that you alone are responsible for . . . the 5C Elements (see chapter 1). They want to see that you are appropriate, use good judgment, show concern for others, have a sense of duty about your obligations, and demonstrate fortitude when the going gets tough. Do you do all of these things well, or do you sometimes fall short in some way? No one is perfect, but if you do all of the 5C Elements consistently well, you earn trust because you communicate that you handle people, activities, and situations with integrity and trust. Although it is difficult to simultaneously do all of the 5Cs well all of the time, it is what behaviorally aware individuals strive to achieve.

What can you do to communicate more effectively, that is, behave in a manner that demonstrates integrity and trust? One way is to look for evidence of behavioral patterns that are consistent with the 5C Elements, or are antithetical to the 5C Elements. Everyone leaves behind clues about the way that they conduct themselves. Here are some examples of how people's behavioral patterns reveal that the 5Cs are not part of their modus operandi (the way they conduct themselves).

When you think about and evaluate communication effectiveness, it is relative to the 5C Elements. Each one of us filters all available communications through a trust sifter looking for behavioral evidence of appropriate communications, sound judgment when we make choices, reliable committed behavior, care and concern for others, and fortitude when dealing with challenging situations. As you begin to look at your behavior, you will begin to see that there are many different people (audiences) with whom you communicate. If it is your sincere wish to maintain good relationships with all of your people (audiences), the messages that you communicate and the way that you communicate are the means through which you will maintain and build those relationships. Let us look at three examples to see how the 5C Elements can be used to assess behavioral evidence.

In order for individuals to be viewed as being considerate of others, there must be an absence of inconsiderate behavior toward others. Patterns of disrespect, belittling, demeaning, abuse, or undermining others regularly would be evidence of an inconsiderate person. So, the fourth-grade math teacher who calls a student "stupid" in front of her entire class, or the rude and nasty radio and television talk-show personalities who berate others for not agreeing with their point of view, or the parent who regularly reprimands their children publicly are all exhibiting behavior that would be indicative of an inconsiderate person.

Similarly, for an individual to be viewed as being able to cope well with difficult, changing, or complex situations, there should be an absence of patterns of failing to cope well with these types of situations. For example, the surgeon that yells at the nurse when he is under pressure, or the pilot that freaks out when she encounters heavy turbulence, or the driver that flies into a rage when he is in traffic are all evidence of an inability to cope well with the stress associated with challenging situations. If evidence of patterns of failure to cope emerge, then it is reasonable to infer that the individual may not cope well with similar challenging situations in the future.

Likewise, for an individual to be deemed reliable and committed to an activity (at school, work, home) there should be an absence of patterns of uncommitted behavior. For example, the student that always arrives to class late and leaves in the middle of class, or the plumber that doesn't show up at all, or the roofer that installs a leaky roof are all evidence of uncommitted behavior. Again, it is entirely reasonable to assume that these individuals have other priorities and may not be committed to other types of related activities in the future. It is absolutely reasonable to use past performance to predict future performance.

This is not to say that behavior cannot change. However, it does suggest that unless people genuinely desire to change their behavior, it will probably continue. Remember, communicating effectively is not easy, and the consequences of sending conflicting messages can be severe. That is why it is important to be aware of whom you are communicating with (your audience), the level of concern of each audience (involvement), and what you are communicating both verbally and nonverbally (message). When the evidence shows that your actions do not match your words, you erode trust because you send out contradictory messages.

Personal Communication Policies

In addition to the AIME Model that helps you answer the What? When? How? Why? and Who? questions of communication, you will also create your own set of personal communication policies (PCPs). PCPs are your own self-created communication rules that help you by (1) taking the guesswork out of what you should and should not communicate, which helps ensure communication appropriateness in all situations, (2) establishing your own communication expectations of yourself, (3) reducing your own communication risk, and (4) improving your communication quality. Your personal communication plan will include personal communication policies for the following:

1. Law, ethics, and professionalism

2. Clarity of meaning and conciseness of style

3. Grammar, spelling, punctuation, and capitalization

4. Listening and understanding

5. Formality in written and oral communications

Let us take a look at each of these.

1. Personal Communication Policy for the Law, Ethics, and Professionalism

    1.1. Ensures that in public your written and oral communications are ethically and legally sound. Failure to comply with this standard communicates a breach of established criminal or civil law, or social customs and codes that could be punishable by incarceration, fine, or social sanctions that will make it difficult to maintain trusting relations with others. This standard is a communication minimum.

    1.2. Examples of unhelpful behavioral patterns for this standard to be avoided:

        1.2.1. Illegal behavior (i.e., discrimination, liable, slander, threats, intimidation, fraud, tax evasion, stealing, and robbery).

        1.2.2. Social behavior (i.e., bias, dishonesty, incivility, disrespectfulness, impoliteness, vulgarity, anger, hostility, aggression, abusiveness, plagiarism, cheating, talking about others, nepotism, favoritism, and off-color jokes).

1.3. PCP statement

    1.3.1. Your communication personal policy for the law, ethics, and professionalism:

_____

_____

_____

_____

_____

_____

2. Personal Communication Policy for Clarity of Meaning and Conciseness of Style

    2.1. Ensures that written and oral communications coherently get to the point. Enhances communication comprehension, credibility, objectivity, and accuracy. Failure to comply with this standard diverts audience attention away from the main point of the communication and instead conveys an inability to articulate conceptually complex or nuanced ideas in a sophisticated and succinct manner.

    2.2. Examples of unhelpful words, phrases, or mannerisms in oral or written communication that do not add meaning in academic, professional, and public contexts, including discussion posts, social media, blogs, emails, letters, memorandums, academic papers, written homework assignments, and voicemails..

        2.2.1. Examples of unhelpful words, phrases, and mannerisms to be avoided (after you read the sentences, please reread them without the bolded type to see how eliminating meaningless wording improves the sentences):

            2.2.1.1. You know and Like: "I **like** went on an interview on Monday **you know**."

            2.2.1.2. Very: "I attended a **very** cool class the other day."

            2.2.1.3. Totally: "I think that it's **totally** admirable that you were able to overcome so much adversity in your life."

2.2.1.4.   Literally: "I **literally** studied for the test for only one day."

2.2.1.5.   For sure: "I **for sure** will never do that again."

2.2.1.6.   OK and So: "**OK so** he then became very rude in the meeting."

2.2.1.7.   Yes: "**Yes** that seems right to me."

2.2.1.8.   Really or Very: "She was **really very** qualified for the position."

2.2.1.9.   So and Basically: "**So** he **basically** was unable to complete the test in the time allowed."

2.2.1.10.   Of course: "I **of course** passed the course with a very good grade."

2.2.1.11.   All right: "**All right** we are now going to move into chapter 5 of the text."

2.2.1.12.   Perfectly: "That's **perfectly** fine; we can sign the papers now that we've negotiated this final part of the agreement."

2.2.2.   Examples of wordiness to be avoided in academic, professional, and public contexts, including discussion posts, social media, blogs, emails, letters, memorandums, academic papers, written homework assignments, and voicemails. (after you read the sentences. Please read the revised sentence to see how eliminating unnecessary words improves the sentences):

2.2.2.1.   Wordy: "Can you please note this **as being** an excused absence?" Revised: "Can you please note this as an excused absence."

2.2.2.2.   Wordy: "**In spite of the fact that** she missed the train, she was **able to be** on time for class." Revised: "**Although** she missed the train, she was on time for class."

2.2.2.3.   Wordy: "**Sharon's accusation of** her husband's infidelity **was unfair.**" Revised: "Sharon unfairly accused her husband of infidelity."

2.2.2.4.   Wordy: "Dave is very tall **for his height**." Revised: "Dave is very tall."

2.2.2.5.   Wordy: "**I am of the** opinion that college classwork should not be graded." Revised: "**My** opinion is that college homework should not be graded."

2.2.2.6.   Wordy: "**The fact of the matter is that** she does a good job despite a challenging home life." Revised: "She does a good job despite a challenging home life."

2.2.2.7.   Wordy: "The professor did not **give any indication** of his grading policy." Revised: "The professor did not **indicate** his grading policy."

2.2.2.8.   Wordy: "This sentence is **definitely** wordy." Revised: "This sentence is wordy."

2.2.2.9.   Wordy: "This **particular** part of the book **is excessively** wordy." Revised: "This part of the book is wordy."

2.2.2.10.   Wordy: "**Due to the fact that** this is not an English textbook, this is only a **very** small list of examples of wordiness." Revised: "**Because** this is not an English textbook, this only includes a small list of examples of wordiness."

2.3. PCP Statement

2.3.1.   Your personal communication policy for clarity of meaning and conciseness of style:

_____

_____

_____

_____

_____

3. Personal Communication Policy for Grammar, Spelling, Punctuation, and Capitalization

    3.1. Ensures that written communications comply with minimum writing conventions. Enhances communication comprehension, credibility, and accuracy. Failure to comply with these standards diverts audience attention away from the primary messages and conveys carelessness, or an inability or unwillingness to meet minimum academic and professional writing standards.

    3.2. Examples of grammar, spelling, punctuation, and capitalization to be avoided:

        3.2.1. "hey i was wondering if you could send me the homework and everything else that we did in class and again i am sorry that i could not be there but if you would send me the homework for monday and last monday and wednesday please so that i can get what we did in class and so i can study the things and know what we did thank you that would be great thankyou see you on monday and sorry that i could not e there."

    3.3. PCP Statement

        3.3.1. Your personal communication policy for grammar, spelling, punctuation, and capitalization:

_____

_____

_____

_____

_____

4. Personal Communication Policy for Listening and Understanding

    4.1. Ensures comprehension and empathy for others' points of view. Failure to listen to what is communicated creates misunderstanding because it conveys an inability to understand or unwillingness to understand others' opinions, thoughts, and ideas.

4.2. Examples of listening and understanding communication patterns to be avoided:

    4.2.1. Talking instead of listening

    4.2.2. Uncontrolled emotions

    4.2.3. Interrupting

    4.2.4. Changing the subject

    4.2.5. Disinterest

    4.2.6. Silent and unresponsive

    4.2.7. Not finding common ground

    4.2.8. Failure to ask questions

    4.2.9. Closemindedness

    4.2.10. Avoiding eye contact

    4.2.11. Not writing things down

    4.2.12. Lateness or not showing up

    4.2.13. Leaving early

    4.2.14. Distracted

    4.2.15. Looking at the clock on the wall, computer screen, or cell phone when someone is talking

4.3. PCP Statement

    4.3.1. Your personal communication policy for listening and understanding:

_____

_____

_____

_____

_____

_____

5. Personal Communication Policy for Formality in Written and Oral Communications

5.1. Ensures formal written and oral communications are accurate, objective, and respectful. Failure to comply with this standard trivializes communication, conveys impropriety, subjectivity, and superficiality of understanding.

5.2. Examples of written and oral communication patterns for this standard to be avoided:

    5.2.1. Disrespect

    5.2.2. ALL CAPS

    5.2.3. Negativity

    5.2.4. Informal language and slang (examples): "heyyyy," "hey," "i," "eye'm," "u," "lol," "thats," "ty," "omg," "hi," "howdy," "emojis," "cool," "awesome," "you betcha," and "honey do list"

    5.2.5. Use of jargon including industry-specific buzzwords, use of abbreviations, and acronyms without introducing term definitions

    5.2.6. Inappropriate humor

    5.2.7. Bias related to gender, age, political, race, and health

5.3. PCP Statement

    5.3.1. Your personal communication policy for formality in written and oral communications:

_____

_____

_____

_____

Now that you have your own personal communication policies, you have another tool to help you take the guesswork out of communicating in formal and informal settings, reduce your own communication risk, and improve your communication quality.

Communication Effectiveness: A Self-Assessment

One of your most important individual responsibilities is to communicate effectively. This chapter acquaints you with what needs to be done in order to communicate effectively. The work has been organized and presented so that you should be able to achieve mastery of nonverbal, verbal, and written communication fundamentals.

This chapter also includes an introduction to the five personal communication standards and the AIME Model. Each of these topics has been introduced and its underlying ideas reemphasized with examples. In addition, you were given an opportunity to develop your own personal communication policy statements for each standard and to personalize the AIME Model to your particular situation.

When you evaluate your own communication effectiveness, you will be able to compare your own performance to these new predetermined standards defined in this chapter. Assessing your communication effectiveness is important because it provides you with your own policy-based measurement of how your communication comports with sound communication theory and practice. This gives you an opportunity to critically think about your own communication, which can help you understand what you are doing well and areas that you might want to improve. To see if you are consistently sending messages that are in your best interest, please take a few minutes to complete table 4.2.

Using the behavioral observation scale (table 4.3) as a guide, write in the rating column the number corresponding to the degree to which you consistently exhibit the behavior described in the statement. Note, there are

Table 4.2. Communications Effectiveness Behavioral Observation Scale Self-Assessment

5	4	3	2	1
Role Model		**Meets Expectations**		**Below Expectations**
Can be trusted to independently and willingly craft verbal, written, and nonverbal communications that are appropriate and aligned with audience expectations. expectations.		With guidance from others, is willing to work on the responsibility of crafting verbal, written, and nonverbal communications that are appropriate and aligned with audience		Even with guidance from others, is unwilling to work on the responsibility of crafting verbal, written, and nonverbal communications that are appropriate and aligned with audience expectations.

Source: Author-created.

Table 4.3. Behavioral Observation Scale

5 = Almost always performs as described by the Role Model standards.
4 = Sometimes performs as described by the Role Model standards and sometimes performs as described by the Meets Expectations standards.
3 = Almost always performs as described by the Meets Expectations standards.
2 = Sometimes performs as described by the Meets Expectations standards and sometimes performs as described by the Below Expectations standards.
1 = Almost always performs as described by the Below Expectations standards.

	Action Statement	Rating
1	I choose the best medium to communicate before I communicate (face to face, phone call, text message, voicemail, memo, email, letter).	
2	I take time to properly construct voice, text, and email communications before I communicate.	
3	I identify the most important messages that I am trying to communicate before I send out messages.	
4	I try to read the nonverbal cues of others and myself before I communicate.	
5	I consider my level of involvement with each audience when I communicate (High, Medium, or Low).	
6	I identify what's most important to me and the points of view of audiences when I communicate.	
7	I tailor my messages to ensure that the tone and content are appropriate to audiences when I communicate.	
8	I consider how my messages will impact my audience and myself when I communicate.	
9	I actively listen by asking questions and demonstrating attention to and conveying understanding of the comments and questions of others when I communicate.	
10	I control my emotions and remain positive even when demands are placed on me when I communicate.	
11	I make sure that my choice of nonverbal, verbal, and written communications are the same message when I communicate.	
12	I communicate clearly, using appropriate style, format, grammar, and tone.	
13	I choose my actions and words carefully to be respectful of others when I communicate (even when I'm upset).	
14	I make sure that my actions and words are timely when I communicate.	
15	I think about how my nonverbal, verbal, and written communications will impact my character, relationships, and future when I communicate.	

Source: Author-created.

no right or wrong answers. All that is important is that you indicate how consistently you exhibit the behavior described in the action statement.

Now transfer your answers for each statement into the corresponding space in table 4.4.

Table 4.4. Communication Behavior Mapping Table

Item (n)	Behavior	AIME	Behavior Rating	AIME Average
1	Communication	Audience		
2	Communication	Audience		
3	Communication	Audience		
4	Communication	Involvement		
5	Communication	Involvement		
6	Communication	Involvement		
7	Communication	Involvement		
8	Communication	Message		
9	Communication	Message		
10	Communication	Message		
11	Communication	Message		
12	Communication	Message		
13	Communication	Message		
14	Communication	Message		
15	Communication	Evidence		
Average				

Average = Σ of Behavior Rating/15: [   ]

Source: Author-created.

Greater than 4: If your average is between 4 and 5, you are a good communicator, you avoid communication problems, and you require little guidance to communicate appropriately.

Between 3 and 4: If your average is greater than 3 but less than 4, with guidance you can communicate appropriately, but occasionally you may be sending some messages that conflict with your goals.

Less than 3: If your average is less than 3, you sometimes communicate appropriately, but occasionally, even with guidance, you fail to communicate appropriately.

Take your averages for this unit, calculate the new average of averages, and input that information into your employability profile.

1	2	3	4	5
Below Expectations		**Meets Expectations**		**Role Model**
Even with guidance from others, fails to provide evidence of behavioral understanding of the 5C Elements and cannot be trusted with responsibility, and is unwilling to work on the responsibility of self-management.		With guidance, provides evidence of behavioral understanding of the 5C Elements and can be trusted with responsibility.		Independently and willingly provides evidence of behavioral understanding of the 5C Elements and can be trusted with responsibility.

Where:

5 =	Almost always performs as described by the "Role Model" standard.
4 =	Sometimes performs as described by the "Role Model" standard and sometimes performs as described by the "Meets Expectations" standard.
3 =	Almost always performs as described by the "Meets Expectations" standard.
2 =	Sometimes performs as described by the "Meets Expectations" standard and sometimes performs as described by the "Below Expectations" standard.
1 =	Almost always performs as described by the "Below Expectations" standard.

Communication
Trust a person to convey messages appropriately.

- Audience
- Involvement
- Message
- Evidence
- COMMUNICATION MEAN

- BEHAVIORAL COMPETENCY RATING (MEAN OF MEANS)

Choices
Trust a person to use good judgment.

- Communication
- Commitment
- Coping
- Caring
- Choice
- CHOICE MEAN

Commitment
Trust a person to be dutiful.

- Dependability Attendance
- Dependability Accountability
- Dependability Contribution
- Hard Work Time Deliberate Practice
- Hard Work Delayed Gratification
- Hard Work Effort Energy
- Hard Work Effort Determination
- Hard Work Effort Stamina
- Quality Measure of Excellence
- Quality Continuous Improvement
- COMMITMENT MEAN

Coping
Trust a person to demonstrate fortitude during difficult times.

- Coping Change Demonstration
- Coping Adversity Self-Awareness
- Coping Adversity Self-Restraint
- Coping Adversity Self-Improvement
- Coping Complexity Capacity
- Coping Complexity Capability
- Coping Complexity Activities
- COPING MEAN

Caring
Trust a person to show concern for others.

- Caring Civility Listening
- Caring Civility Courtesy
- Caring Civility Consideration
- Caring Helpfulness Concern
- Caring Helpfulness Cooperation
- Caring Helpfulness Compromise
- Caring Conscientious Thoughtfulness
- Caring Conscientious Carefulness
- Caring Conscientious Fairness
- Caring Common Good Respect
- Caring Common Good Equity
- Caring Common Good Goodwill
- CARING MEAN

Think about It

In 1606 William Shakespeare wrote, "Mend your speech a little, lest you may mar your fortunes." As Shakespeare understood four centuries ago, communicating effectively is fundamental to human success. The communication behavior mapping table shows you how appropriately you communicate to others. Do you communicate appropriately to others? If not, why not?

Changing Habits

How can you employ Fogg's Behavior Model tiny habits (see chapter 1) to improve how you communicate with people? As you think about changing your habits, think about framing the tiny habit using Dr. Fogg's formula:

Format for a tiny habit:

After I (insert existing behavior),

I will (insert new tiny behavior).

Please take a few moments and try to come up with one tiny communication habit that you can use to help you improve how you communicate. Remember to use the format, "After I (insert existing behavior), I will (insert new tiny behavior)."

After I _____ ,

I will _____ .

Communication Personal Policy Contract

To help you achieve your behavioral goals, you will be writing them down to create personal policy contracts like the following one. By signing and dating the personal policy contract, it becomes an obligation to yourself that cannot be broken. Please attach additional pages if more space is needed.

Communication Goals

Goals	Communication goal(s) that will guide how I communicate in college: _____ _____ _____ _____
Personal Policies	Personal policies I will follow when I communicate with others: _____ _____ _____
Public Commitments	Public commitments that I will make to regularly measure how I am doing regarding my communication goals and personal policies. I will send my goals, personal policies, and quick weekly progress reports to a supportive friend and the professor. _____ _____ _____ _____
Signature: _____ **Date:** _____	

Key Terms

- AIME Model
- Audience
- Audience Profile
- Audience Types
- Evidence

- Involvement
- Messages
- Personal Communication Strategy (PCS)

Discussion Questions

1. Explain the AIME Model. Please define each of the variables in the model?

2. What are the five questions that a well-defined personal communication strategy should answer?

3. Explain the five personal communication policies and why each of them is important.

4. Clarity of meaning and conciseness in style are important when you communicate in formal academic and professional settings. Explain why they are important and give three examples of written communication that violates this policy.

5. Define the terms *audience type* and *audience profile*. What is the distinction between a formal audience type and an informal audience type?

6. Explain how listening and understanding reduces the likelihood of communication problems?

7. List some of the challenges that you face when you use electronic forms of communication to communicate.

To Sum Up

- A well-defined personal communication strategy helps you answer questions like:

   o Whom am I communicating with?

- o How should I communicate with them (nonverbal, verbal, written)?

- o How should I communicate with them?

- o When should I communicate with them?

- o What should I communicate about myself?

- The AIME (Audience, Involvement, Message, Evidence) Model helps you:

  - o Identify the different audiences that you interact with and their unique characteristics

  - o Outline your level of involvement with each audience type

  - o Identify the messages that each audience type will be looking for from you

  - o Analyze how your actions are evidence that substantiate claims that you make about yourself

- Your personal communication strategy will include personal communication policies for the following:

  - o Law, ethics, and professionalism in public settings

  - o Clarity of meaning and conciseness of style

  - o Grammar, spelling, punctuation, and capitalization in formal and professional settings

  - o Listening and understanding

  - o Formality in written and oral communications in academic and professional settings

- Your verbal and written communication should always be supported by your nonverbal communication to build integrity and trust with others.

- The communication effectiveness self-assessment and behavior mapping table help you quantify how effectively you are communicating with others.

Changing tiny habits can help you to improve the way you communicate.

Section III

CHOICE

How to understand, communicate, and assess judgment-based trust regarding the quality of decision-making and an introduction to decision-making prioritization methodology

5

UNDERSTANDING JUDGMENT AND CHOICES

After reading this chapter, you should be able to:

- Define what laws and personal policies are and the differences between the two terms.

- Explain what the age of responsibility is and define responsibility.

- Understand the link between consciousness and choosing, and how choosing is related to our well-being individually and collectively.

- List the five variables in the framework for the choosing model.

- Define the values model and the importance of aligning choices with your values.

- Explain the terms *situational awareness* and *situational blindness* and how they relate to making good choices.

- Understand why you have more control over your behavior than you might think, and how you can change your behavior tomorrow by changing your choices today.

Understanding Choice

We are our choices.

—Jean-Paul Sartre

Why Do Choices Matter?

If you have ever seen an out-of-control political protest or sporting event, or almost been crushed by zombie-like concertgoers, or were stuck in a maddening traffic jam for hours, then you can understand the need for social order. We can define **social order** as *individuals and groups willingly abiding by rules that govern their public conduct to keep individuals and society safe, secure, and stable.* The key word in that definition is willingly. Not willingly following laws is not self-managing behavior.

Social Order: Individuals and groups willingly abiding by rules that govern their public conduct to keep individuals and society safe, secure, and stable.

Laws: Macroscale rules that societies develop and willingly follow for maintaining social order.

Laws are *macroscale rules that societies develop and willingly follow for maintaining social order.* Personal policies are microscale rules that individuals develop and willingly follow to achieve goals within societies. Stated another way, laws manage behavior at a societal level; personal policies manage behavior at an individual level. For example, the law against stealing a loaf of bread applies to society as a whole (no one is supposed to steal), whereas your own decision not to steal is specific to you. You may decide to refrain from doing something that is perfectly legal for others to do; for example, it may be your personal policy to always wear a raincoat when it's raining, but others might not follow your lead.

When a society governs itself, it:

- Collectively determines the rules of how it will function based on a vision of the type of people they want to be.

- Codifies those rules into laws.

- Willingly follows those laws without having to be asked.

- Enforces compliance of the laws through large-scale policing.

When individuals govern themselves, they:

1. Self-determine the rules for how they will function, based on the person they want be.

2. Self-codify those rules into personal policies.

3. Willingly follow those rules without having to be asked.

4. Self-enforce compliance of these rules when they make choices.

If people need to be asked to follow either laws or rules, they are not self-managing. Perhaps the best place to understand the role that our individual and collective choices play in our lives is to look at the link between our choices and consciousness.

Choices and Consciousness

It is midnight and your decision-making begins: Do you go to bed, continue studying, submit your homework, turn the light off, play a video game, watch TV, party with your friends, pull the curtains down, cross your legs, take a shower, brush your teeth, put your clothes in the hamper, drop your cloths on the floor, text your friend, set the alarm, brush your teeth, floss, set up the coffee maker, read in bed, sleep on your left side, right side, back, stomach, knees touching, get a snack? And so, it goes, on and on and on, every day for your entire life. Researchers estimate that the average adult makes an astounding thirty-five thousand decisions each day.[1] That works out to more than two choices per second (86,400 seconds per day divided by 35,000 choices per day). And because you are sleeping for about one-third of the day, you actually make even more than two choices per second during your waking hours. To put that number into perspective, the average adult only takes twenty-two thousand breaths each day.[2]

Despite being the most important determinant of our individual and collective destiny, there is no formalized education or instruction that teaches people what good judgment is or how to make those thirty-five thousand daily choices good ones. As we discussed in the introduction, it is not unreasonable to argue that the purpose of education is twofold: (1) to help all people (individually and collectively) fulfill their unrealized potential; and (2) to give all people the tools that they need to leave the world a better place than they found it. How do we individually and collectively fulfill these worthy goals without recognizing or even seeing the strong influence that decision-making plays in the destiny of individuals and societies? The ability to see things is sometimes hardest when what we cannot see is in plain view directly in front of us. This story underscores that simple fact:

> There are these two young fish swimming along and they happen to meet an older fish swimming the other way, who nods at them and says, "Morning, boys. How's the water?" And the two young fish swim on for a bit, and then eventually one

of them looks over at the other and said, "What the hell is water?"[3]

We make so many choices each day that we may not even realize that everything that we do when we are conscious involves some sort of choice. Our choices are like the water in which the fish swim; it's there, but they are not thinking about it constantly, just like we don't think about the air that we breathe. The act of choosing between different alternatives is so difficult to see because it is inextricably linked to our consciousness.

Consciousness can be defined as *an awareness of and response to situations that we experience.* Our choices are predictive responses to situations. At college, choices are how students interact with the reality of college. College students may begin to see how everything that they do requires some sort of decision. Although many of the choices are routine (cream in your coffee, color of your socks, hairstyle, room color) and can be made without much thought, other choices are life impacting and can be life changing (college, marriage, career). Choices are an omnipresent aspect of college. Every moment of the day students make choices.

No one else is walking in your shoes, so no one else can make your choices for you. What you think involves making choices. How you communicate to faculty and other students involves making choices. How committed you are to college-related activities (going to class, doing homework, following through on group projects) involves making choices. How caring you are to others (faculty, transfer students, other college personnel) involves making choices. How well you cope with difficulty (academic complexity, financial problems, low grades) involves making choices. Even how you make choices (do you take academic advice from trusted sources such as academic advisors, faculty, and parents or friends) involves making choices. In other words, students cannot not make choices. Not making a choice is a choice.

Equally important, the choices you make transmit information about what is important to you. As such, your choices in college not only define you to yourself; they also define you to others (i.e., faculty, transfer schools, potential employers). Because college is such an expensive and life-changing experience, you should make choices that maximize your chances of doing well in this high-stakes opportunity. You can begin by taking a moment to realize that everything that you do when you are a conscious in college involves some sort of choice.

Consciousness: An awareness of and response to situations that we experience.

Think about It

What are some of the thirty-five thousand daily choices that students make that maximize their chances of staying in college? What are some choices that students make that minimize their chances of staying in college?

Choices That Maximize College Success

_____

_____

_____

_____

_____

_____

Choices That Minimize College Success

_____

_____

_____

_____

_____

_____

Choices and Responsibility

At what point do people become responsible for their choices? At what age should conscious decision-making start and acting on impulse stop? Let's begin to answer these questions by examining the difference between infant and adult behavior.

Infants are **behaviorally impulsive**. That is to say, infant *behavioral actions are done without forethought*, because infants are oblivious to abstract concepts like risk, consequences, and responsibility. Infants are not critical thinkers, which means that infants do not have the ability to carefully think about ideas and concepts that exist beyond what is experienced with the five senses (seeing, hearing, touching, tasting, smelling). If infants cannot see it, hear it, touch it, taste it, or smell it, they do not react to it. **Critical thinking** is defined as the *analysis of available facts, evidence, observation, and arguments to form a judgment.*[4] Because infants cannot think critically about what they are experiencing and doing, they cannot solve problems and make predictions about what will happen

Behaviorally Impulsive: Behavioral actions that are done without forethought.

Critical Thinking: Analysis of available facts, evidence, observation, and arguments to form a judgment.

in the future by making certain choices. For example, infants cannot understand phenomena like impulsiveness, appropriateness, behavioral cause and effect, behavioral norms, standards and patterns, behavioral consequences, and behavioral rules.

Because infants are not cognitively developed enough to think critically about what they are doing, they are not responsible when their behavior violates behavioral norms. Responsibility is defined as having a palpable sense of duty about one's obligations to others. For example, when a baby screams at the top of their lungs while on a seven-hour flight from New York to London, air marshals are not called in to arrest and remove them from planes because it would presuppose that they are familiar with concepts like behavioral norms, personal policies, and behavioral rules. How can infants flout rules with flagrant disregard if rules are incomprehensible to them?

Unlike infants, college students are expected to have developed the ability to comprehend reality and analyze available facts, evidence, and arguments to form judgments. As such, college students should have a fairly well-developed understanding of behavioral rules, and also behavioral cause and effect. College students should also be able to accurately predict the effect that their behavioral choices will have on themselves and others. The ability to forecast what will happen in the future if we make certain types of behavioral choices is a behavioral hallmark of maturity and adulthood. College students are considered adults.

College students are legally responsible for behavioral consequences when they reach eighteen years of age. As such, college students are expected to think about what they are doing and adjust their behavior before they make choices because they are responsible and accountable for every choice that they make in college. They are responsible and accountable for reading all assignments, studying, doing homework, writing their own papers, and performing well on exams.

Society expects college students to appropriately adapt their behavior to the environment. Colleges also expect their students to appropriately adapt their behavior to life in college. Unlike infants, mature adults cannot SCREAM AT THE TOP OF THEIR LUNGS on planes just because they are uncomfortable or upset or when things do not go their way. Air marshals would be called in to remove and arrest screaming adults from planes for this type of behavior. Unlike infants, college students cannot SCREAM AT THE TOP OF THEIR LUNGS just because they are uncomfortable or upset or when things do not go their way.

Photos 5.1 and 5.2. A baby screaming uncontrollably is not held responsible for their actions, whereas an adult would be. *Photo 5.1 Source:* Dave Buchwald; Creative Commons Attribution-Share Alike 3.0 Unported. *Photo 5.2 Source:* Depositphotos.

Think about It

Juan arrived at college with great expectations. But when he started attending classes, he had difficulty completing the work or even understanding the topics that were being taught. He panicked because he didn't know how to address this situation and began skipping classes. Before the first semester was over, he had dropped out of school, feeling like he had failed at one of his key goals.

Like Juan, many first-time freshman students are not successful in college. Between the fall semesters of 2019 and 2020, 24.1 percent of all first-time, full-time freshmen dropped out of college.[5]

In your view, why do you think that so many students are not successful? Does the statistic surprise you? Explain your answer.

_____

_____

_____

_____

_____

_____

A Framework for Choosing

Ideally, good choices are informed by a number of factors. Making any choice before critically thinking about and then validating these factors prior to choosing is nothing more than **guesswork**, which is defined here as *knowingly making a choice with little or no information*.

Good judgment and sound choices are informed by your: goals and intentions, situational awareness, values and ethics, reasoning, and personal policies. In a reason-based world, these variables are organized and considered before choices involving actions and words are made.

Figure 5.1 outlines the framework within which you can gather, organize, and analyze information prior to choosing between different alternatives. Each factor plays an essential part in determining the best choices, which should be done before you make any choices, not after. Remember, the truism is "ready, aim, fire" not "fire, ready, aim." If you are not consciously analyzing these factors prior to making choices, you are operating in a state of **situational blindness**, which is defined here as *lacking the information required for understanding, discernment, and comprehension of meaning*. Ignoring these factors when you make choices is just as bad as driving a car with your eyes closed. Choices made in the absence of understanding, discerning, and comprehending meaning are situationally blind. Although hindsight is twenty-twenty, the formation of judgments and decisions based on situational blindness is often at the heart of poor decision-making and feelings of regret. Let's review each of these factors.

Guesswork: Knowingly making a choice with little or no information.

Situational Blindness: Lacking the information required for understanding, discernment, and comprehension of meaning.

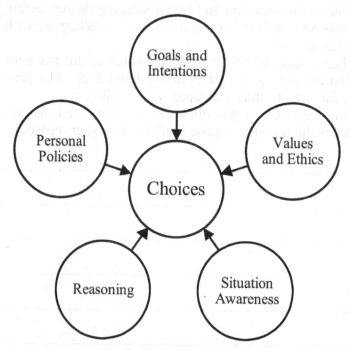

Figure 5.1. A Framework for Choosing. *Source:* Author-created.

Goals and Intentions

Goals are defined here as *future-oriented ambitions that you would like to achieve, and that would bring you a sense of satisfaction with yourself and minimize regret.* Goals are destinations on the map of life. For example, imagine that you are looking at a map of the world and you are in New York City, and you want to go to Los Angeles. Los Angeles would be your goal.

The goal of choosing is to (1) help individuals actualize their unrealized potential and, in doing so, (2) bring about a sense of individual satisfaction with their life circumstances. The choices that you will be making in college and beyond will take you to a future reality of your own making. Choices that would take you to destinations that are contrary to these two worthy goals—that actualize within you feelings of bitterness, anger, and dissatisfaction with your life circumstances—are antithetical to your own self-interest because they lead you away from your desired future reality. Nobody wakes up in the morning and says to themselves, "I'd really like to skip getting dressed today."

Choices are the mechanisms that help all people actualize their goals by bringing about a state of fulfillment or contentment with life's circumstances and avoid feelings of regret, worry, and longing for something better than what they have achieved. Have you ever reflected on your own choices? Have you ever thought about your choices relative to the long-term goal of well-being and contentedness with yourself? Have you ever asked:

- How can I make choices today that are linked to my goals of tomorrow?

- How can I prioritize different alternatives when I make choices?

- How can I change my behavior?

- How can I tell if my choices are good or bad?

If you have asked yourself these questions, what have you done about answering these questions? This section gives you the tools that you need to examine and assess your own choices in a precise and valuable way. This section is also intended to help improve the quality of your choices and answer such questions as:

- How good is my judgment?

- How good are my choices?

- How good can my choices be?

Goals: Future-oriented ambitions that you would like to achieve, and that would bring you a sense of satisfaction with yourself and minimize regret.

These types of questions will help you develop and continuously improve your own judgment by aligning your daily choices with your goals and aspirations. Importantly, these types of questions will also help you predict and steer clear of many of the avoidable struggles that are associated with making choices that are uninformed by your own self-created rules and personal policies.

Think about It

Emily is looking for a lab partner to work with in her first-year chemistry class. She approached three other possible partners, Juan, Betsy, and Miguel. How could she evaluate who would be the best partner for her? She'll want to know if she can trust her partner to be reliable, trustworthy, and capable to determine if it is in her best interest to be involved with them. She will be looking for answers to questions like:

- Is this person a good decision-maker?
- Is this person fair-minded?
- Is this person respectful of others?
- Is this person easy to work with?
- Is this person reasonable? Or temperamental?
- Is this person someone I want to be involved with?

Think about the impression you make on others. Can you honestly answer "yes" to all, some, or none of these questions? Importantly, would other people that interact with you honestly answer "yes" to all, some, or none of these questions about you? If you answered "no" to any of these questions, can you give examples of things that you have done that would bring people to that answer?

_____

_____

_____

_____

If others consider you to be respectful, fair, easy to work with, appropriate, reasonable, levelheaded, and evenhanded, then they will be more likely to trust you and form meaningful professional and personal relationships with you. Most people will never confront you or tell you directly that you are difficult or unpleasant to be around; they will just reduce their involvement with you. You have to be conscious of the impact your behavior has on other people.

Your **intentions**, on the other hand, are *choices that actualize your now-oriented ambitions in the present and are concerned only with your current state of being*. Whereas goals are the destination, intentions are roads on the map of life that can lead you closer to or further away from your desired future reality. Continuing with the map example. If you are in NYC and you decide to take I-95 North toward Maine, you have chosen a route that will take you further from LA. The most efficient way to get to LA from NYC is to immediately head west.

Choices are informed when they align with long-term goals. As we discussed earlier, intentions are now-oriented ambitions and primarily associated with short-term thinking. Informed choices are more strategic in nature and are made with long-term goals in mind. As such, informed choices would tend to err on the side of **long-termism**, which we can define here as *concentrating on your long-term objectives, such as maximizing well-being and minimizing long-term regret, at the expense of your short-term desires*. The opposite of long-termism is **short-termism**, which would be to *make choices that maximize your short-term objectives, at the expense of your long-term ambitions*.

Chenglei has the long-term ambition to do well in college, graduate with distinction, and get a well-paying job when she graduates, but she might also have short-term desires to go out and party with friends before her school work is done. Although these two competing desires can simultaneously coexist within her mind, they cannot both be fulfilled because they are antithetical to each other. If she chooses to go out and party with friends instead of doing her homework or studying for tests, she is guilty of short-termism because she is prioritizing her now-oriented ambitions ahead of her future-oriented ambitions. It will only become obvious that short-termism is poor personal policy in college when the student does poorly in college.

Another nonacademic example of short-termism is building a house in a floodplain. Hiromi wants to build a beautiful grand house, but the only affordable building site is in a floodplain. If he chooses to purchase the site and build his house in a floodplain instead of waiting for an affordable location in an area that does not flood, Hiromi is prioritizing his short-term ambitions ahead of his long-term well-being. It will become painfully obvious that building a house in a floodplain was not a great idea when it floods and his investment is lost.

The thing that is so problematic about poor strategic choices is that they are all difficult to recover from, which makes them all high-stakes choices. Graduating with a low grade point average (GPA) requires the same amount of money and time (sometimes even more) than it does to

Intentions: Choices that actualize your now-oriented ambitions in the present and are concerned only with your current state of being.

Long-Termism: Concentrating on your long-term objectives, such as maximizing well-being and minimizing long-term regret, at the expense of your short-term desires.

Short-Termism: Choices that maximize your short-term objectives, at the expense of your long-term ambitions.

graduate with a high GPA. You cannot get the investments in time and money back. It takes the same amount of time and money (the cost of the land will be less) to build a house in a floodplain as it does to build a house in a location that does not flood. How do you fix a poor GPA or a house that is in a floodplain? Who owns those decisions?

Is there a way to balance long-term and short-term ambitions? Yes. By prioritizing your day so that you complete the most important activities before doing less important ones, you can satisfy both your long-term and short-term ambitions. For example, try to get all of your schoolwork done first thing, when you wake up. To achieve this goal, you may need to get up very early in the morning and consume many gallons of coffee. However, this will benefit you in two ways: (1) Your brain will be fresher because you will have just woken up, which will make knowledge acquisition easier; and (2) You will knock off the most difficult thing that you need to do first, which will help you enjoy the rest of your day more. This is a good personal policy.

Think about It

Compare these two images of college students pursuing their goals.

Which group appears to be pursuing their long-term versus short-term interests? How successful in school (and life) do you think each of these people will be? Explain your answer.

_____

_____

_____

_____

_____

If you prioritize your long-term interests ahead of your short-term ones you are not taking "all the fun" out of your day. You are just delaying your short-term interests until the important work of securing your future well-being is completed. To do the opposite, to consistently demonstrate patterns of prioritizing now-oriented ambitions ahead of future-oriented ambitions is akin to building your life on a floodplain. It is shortsighted and will lead to regret.

Values and Ethics

Your choices are informed when they align with your values and ethics. **Values** are the *underlying set of principles (or rules) that govern your thinking, judgment, behavior, and ultimately every choice that you make.* Your values represent what you believe to be is right, fair, and just in the world. Your values are what:

1. Is important to you

2. Defines your purpose and character

3. Brings you long-term sense of well-being

Values: Underlying set of principles (or rules) that govern your thinking, judgment, behavior, and, ultimately, every choice that you make.

Your values can be represented by the Values Model (see figure 5.2).

Making choices that do not align with your values is, by definition, bad judgment precisely because they are contradictory to the three key elements of the Values Model. Making choices that do not align with your values can only bring you temporary or false happiness, but it does so at the expense of your longer-term contentment and well-being. When your choices in the present are not in alignment with your values, you may feel guilty about the obvious contradiction between your choices and your values.

People are different. Each one of us is born with our own unique brains, presumably so that we can think for ourselves. As such, the values that are important to you, define your purpose and character, and bring you a long-term sense of well-being may also be unique to you. As such, only you can define the values that will bring you true contentment and well-being in life.

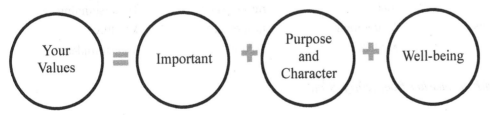

Figure 5.2. Values Model. *Source:* Author-created.

Think about It

Take a few minutes and carefully go the through this list of values and jot down or circle three values that are (1) important to you, (2) define your character and purpose, and (3) bring you long-term well-being. After you have identified the three values, please take some time and write down why each meets these three criteria. If the values that are important to you are not on this list, please feel free to create your own.

Values List

Accountability	Decisiveness	Graciousness	Motivated	Risk-taker
Achievement	Dedicated	Happy	Nice	Romantic
Adaptability	Dependable	Hard worker	Objective	Satisfied
Admirable	Determination	Harmony	Open-minded	Self-aware
Altruism	Dignity	Healthy	Optimistic	Self-reliant
Ambitious	Disciplined	Helpful	Orderly	Self-respect
Appreciative	Discretion	Heroic	Organized	Selfless
Articulate	Diversity	Honesty	Patient	Sensitive
Assertive	Effective	Honorable	Patriotic	Service-minded
Balanced	Efficient	Hopeful	Peaceful	Smart
Benevolence	Eloquent	Humble	Persevere	Sociable
Brave	Empathic	Idealism	Persistent	Spiritual
Calm	Endurance	Imaginative	Playful	Stable
Candor	Energy	Independent	Poised	Steady
Capability	Equality	Influencer	Polite	Strong
Careful	Excellence	Innovative	Positive	Structured
Caring	Fair	Insightful	Practical	Studious
Challenge	Faithful	Integrity	Principled	Successful
Commitment	Family	Intelligent	Productive	Sympathetic
Common sense	Famous	Inventive	Professional	Teamwork
Community	Farsighted	Kind	Protective	Thankful
Compassion	Foresighted	Knowledgeable	Punctual	Thorough
Competence	Forgiving	Leader	Rational	Thoughtful
Compromise	Forthrightness	Likable	Realistic	Tolerant
Conscientious	Fortitude	Logical	Reasonable	Traditional
Considerate	Friends	Loving	Relaxed	Trustworthy
Courage	Fun	Loyal	Reliable	Truthful
Creativity	Funny	Mature	Respectful	Understanding
Credibility	Generous	Moderation	Responsible	Wealthy
Decency	Gentle	Modest	Secure	Well-rounded

Adapted from a list by and with permission from Jeffrey Scott.

Value 1 _____

Important: Why is this value important?

_____

_____

_____

Purpose and character: How does this value signify your purpose and character?

_____

_____

_____

Well-being: How do you think that this value will bring you long-term well-being?

_____

_____

_____

Value 2 _____

Important: Why is this value important?

_____

_____

_____

Purpose and character: How does this value signify your purpose and character?

_____

_____

_____

Well-being: How do you think that this value will bring you long-term well-being?

_____

_____

_____

Value 3 _____

Important: Why is this value important?

_____

_____

_____

Purpose and character: How does this value signify your purpose and character?

_____

_____

_____

Well-being: How do you think that this value will bring you long-term well-being?

_____

_____

_____

Ethics: The prioritization of values when you make a choice.

Many situations are complex and require choices that involve more than one value. This is where personal ethics becomes involved. **Ethics** can be defined as *the prioritization of values when you make a choice*. In ethics you must choose between competing values by ranking one value over other values. Some choices are easy and some are not. For example, would you steal to feed your family? If you would, you are prioritizing your family's health above the law. Ethical decision-making forces you to select one value over all other values and possibly compromise beliefs that are important to you. These choices can affect how you see yourself and influence the way others see you too. When the choice is difficult, you may feel caught between a rock and a hard place.

Think about It

Would you lie under oath in a court of law to protect a friend after you saw him do something illegal if you knew that you would be fined or go to jail? If you knew that you wouldn't get caught, would your answer change? Please explain your answer.

_____

_____

_____

What would you do if a cashier accidentally gave you an extra $1.00 in change? Would you give it back, or would you keep the extra buck? Explain your answer.

_____

_____

_____

Your Choices in College and University

Every choice that you make has message value. By making sure that your choices are conveying messages that are honorable, virtuous, and morally good, you will be in a better position to communicate with integrity and trust, which are building blocks of long-term well-being. As discussed previously, without trust, meaningful and healthy long-term relations between yourself and others, regardless of context (i.e., state and local governments, countries, religions, sexual orientations, races, and genders), are not possible because feelings of safety, belonging, forgiveness, openness, and goodwill cannot take root. As discussed in chapter 4, trust is the foundational principle that holds all relationships together. If other people trust you, they will feel safe around you and be more willing to associate and be involved with you. The opposite is also true. If others do not trust you, they may not willingly want to interact or associate with you. They may not come right out and say anything to you, they just will not let you into their lives.

Keep in mind that your choices can communicate trust to one type of person but not to others. For example, if you cheat on an exam, you might be admired by others who see nothing wrong with cheating to get ahead, while those who feel that you are taking advantage of the students who studied hard and passed the test on their own merit might not want to have anything to do with you.

Think about It

Trust is very difficult to build and extremely easy to destroy. Take a few minutes and think about the people in your life. Identify the person you most trust. Why do you trust that person? After you have figured out whom you trust and why, try to identify a person that you don't trust. Why don't you trust him or her? Is your opinion of that person the result of his or her actions or words?

Who Do You Trust Most and Least?

Who is a person you trust most? _____
What are the personal qualities that you like most about that person?

_____

_____

_____

Who is a person you trust least? _____
What are the personal qualities that you dislike most about that person?

_____

_____

_____

In this exercise, we have identified many different behavioral traits, some trustworthy and some not so trustworthy. If a person communicates that he or she is a liar, bigot, disloyal, lazy, unreliable, mean, or abusive, they will become defined by those behavioral qualities. By contrast, those who are consistently honest, loyal, fair-minded, hard-working, reliable, and respectful of others tend to be trusted by others. You expect people to behave in certain ways; one person lives up to your expectations and the other does not.

Just as you expect others to behave in certain ways, others will have expectations of you. They will be looking for behavioral evidence that they can trust you. People will be more apt to help and support you if they trust you. Years from now, if your professors are asked to list the students they trust most and least, which list will you be on? If you believe that you will be on the trusted list, what behavioral evidence can you provide to support your belief?

What Type of Person Do You Want to Be?

Making choices that are good for you begins with an understanding of the type of person you want to be. If you want to be a trustworthy person, then your choices should be worthy of trust. For example, if you want your professors to get a favorable impression of you, show up to class on time and do your homework. Showing up to class is a choice of action that others will use to describe the type of person that they see and/or experience. The type of person you want to be is a destination or endpoint toward which your judgment and choices should take you. In the same way that you cannot chart a course to an unknown destination, you cannot make the best choices for yourself if you do not know the type of person that you want to be. Do you understand the behavioral traits that define your character?

Think about It

Try to imagine that all your college professors had a meeting about you and that you could eavesdrop on that meeting. What would you hope they would say about you? (What you hope they would say might not be the same as what they would actually say.)

Let's imagine that they note the three values that you already selected as being key to your own character. Using just one sentence, starting with "I would hope they would say that I was . . . ," please write down your character statement or personal policy that you would like to guide your behavioral conduct and decision-making going forward.

Tip: What would your professors say about you to transfer schools or future employers? What qualities would bring you well-being and contentment?

Personal Quality 1 _____
Character statement: I would hope they would say that I was . . .

_____

_____

_____

Personal Quality 2 _____
Character statement: I would hope they would say that I was . . .

_____

_____

_____

Personal Quality 3 _____
Character statement: I would hope they would say that I was . . .

_____

_____

_____

It is never too late to become the student that you want to become. How you choose to interact with the rest of the world is up to you. Your own daily choices will determine your character and the type of person you become. Choose wisely because choices communicate your character to others.

Situational Awareness

Everything that you do in college requires your full and undivided attention. In fact, an important prerequisite of good judgment and good decision-making is **situational awareness**. This is *the ability to accurately comprehend the meaning of environmental factors at a given time and place and accurately predict the future consequences for ourselves and others*. When you comprehend the meaning of the circumstances in which you find yourself, you are aware of yourself within these situations and can begin to predict what might happen in the future when you make

Situational Awareness: The ability to accurately comprehend the meaning of environmental factors at a given time and place and accurately predict the future consequences for ourselves and others.

choices (or do not make choices). When you consciously sift through situational factors to gain insight into your circumstances and then make thoughtful choices from different alternatives, you become responsible for your choices and affect the direction of your life.

Driving safely is an example of an activity that requires situational awareness. When you drive a car at 65 miles per hour, life comes at you at 95.3333 feet per second. It is easy to see life careening toward you when you drive. Yet, despite the obvious need for situational awareness when we drive, the World Health Organization estimates that approximately 1.3 million people are killed on roadways every year around the world.[6] Traffic fatalities are a leading cause of preventable death globally every single year. Even in situations that demand situational awareness, such as driving, many adults make choices that compromise their own capabilities. Drivers impair their own situational awareness when they drive under the influence of drugs and alcohol, drive and text, drive and eat, drive and fiddle with the radio, speed, or engage in road rage. These adults drive without an appropriate level of appreciation for the risks associated with driving heavy vehicles, filled with combustible fuel, at high rates of speed.

While it is easy to see life coming toward you through the windshield when you are driving a car, it is not so easy when you are not driving. Life is still coming toward you, but at an imperceptibly slower speed. You can think of college, work, and relationships as types of slow-moving vehicles on the road of life. They also require your full and undivided

Photo 5.3. It's easy to predict the outcome of the impact of lack of situational awareness when you're driving a car; it's less obvious if you're not aware of changes as they are occurring in your life. *Source:* Shuets Udono; Creative Commons Attribution-Share Alike 2.0 Generic.

attention in order to be situationally aware, which is a prerequisite for sound decision-making. College, work, relationships—indeed, life itself—requires your full and undivided attention.

There are behaviors that are controlled by our biology, including fight or flight responses, blinking, and knee-jerk reactions. All of these behaviors occur without our thinking. For example, a loud explosion might lead you to run quickly in the other direction; it is a natural reaction to flee imminent danger. However, many behaviors are learned responses to circumstances. Even though it feels like your emotions and behaviors are biologically hardwired, they actually are not. According to world-renowned neuroscientist Dr. Lisa Feldman Barrett, our brains ceaselessly regulate all activity within our bodies in response to what is happening in the outside world in order to protect us.[7] They do this by continuously receiving information from the present moment through the five senses (taste, smell, hearing, seeing, and touching), and then comparing what is happening now to what has been experienced in the past, to make predictions about how best to proceed in the future in order to keep you alive and well. Everything that you do, and everything that you experience, is a constructed reaction created in real time that your brain orchestrates in response to what is happening in the world and inside of yourself. According to Dr. Barrett, your brain processes all of this every second of every day and then draws on past experience to react to what is being experienced in the present moment.

Suppose it is your first day of college and you walk into a classroom. Your brain experiences the classroom through all of your five senses. It then takes that information and compares it to what you have experienced in the past in classrooms. These past experiences are then applied to the present situation to help you thrive (or not) in these new circumstances. Those past classroom experiences inform everything (thoughts, emotions, and behaviors) about how you react to the present. This happens over and over and over again, thirty-five thousand times a day, for your entire life.

What does this mean for you? Dr. Barrett's research provides scientific evidence that proves you have much more control over your emotions and behavior than previously thought. Her work establishes a scientific basis for the establishment of a philosophy of self-management. By being more aware of and thoughtful about what you do today, you will be teaching your own brain how to better predict and make better choices tomorrow, because what you do today will become the point of reference for future decisions. You will be creating within your own mind a new and improved reference point that your brain will draw upon when it makes future predictions and choices. Better choices today are the building blocks of a better tomorrow.

Think about It

Suppose that you are home and your home (landline) telephone rings. The instant you hear the ring, your brain might associate that sound with past calls from telemarketers. Your brain might then make a prediction that the call is a telemarketer, which might then inform your decision not to answer the telephone. But, what if your current situation is different? What if your mother is in emergency surgery and the phone rang? Would that bit of information change your decision to pick up the phone?

_____

_____

_____

_____

_____

Your choices are informed by two types of situations: (1) your past experiences with similar situations, and (2) the current situation in which you find yourself. It is both past experience and current experience that give your brain the context and meaning required to make an informed prediction about what choice to make. Without either of these inputs, your brain is in a state of situational blindness and the probability that your decision will be sound is compromised. Your choices become nothing more than uninformed guesses.

The good news from Dr. Barrett's neuroscience research is that you have much more control over your behavior than you might think.[8] Because most behavioral choices are learned through experience, practice, and routine, they can also be changed in these same three ways.[9] By changing what you do (or experience) in the present, you are creating a new type of past experience that your brain will use to create a new frame of reference that you can use to practice this new behavior and then incorporate it into your routine.

Think about It

Martin wasn't doing well on his homework for his Intro to Psychology course. He decided that he would change the way he approached this task. While he previously was tackling his homework late at night after partying with his friends, he decided to do his homework first thing in the morning. While he had previously done his homework before reading the assigned text, he decided now to read the text first. Finally, while he had previously been listening to music while completing his homework, he now worked in silence. What do you think the outcomes of these decisions will be on his grades?

Because you have more control over your behavior than you think, are there new ways that you can approach your school work now, so that your brain's frame of reference tomorrow is aligned with your goals in college?

_____

_____

_____

_____

_____

_____

_____

Reasoning

If aliens from another planet arrived on earth and asked, "What is the most important thing that all human beings have in common?" We might answer their question with "Every human being has a brain." Your brain is the self-managing mechanism with absolute responsibility for your: (1) health, safety, life, and destiny; (2) vital organs including your heart, glands, liver, and kidneys; (3) vital systems including your nervous, cardiovascular, respiratory, digestive, and reproductive systems; (4) senses including seeing, touching, tasting, hearing, and smelling; (5) personality, emotions, listening, and speech; (6) routines, reactions, mannerisms, and behaviors; (7) thinking, prioritizing, and choices; and ultimately (8) well-being and contentedness. Although much of this massive workload is ceaseless brain activity that happens without our awareness, much of what our brains do is done consciously and intentionally.

Reason-Based Choices:
Purposely and critically thinking and then making informed predictions about what will happen in the future by making choices.

Choices are informed when they are purposely validated by reason. Reason-based choices involve critical thinking or the analysis of available facts, evidence, observation, and arguments to form a judgment.[10] **Reason-based choices** solve problems *by purposely and critically thinking and then making informed predictions about what will happen in the future by making choices.*

It is worth repeating that choices made without understanding, discernment, and understanding of the available information are situationally blind. Again, the information is what separates sound decision-making from guesswork. The formation of judgments and decisions without thoughtfully analyzing facts, evidence, observations, and arguments is often at the heart of poor decision-making and feelings of regret.

Think about It

Xavier was busy playing soccer during the fall semester, so he failed to complete his studying every day for his calculus class. He figured he could catch up after soccer season was over. However, when it came time to study for his first exam, he realized he couldn't possibly read all the material and complete the assignments that he skipped. Not surprisingly, he failed the test. He had put off doing the work he knew needed to get done to fulfill his desire to play a sport. He procrastinated rather than keeping up with his homework.

All students know that studying every day is better than procrastination, yet many students procrastinate. Procrastination is an example of an emotion-based choice. Do you procrastinate? If so, who controls your decision to procrastinate? Are you in control of your emotions, or are your emotions in control of you? Explain your answer.

_____

_____

_____

_____

_____

_____

Making a Personal Policy

Choices are informed when they purposely align with your self-created personal policies. Personal policies are small-scale rules that you develop to govern your conduct and keep yourself safe, secure, and stable. Personal policies are powerful tools that define the boundaries within which you will conduct yourself in specific situations. If you have effective personal policies, it will be easier to make decisions in situations that might create feelings of disappointment and regret. The purpose of these situation-specific or people-specific rules is to remove the ambiguity (as much as possible) about how you will respond when you find yourself in challenging circumstances that might compromise your own long-term goals. For example, sometimes college students have a hard time balancing their social and academic lives. By establishing personal policies about how you will handle situations involving the conflicting priorities of homework and studying with partying and having fun with friends, you establish in advance your own rules for how you will handle these types of situations.

Three-Step Process for Creating Personal Policies

In college you will experience all kinds of situations, including challenging situations and people that may trigger feelings of anger, fear, worry, anxiety, confusion, and self-doubt. When the inevitable happens and you are faced with these types of difficult feelings, it is helpful to have a predefined game plan for how you will respond so that you can push forward despite these feelings. Creating personal policies is a discipline that is actually quite easy to do because it only involves three steps:

STEP 1

The first step in creating personal policies is to create a list of situations and people that make you feel upset and create a sense of dread within you. Because dread involves suffering and pain, it is a feeling that most people want to avoid at all costs. But not all dreadful situations are created equally. Some dreadful situations can and should be avoided, while others cannot and should not be avoided. So, the first step in creating personal policies for these types of events is to list all of the situations and people that trigger dread and then categorize them as important or unimportant:

- Unimportant dreadful situations or people play no role in your academic goals and therefore can and should be avoided because they are impediments to your academic progress. You can think of these as low-involvement matters for you.

- Important dreadful situations or people play a big role in achieving your academic goals and cannot and should not be avoided. You can think of these as high-involvement matters for you.

Be careful to phrase each problematic situation or person in the form of a statement that you would like to avoid. Here are some examples. This is not an exhaustive list by any means, but what it suggests is that there are many types of challenges that college students face.

Dreadful situations or people that you can and should avoid:

- socializing too much

- experiencing peer pressure

- experiencing impolite or rude people

- experiencing unwelcome advances

- not getting enough rest

- experiencing social media bullying

- experiencing disrespectful or impolite students and professors

_____

_____

_____

_____

Dreadful situations or people that cannot and should not be avoided but that you would like to avoid:

- required to do a speech in class

- getting to class late

- not going to class

- not studying

- not doing homework

- not giving enough time to study for tests

- experiencing demanding professors

- not writing papers well

_____

_____

_____

_____

_____

STEP 2

Now that you have lists of situations and people that you dread; the second step is creating the actual policies. Because you have listed each of these situations and people in the form of a statement, you have already completed one half of the policy statement because the policy statements will be framed as follows: "In order to reduce feelings of dread when I am (insert dread statement here), I will (insert new personal policy)."

Examples of personal policies:

- In order to reduce feelings of dread when I am required to do a speech in class, I will practice my speech by facetiming my parents.

- In order to reduce feelings of dread when I am getting to class late, I will set my alarm thirty minutes prior to class to remind me to get to class on time.

- In order to reduce feelings of dread when I am not studying, I will get my studying out of the way first thing when I wake up.

- In order to reduce feelings of dread when I am not doing well on exams or quizzes, I will talk to my academic advisor and ask for tutoring help.

- In order to reduce feelings of dread when I am socializing too much, I will only go out on Friday and Saturday nights.

Situation 1

In order to reduce feelings of dread when I _____
_____ ,

I will _____
_____ .

Situation 2

In order to reduce feelings of dread when I _____
_____ ,

I will _____
_____ .

Situation 3

In order to reduce feelings of dread when I _____
_____ ,

I will _____
_____ .

Situation 4

In order to reduce feelings of dread when I _____
_____ ,

I will _____
_____ .

Situation 5

In order to reduce feelings of dread when I _____
_____ ,

I will _____
_____ .

STEP 3

Now that you have formalized your personal policies in writing, the last step is to publicly commit to them by sharing and reviewing your written policies with a trusted advisor. That person can be a parent, grandparent, sibling, friend, professor, colleague, or advisor.

Key Terms

If you learn to understand these words and phrases thoroughly—if you can explain each one and use it correctly—your ability to make sound choices will become much easier for you.

- Behaviorally Impulsive
- Consciousness
- Critical Thinking
- Ethics
- Goals
- Guesswork
- Intentions
- Laws

- Long-Termism
- Reason-Based Choices
- Short-Termism
- Situational Awareness
- Situational Blindness
- Social Order
- Values

Discussion Questions

1. What is the distinction between laws and personal policies? Define each.

2. In what ways are your choices and consciousness inextricably linked? Explain your answer.

3. Can adults behave like children? What are the main behavioral differences between children and adults?

4. Name, define, and provide examples of the Framework for Choosing Model.

5. The Values Model has three variables. Explain and provide examples of each variable.

6. Explain the term *situational blindness* and how that relates to making choices. Please use examples to explain your response.

7. Explain the three-step process for creating personal policies. Please provide examples to illustrate each step.

To Sum Up

- If you need to be asked to follow laws and personal policies, you are not self-managing.

- Your choices and your consciousness are linked.

- Decision-making is an organized and intentional approach to assessing the consequential effects of choices on one's life.

- The Framework for Choosing involves your:
  o Goals and Intentions
  o Values and Ethics
  o Situational Awareness
  o Reasoning
  o Personal Policies

- Just as you expect others to behave in certain ways toward you, others will have expectations of you. They will be looking for behavioral evidence that they can trust you.

- Values and ethics play key roles in the decision-making process.

- The Values Model involves what is important to you, your purpose and character, and your well-being.

- You have much more control over your behavior than you think and therefore are more responsible for the choices that you make.

- Your choices define your character.

6

CHOICES AND CONSEQUENCES

After reading this chapter, you should be able to:

- Explain the principles of causality and self-determination.

- Describe how to assess the costs and benefits of choices and consequences.

- Explain the difference between consequential costs and consequential benefits.

- Understand how value maximization and key performance indicator metrics are linked to well-being and contentedness.

- Explain the Consequence Prioritization Framework Model.

- Describe the three variables that affect the Rule-Breaking behavior model.

- Understand the difference between mistakes and bad choices.

Understanding Choices and Consequences

Post hoc, ergo propter hoc.

—Latin proverb

The Latin proverb "Post hoc, ergo propter hoc" translated means "After this, therefore, because of this." There is a simple cause and effect relationship between your choices and your consequences. Stated more simply, your choices are the cause of your consequences, and your consequences are the effect of your choices.

In self-management, the **principle of causality** states that *your consequences are always caused by your choices*. In a sense, regardless of context, you make choices because you want something to happen in the future. The future can be one minute from now, or forty-five years from now. Attached to each one of your thirty-five thousand daily choices are thirty-five thousand daily consequences.

This cause and effect relationship between choices and consequences is true, regardless of your circumstances. Your choices can have good or bad consequences. Your choices can have consequences that turn good circumstances into bad ones, and also turn bad into good circumstances. Your choices can also have consequences that turn good into great circumstances, and bad into worse circumstances. For example, you can come from fortunate circumstances and be academically dismissed from college. You can also come from unfortunate circumstances and thrive academically in college. At the same time, it is also possible to come from fortunate circumstances and thrive academically, and also come from unfortunate circumstances and be academically dismissed. The long and short of it is this: your academic choices will be the cause, and therefore, the effects of your academic consequences.

Principle of Causality: Your consequences are always caused by your choices.

Photo 6.1. These friends are enjoying the bacon and eggs that they ordered off the diner's menu; their breakfast is the consequence of their order. *Source:* Virginia State Parks staff, Creative Commons Attribution 2.0 Generic.

A nonacademic example of the principle of causality would be that ordering food always precedes its delivery at restaurants. The cause of the food being delivered is the ordering of the food; the effect of ordering the food is the delivery of the food. Continuing with the restaurant example, suppose you and a friend meet for brunch. You find a booth, review the menu, wait patiently for someone to take your order, give the waitstaff your order, eat your western omelet with coffee and orange juice after it is served, pay the restaurant, tip the waitstaff, and hopefully have enjoyed the whole experience.

Your order is **premeditated and intentional**, which means that you reviewed your menu options and thought about what you wanted to eat before you made your menu choice. When you order at restaurants, you are choosing the future consequence that you desire. Restaurants make this process easy because the consequences that you receive are: (1) clearly listed on the menu, (2) neatly categorized (i.e., wine lists, appetizers, salads, fish, chicken, beef, dessert), and (3) purposely limited to the menu options. You choose your consequence.

> **Premeditated and Intentional**: Choices that are made that involve preplanning and thought before taking action.

Outside of restaurants, however, reality has no clearly published menu of consequences that are neatly categorized and purposely limited so that you can review them before you make your many daily choices. In fact, reality has three defining characteristics that are antithetical to the way consequences are presented on restaurant menus. In reality, you have:

1. An unlimited list of consequences from which to choose.

2. The freedom to choose any consequence that you desire.

3. To always choose a consequence; consequences always follow choices. Remember, not choosing is a choice that has consequences as well.

Reality gives you all of the tools required for **self-determination**, which means that you:

1. Have absolute power over your choice of consequences.

2. Have much more control over your destiny than you think.

3. Cannot not choose your consequences and your destiny.

> **Self-Determination**: You (1) have absolute power over your choice of consequences; (2) have much more control over your destiny than you think; and (3) cannot not choose your consequences and your destiny.

Reality does not allow you to walk away from the responsibility of choosing your consequences, because you cannot not make choices. What all of this means for you is that you are solely responsible for your fate, precisely because you control the most powerful regulating mechanism of self-determination, your own choices.

Because consciousness, choices, and consequences are all impossible to separate, when you make your daily choices, you are always making choices that have consequences on your future, both short-term and long-term. Granted, many of these are routine choices that you may not even consciously realize that you are making, but those types of automatic or habitual choices are also choices that you self-determine, make, and impact your destiny.

Here is the thing: In the same way that you cannot not communicate, and you cannot not make choices, you also cannot not exercise self-determination. You are exercising self-determination right now. Reading this passage is an example of self-determination. You could have chosen to do something else, but you are not. Unless you are dead or in jail, you never give up the power of choosing your consequences, which means that you are never not making choices that have present and future consequences. Doesn't it make sense to approach the way that you make choices in a very organized and intentional way so that you can: (1) avoid making wrong decisions; (2) align your choices with your values and ethics; (3) align your short-term intentions with your long-term goals; and (4) increase the probability of achieving your purpose, which in all likelihood is related to your long-term well-being and contentedness?

Assessing the Costs and Benefits of Choices and Consequences

In college, you will never have an unlimited amount of money and time to draw upon to successfully complete your education. Most likely, you will be operating in conditions of **scarcity of resources**, which can be defined as *circumstances when the demand for your time and money is greater than your supply of time and money*. It requires no talent, behavioral or otherwise, to accomplish objectives with an unlimited amount of money and time. Anyone can accomplish anything with an unlimited amount of these resources.

As an effective self-managing college student, you must properly monitor and manage your limited amount of money and time to ensure that what you are spending of these finite resources does not exceed your budgeted amount of each of these assets. You only have one brain, twenty-four hours each day, and a limited financial budget within which to accomplish your daily academic goals. How do you manage your time, money, and mental energy in conditions of scarcity? One way is to intentionally determine the benefits and the costs of the things that you do, and then try to figure out the reasons why you do them. The logic behind completing this inventory and comparative cost-benefit analysis is that

Scarcity of Resources: Circumstances when the demand for your time and money is greater than your supply of time and money.

whenever your money, time, and mental energies are consumed, they should be in support of your long-term goals.

In college, your long-term academic goals may be to transfer, go to graduate school, or get a good job that pays well. Some of the activities that you do will support your academic goals much more than others. By objectively analyzing what you do each day in terms of money, time, and mental energy, you can then develop a rating and ranking system to prioritize what you do in order of importance so that what you do in the present aligns well with what you want to accomplish in the future.

Some choices and consequences align well with your long-term goals in life, and some may not. The choices and consequences that are aligned with your long-term goals are of greater value to you than those that do not. Specifically, they have value to you and they have value to others who experience the impact of your choices and consequences.

The end goal in choosing your consequences is **value maximization**, which is defined *as the increase of the total long-term value of your choices and consequences to you.* **Total long-term value** is defined as *the sum of the value of all of your choices and consequences to you.* In self-management, value maximization is *measured by the degree to which the choices and consequences align with your long-term purpose, values, and goals*—the degree that the consequences of your choices help you achieve contentment and well-being (versus regret).

Contentment and well-being then, are examples of **key performance indicators (KPIs)** of a successfully self-managed life. KPIs are *measures (indicators) of your performance over time toward a specific objective*, in this case contentment and well-being. Contentment and well-being are similar and can be defined as *subjective measures of the state of mental satisfaction that results from being happy, satisfied, and at peace with the choices that you have made throughout your life.* Contentment and well-being are subjective measures of the quality of your own existence and are a function of the quality of your own choices and the consequences that always follow. Contentment and well-being are consequences of a life well lived.

For example, would you rather be an embittered, lonely billionaire that is in poor health, or a happy, faithful, financially secure spouse or partner, with kids and good health? What you think and how you feel depends on your choices and how well that they align with your values. Remember, you will define yourself by your choices, and those very same choices will define you to others. If you allow externals like money, power over others, immediate gratification, and satisfying your own short-term desires to dominate your thinking and be prioritized over your values and long-term purpose and goals, you may be unwittingly sacrificing your own view of yourself that no amount of money can buy back.

Value Maximization: Measured by the degree to which the choices and consequences align with your long-term purpose, values, and goals.

Total Long-Term Value: The sum of the value of all of your choices and consequences to you.

Contentment and Well-Being: Subjective measures of the state of mental satisfaction that results from being happy, satisfied, and at peace with the choices that you have made throughout your life. Contentedness and well-being are consequences of a life well lived.

Key Performance Indicators (KPIs): Measures (indicators) of your performance over time toward a specific objective.

Think about It

Nineteenth-century British novelist Charles Dickens reduced this equation to a simple statement in his classic work *David Copperfield*:

> Annual income twenty pounds, annual expenditure nineteen and six, result happiness. Annual income twenty pounds, annual expenditure twenty pounds and six, result misery.

In other words, if your expenses are $19.60 (to put it in dollars and cents) and your income $20.00, you'll be able to cover your costs; but if your costs are $20.60 and income only $20, you will have to scramble to make up the difference. Reduced to simple financial terms, Dickens says that if your expenses are less than your income, you will be happy, whereas if your expenses are greater than your income, you will suffer.

Do you agree with Dickens's statement? How might this be translated to other accountings based on the decisions you make in life?

So how do you begin your journey to long-term contentedness and well-being? You begin by intentionally and ceaselessly trying to analyze your daily choices to make sure that they are aligned with your purpose, values, and goals. That is because every single choice that you make is either: (1) aligned with your purpose, values, and goals; or (2) not aligned with your purpose, values, and goals. Valuing your choices and their consequences starts by understanding that everything that you do requires that you choose a consequence. For example, in college you choose when to get up, when to go to bed, what to eat, how much to eat, when to study, when to exercise, when to go out, how much to drink. Every one of those choices has a consequence. If you choose to go to bed at 3:00 a.m. and you have to get up at 6:00 a.m., the consequence of that decision will be that you will be tired the next day. If you choose not to study for a test, the consequence will be a low grade on the test. You can think conceptually of **choosing** as *an organized and intentional approach to assessing its consequential effects on your purpose, values, and goals.*

Every choice involves competing consequential results. It is helpful to think of consequences as competing for your attention. They jump up and down saying, "Pick me, pick me." But why should you pick one consequence over another consequence? That is where having a ceaseless and intentional approach to choosing consequences is essential.

The main goal of choosing is to increase the probability that benefits of the consequences that you choose will outweigh the costs, or the benefits lost, of the consequences that you did not choose. So, intentional and organized choosing is fundamentally a **cost-benefit analysis**, which can be defined as *an analytical process of determining which choices and consequences to make and forgo*. You can divide choices and consequences

Choosing: An organized and intentional approach to assessing its consequential effects on your purpose, values, and goals.

Cost-Benefit Analysis: An analytical process of determining which choices and consequences to make and forgo.

into two types: (1) the choices and consequences that you select, and (2) the choices and consequences that you forgo. Each of these consequence types has associated benefits and costs. The benefits and costs associated with the consequence that you select are called beneficial consequences. It is important to note that you receive all of the benefits and incur all of the costs associated with the consequences that you select, and you also incur all of the benefits and costs associated with those that you do not select.

Consequential benefits can be defined as *the potential impact (good and bad) that is received when an opportunity is chosen. Consequential benefits are always associated with a choice that you have made.* Whereas, **consequential costs** can be defined as *the potential impact (good and bad) that is lost when a consequence is not chosen.* Consequential costs are always associated with a choice that you have not selected. You never receive the benefits of choices not chosen.

There are two goals of this type of consequential cost-benefit analysis: (1) to increase the probability that the positive impact of decisions made (consequential benefits) is greater than the future consequences of decisions not made (consequential costs); and (2) to help you avoid making bad or wrong decisions. Your ability to correctly judge the potential future consequences on your life is fundamental to making good choices.

Consequential Benefits: The potential impact (good and bad) that is received when an opportunity is chosen. Consequential benefits are always associated with a choice that you have made.

Consequential Costs: The potential impact (good and bad) that is lost when a consequence is not chosen. Consequential costs are always associated with a choice that you have not selected.

Think about It

Renee is sitting at her desk in her dorm room, getting ready to study for the midterm exam that she is taking the next morning. Her friend, Ellie, comes into the room and tells her that a bunch of her friends are planning to go out dancing and encourages her to come along for the fun.

Faced with the decision whether to stay home and study (something she doesn't enjoy) or go out and join her friends (for a fun evening), Renee doesn't know what to do.

Facing this choice, how could Renee perform a cost-benefit analysis to determine the best course of action? What are the likely consequences of each choice? Which choice would better serve her ultimate goal of succeeding in class?

_____

_____

_____

_____

_____

Good Choices: Intentional prioritization and selection of more consequential matters ahead of less consequential ones.

Good Judgment: Consistently prioritizes more consequential matters ahead of less consequential ones when making choices.

Some choices will be much more consequential than others because they have the potential to produce good or bad life-altering effects. Going to college, completing college, marriage, having children, smoking, texting while driving, robbing a bank, committing fraud, dropping out of college, or driving while intoxicated are all examples of life-altering choices.

In general, choices that have more significant consequences (i.e., the power to affect the outcome of our lives) should be prioritized ahead of those that have less consequential impact. **Good choices**, then, can be thought of as *intentional prioritization and selection of more consequential matters ahead of less consequential ones*. To do otherwise—to prioritize less consequential matters ahead of more consequential ones—is bad judgment and, by logical extension, poor decision-making. So, by extension, someone who uses **good judgment** *consistently prioritizes more consequential matters ahead of less consequential ones when making choices*.

Because you have the power of self-determination that gives you unrestrained freedom of choice, you have the power and right to do whatever you please. You also have the power and right to make choices that will have good and bad consequences. For example, you have the power to choose to study, and you also have the power to choose to avoid studying. Viewed through the lens of this framework, the quality of your choices and judgment becomes clear. If you demonstrate patterns of independently, willingly, and consistently prioritizing more consequential matters ahead of less consequential matters, you communicate common sense and good judgment.

While this logic may not be true in every circumstance, it does hold up in most situations. One exception to this framework are heroic acts made on the spur of the moment, such as rushing into the water to save a drowning swimmer, or rushing into a burning building to save a family. Heroes choose risky behaviors that endanger their own lives to help others. They are admired because of their courage in the face of existential threats to their own lives.

Individuals who seem to chronically prioritize less consequential matters ahead of more consequential matters communicate a lack of judgment that may expose themselves and others to unnecessary risks and problems. For example, if you prioritize texting a friend while driving ahead of your personal safety, you are prioritizing your short-term desire to reach out to a friend over your personal safety. As such your choice not only endangers you, but it also endangers other drivers on the road. Distracted driving is the number one cause of accidents and traffic fatalities on the road, which is evidence of chronic poor judgment on a macrolevel societal scale.

Macrolevel problems like distracted driving are always made by trillions of microscale individual choices. We've already listed many student-related examples that have both microlevel and macrolevel implications for higher education (not attending class, coming to class unprepared, studying for an exam at the last minute) and that can lead to poor student achievement. Each of these microlevel student choices has consequences for the student, but also has macrolevel consequences for university and college, state and local governments, counties, and the planet.

A key problem faced by students—and indeed many others at all stages of life—is procrastination, or "putting off to tomorrow what you could do today," as the old saying goes. **Procrastination** can be defined as *the act of delaying or postponing important matters until after you have done less important ones*. Procrastination may have many causes; you might be surprised to learn that it is often a symptom of poor self-confidence. Afraid that you will fail, you put off even trying, and thus set yourself up for the failure that you fear! Getting ahead of the curve—beginning work early on an assignment that may not be due for several days or weeks, for example—can give you time to refine your work and better position you for success. You'll also avoid the anxiety caused by waiting until the last minute to complete the assignment—including pulling the dreaded "all-nighter" that almost always adds to your overall stress.

Procrastination: The act of delaying or postponing important matters until after you have done less important ones.

Consequence Prioritization Framework

What are the distinctions between more consequential and less consequential matters? We can think of consequences at three levels of importance; they can be important to your:

1. Existence

2. Purpose

3. Lifestyle

The priority levels and definitions of each decision-making level are defined in table 6.1.

Table 6.1. Consequence Prioritization Framework

Consequences to	Definitions	Matter(s) to
Existence	Failure to prioritize these matters ahead of all others can take away your ability to exercise self-determination (i.e., make choices).	• Health • Safety • Freedom
Purpose	Failure to prioritize these matters ahead of less consequential ones can compromise your values and hurt your ability to fulfill your life purpose and goals.	• Character • Relationships • Security
Lifestyle	Failure to priorities matters ahead of less consequential matters will only result in a diminished lifestyle.	• Free time • Material possessions • Leisure activities • Everything else

Source: Author-created.

Think about It

In the following chart, indicate whether you believe the course of action will impact the person's existence, purpose, or lifestyle. For each of your selections, give a short rationale. Remember, there are no right or wrong answers.

Action	Existence	Purpose	Lifestyle
Xiùyīng runs into a burning building to save an elderly couple trapped inside.			
Rationale for your selection:			
Ned orders two beers at lunch right before his biology exam.			
Rationale for your selection:			
Deiondre decides to go out partying rather than staying at home to study.			
Rationale for your selection:			
Fred wins the lottery and uses the $1,000 to buy all his friends a fancy dinner rather than putting it into his savings account.			
Rationale for your selection:			
Xavier drives all night to get home for Thanksgiving even though he pulled an all-nighter the day before.			
Rationale for your selection:			

Consequence to Existence: Health, Safety, and Freedom

You see, touch, taste, hear, and smell our world, experience life, and exist within your body and mind. The quality of your existence depends on your physical person being free and in good working order. Threats to your health, safety, or freedom must be prioritized above all others. When you are healthy, safe, and free, you have the power to exercise self-determination and the opportunity to make choices without hindrance. If your personal choices have consequences that compromise your health, safety, or freedom, you render all other decisions in your life irrelevant. If you are drinking heavily and then get behind the wheel of a car and kill someone, you will lose the right of self-determination. When you commit a crime that leads you to be placed in jail, your choices are made for you. You no longer get to decide what you eat, where you go, who you are with, what clothing you wear, or when you shower. All of those types of choices are made for you.

Smoking cigarettes is another example of a behavior that can have devastating impacts on your health. If as a consequence of smoking cigarettes, you contract lung cancer or emphysema, end up on a respirator for the rest of your life, and you have impacted the quality of your own existence and shortened your own life; you prioritized the pleasure of smoking ahead of your own health. It is important to note that addictive behaviors—such as cigarette smoking, excess alcohol use, or drug use—are not entirely within our self-control. The initial choice may be self-determined, but there are other elements that play into whether this behavior continues or how you ultimately address it.

If the consequences of your choices result in another person's poor health, death, or imprisonment, you have taken away all of these same things from them. Examples of this include the effects of secondhand cigarette smoke; distracted driving; driving while intoxicated; gang and mob violence; police brutality; drug dealing; financial fraud; bullying; road rage and air rage; spousal and child abuse; racism; sexism; ageism; dumping of toxic chemicals into waterways and the ground; and prioritizing profit over the environment, health, and safety of all people.

Think about It

Why do people smoke, text while driving, and commit crimes if they can destroy their own power of self-determination, or that of other people? Explain your answer.

_____

_____

_____

_____

_____

_____

Consequence to Purpose: Character, Relationships, and Security

When existential choices (your personal existence or health) are not at stake, choices with consequences affecting your own character, relationships, and security become the next highest priority. Because you have the freedom and power to exercise self-determination and do so with almost complete impunity, your choices are the main factor that influences your long-term well-being and contentment. If your choices violate generally accepted behavioral norms and values—such as honesty, integrity, trust, selfishness, and politeness—they can not only damage your own view of yourself but can also destroy the connections that bind you to others. If in the pursuit of your own life, liberty, and happiness you compromise your own character, relationships, and security, you may hurt your ability to forge meaningful relationships with others because they may not want to willingly associate with you. Would you willingly want to associate with someone that you thought was dishonest, untrustworthy, selfish, and impolite?

Some examples of these bad behaviors include dishonest behavior such as lying, cheating, and stealing; betraying a partner, friend, or family member; selfishness, impoliteness, and meanness toward others; lack of dependability and accountability; heavy-handedness; boorishness; sexual harassment; insensitivity; laziness; and poor-quality workmanship. Other more specific examples include lying on a résumé about graduating from college; lying about working for a company that you did not work for; and taking advantage of family and friendships for your own personal gain. There are many other examples.

Think about It

Maria really wanted to get a job at a leading website company but the position required that she have majored in a computer or technology related field or at least completed twenty hours of coursework in these areas. She had actually majored in English and had never taken a technology course, but she thought because she used her laptop to log into class and complete assignments it would be OK to say on her application that she met these requirements.

Do you agree with Maria's decision to exaggerate her computer skills and to fudge the fact that she never actually majored in these subjects? Why or why not? Do Maria's actions have an impact on other potential candidates for this position? How would you feel if you did meet the requirements but lost this opportunity to someone who hadn't?

_____

_____

_____

_____

_____

_____

_____

Consequences to Lifestyle: Free Time, Material Possessions, and Leisure Activities

When we are healthy, free, and safe, and our character, relationships, and security are intact, choices involving consequences that can enhance our lifestyle become a priority. These concerns can include the quantity and quality of our material possessions, free time, and leisure activities. Although material possessions, free time, and leisure activities are important, it would be unwise to prioritize them ahead of those that challenge our existence or life purpose. What good are free time, material possessions, and leisure activities if you cannot enjoy them because you are thinking about what you are supposed to be doing?

If you prioritize partying with friends ahead of studying, you cannot fully enjoy the party because you know that you have unfinished work to do. If you are prioritizing your time watching football or basketball ahead of studying for a test or writing a term paper, you are prioritizing leisure activity ahead of your own future security. When you put off important activities to do less important and more pleasurable activities, you are engaged in procrastination. In order to enjoy free time, material possessions, and leisure activities more fully, it is great personal policy to delay gratification by prioritizing your time to address important matters first, so that you can more fully enjoy your free time, material possessions, and leisure activities.

Think about It

For each of the following situations, please indicate whether you believe the person is procrastinating (or putting off doing an important task) or not and then give your rationale, that is, why you think they are either procrastinating or not. Remember there are no right or wrong answers.

Procrastinating or not procrastinating?	Yes	No	Why?
Josephine is a member of her school's track team but only practices the day before each meet, feeling that otherwise she might tire herself out.			
Juan changes the oil and checks the tire pressure in his car every six months, even if he isn't planning a major trip.			
Phillipe had really hoped to take his date to hear BTS when they came to town, but he put off buying tickets until the last minute. He ended up having to pay a scalper $750 for each one!			
Elena woke up early on the first day tickets for the BTS concert went on sale to be sure she'd be first in line and was able to snag two front-row seats for just $75 each!			

Rules and Consequences

Why do drivers intentionally break traffic laws? For example, why do drivers chronically (1) not stop at stop signs, (2) text and drive, (3) drive above the speed limit, (4) drive while intoxicated, or (5) not slow down in construction zones? Likewise, why do college students intentionally break academic policies? For example, why do college students chronically (1) miss class, (2) show up late or walk out of class early, (3) cheat on tests, (4) miss due dates for assignments, or (5) procrastinate and put off writing papers, reading assignments, or studying for tests? What is the difference between drivers breaking a traffic law and students breaking an academic policy?

In all important aspects, both traffic laws and academic policies are similar. They both provide guidelines on what individuals are responsible for to make it easier for people to function well together within their specific contexts. A world without speed limits, stop signs, or traffic signals would be chaos. Similarly, a college without academic policies would be a free-for-all.

So, why do some people intentionally break rules that are designed to make things better for everybody? If the purpose of all rules is to provide guidelines that help create order between people in different contexts, then it would not be much of a stretch to argue that the same behavioral variables that increase the risk of breaking laws might also contribute more generally to an increased risk of breaking rules like academic policies. There are three variables that contribute to an increased risk of rule-breaking behavior in college: (1) opportunity, (2) pressure, and (3) rationalization (see figure 6.1).[1]

Photos 6.2 and 6.3. Running a red light can lead to a bad accident; oversleeping and missing class can also have serious consequences. *Photo 6.2. Source:* David Shankbone; Creative Commons Attribution-Share Alike 3.0 Unported. *Photo 6.3 Source:* Psy3330 W10; Creative Commons Attribution-Share Alike 3.0 Unported.

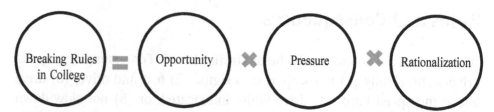

Figure 6.1. The Three Variables That Affect Rule-Breaking Behavior. *Source:*
Author-created.

Opportunity

Opportunity: An
academic circumstance
that gives students the
possibility to break
academic policies without
any consequence.

Opportunity is defined as *an academic circumstance that gives students the possibility to break academic policies without any consequence.* To intentionally break rules in college, students must first believe that they have the opportunity to get away with it. Students may believe that rules are optional and do not apply to them because they might have gotten away with breaking similar rules in high school. This is not to say that high schools do not have rules for attendance, grading, cheating, and other academic-related policies, as they surely do. However, they might have difficulty enforcing academic rules because a formal education is compulsory until the ages of sixteen or eighteen, depending on the state.[2] Because education is considered a legal right, high schools may be required to educate students even if they fail to show up for class or cheat on tests. These students may have been able to disregard academic policies and behavioral rules in the past without suffering any consequences.

Colleges and universities are substantively different than high schools because they are not bound by compulsory education laws. Going to college is a choice, not a legally mandated right. In fact, there are very strict student codes of conduct that deal with poor behavior, excessive absenteeism, chronic lateness, failing academic performance, and cheating. Colleges and universities also have strong policies and procedures, and rigorous, independently reviewed accreditation standards that ensure the academic integrity of their institutions. Students cannot willfully choose to disregard academic policies and procedures without consequence.

Think about It

Eliza signed the honor pledge at her university, which included a statement that she would complete all classwork on her own. Nonetheless, when she had trouble completing the work for her calculus class, she asked her friend Paul if he'd do the work for her. Math was easy for Paul, and he had already aced the class the previous semester so she knew he would be able to do it. Paul hesitated because he knew it was against the honor code, but she was so desperate he decided it was OK to help out because he knew she would not pass the class without his assistance. Plus he was hoping she'd go out with him to the movies.

Did Eliza do the right thing in asking Paul to complete her classwork for her? Did Paul do the right thing by doing the work? Knowing that this was against academic policy, what should be the consequences of their actions?

_____

_____

_____

_____

_____

_____

Pressure

The second variable in the model is **pressure**, which we can define as *the reasons why students break rules*. Rather than try to list and address all of the root causes of why students break rules in college, it is important to understand that feeling pressure to break rules is natural and not always wrong. Going to college and university is a time when you are supposed to ask questions about why society is the way that it is, think about the kind of person that you want to be, what you want to stand for, and possibly even push back when rules, laws, and society are unjust, or have no moral foundation upon which to justify your obedience.

World history is replete with epic, revolutionary, and heroic examples of students feeling pressure to break rules as a way of protesting against societal rules and laws that are unjust. From massive antiwar, civil rights, LGBTQ+, and Indigenous rights protests in the United States, to Tiananmen Square in China, Trisakti University in Indonesia, White Rose Nazi Resistance in Germany, and Greta Thunberg's climate activism, students have sacrificed themselves and sometimes even their own lives in pursuit of a more just and equitable world. So, sometimes questioning rules, taking stands, and righting the wrongs of an unjust world is not only a good thing to do; it is a defining sacred obligation for many students.

Pressure: The reasons why students break rules.

Photo 6.4. Greta Thunberg, outside the Swedish parliament, August 2018. *Source:* Anders Hellberg; Creative Commons Attribution-Share Alike 4.0 International license.

But going to college and university will also force you to change all your old routines and relationships, which can also make you feel confused, uncomfortable, and even stressed-out. These feelings are, for the most part, a natural part of making this transition from one world where you are comfortable and well established, with friends and relationships in place, to a new one. For example, if you played basketball in high school, you may want to play in college. However, you will be playing in a new gym, practicing with new teammates, and have a new coach. They will not have a shared history with you. It will not matter how good you were in high school; the other players will probably be just as good and maybe even better than you. They may even be competing with you for court time or position. The other players will try hard to best you in practice, in the classroom, in the locker room, and in the eyes of the coaching staff. That is the nature of competition.

You might also feel competitive pressures in the classroom. You might have been the best and the brightest in high school, but in college no one that you meet, including your professors, will know how smart you are. They will not really care if you got a high grade on your SAT. Your peers will be fighting to prove themselves, and also filtering everything through their own set of priorities, in the same way that you are. Your professors will judge you based on your current work, not your past success.

This new college environment can trigger within you many internal pressures (see figure 6.2).

Figure 6.2. Some Pressures You May Face in College. *Source:* Author-created.

Although these types of pressures are real and should be addressed, these feelings are not unusual for college students to experience. You may even be coping with a lot of these pressures yourself. Overcoming these feelings, and pushing forward despite having them, is what teaches you that you belong in college. Although there may be some challenging courses that intimidate everyone (i.e., organic chemistry, corporate finance, string theory, and calculus), you should be able to understand almost all academic concepts and subject matter, without seeking tutoring support.

All these negative pressures can trigger feelings that can be confusing. You might think to yourself that you are not "college material." You might even question why so many social forces and pressures are unleashed on you at the same time, and you may begin to feel that college or university is rigged against you and unjust. However, taking negative actions like procrastinating, not showing up, arriving late to or walking out in the middle of class; not doing homework, studying for tests, writing papers; or turning work in late or cheating will not right the wrong of an unjust world. It will only hurt you and your ability to realize your unrealized potential.

You might find comfort knowing that all properly sanctioned colleges and universities are required by national accrediting bodies to have rigorous policies and procedures in place to ensure that you are provided a high-quality education. These policies and procedures are for the common good of all students and ensure the academic integrity of the college or university that you are attending. Examples include policies on attendance, academic performance, testing and grading, curriculum design and oversight, student retention, academic quality assessment, academic dishonesty, student codes of conduct, and many more.

Instead of succumbing to pressures and fears, and walking away from your goal of fulfilling your unrealized potential, please know that these feelings are mostly normal and are the exact feelings that you need to push through in order to grow and develop true confidence in your own abilities. You can do this.

Think about It

Rocco had been a high-achiever in high school academically and was a sports star on the football team. But when he arrived at college, he found the coursework difficult and he failed to even get a place on the freshman team. Far from home and not having many friends, he felt frustrated and angry that he was not doing well. Eventually, he started skipping classes. He dropped out after his first semester.

Why do some students fail to align their behavioral intentions with their behavioral goals? How can you reduce the likelihood that this will happen to you? Please explain your answer.

_____

_____

_____

_____

_____

_____

Rationalization

Rationalization: Using weak, but superficially believable, arguments to justify choices that are not aligned with your own values and ethics, goals, and personal policies.

The third variable in our model is **rationalization**, or _using weak, but superficially believable, arguments to justify choices that are not aligned with your own values and ethics, goals, and personal policies_. You have to rationalize in order to knowingly break rules in college. It's a way for you to justify your own behavior. Rationalizing tries to legitimize choices with excuses that would otherwise be difficult to justify if applied to other people in similar situations.

For example, a student may feel justified in cheating and try to rationalize the decision by arguing that everybody else is doing it. But just because others cheat doesn't mean that you should follow their bad example. Would your own values and ethics, goals, and personal policies allow you to push someone in front of a train because everyone was doing it? Similarly, some students try to explain away excessive absenteeism or chronic lateness by blaming the professor for being boring, excessively rigid, or rude. The professor might in fact be all of those things, but using the professor's poor behavior as your justification to self-destruct presupposes it would be acceptable for everyone to do the same. Is it okay to abandon your own values and ethics, goals, and personal policies because you're dealing with a difficult professor?

Think about It

Jed had been shoveling the snow off the sidewalk in front of his house every time there was a storm. However, after seeing that his neighbors rarely shoveled their walks, he began to think maybe he shouldn't clear his either. After all, it was a lot of hard work and it was cold outside. And no one else seemed to get in trouble with the town for leaving their walks snow-covered. He figured if someone fell on his sidewalk because it was covered with snow and ice it'd be their problem.

How did Jed rationalize his decision not to shovel his walk? Think of some of your own behavior and how you have rationalized it. Do these rationalizations really measure up to your personal values?

_____

_____

_____

Understanding Mistakes and Consequences

I've missed more than 9000 shots in my career. I've lost almost 300 games. 26 times, I've been trusted to take the game winning shot and missed. I've failed over and over and over again in my life. And that is why I succeed.

—Michael Jordan

Human beings are not perfect. The greatest competitors in the history of professional sports made many mistakes. Michael Jordan's lifetime shooting percentage was .493. He missed more than 50 percent of his field goal attempts. In 1941, Boston Red Sox slugger Ted Williams became the last major league baseball player to hit over .400 for an entire year. He did not get a base hit almost 60 percent of the time.

Mistakes can be defined as *unintentional errors that are made during performances*, where **errors** are defined as *unintentionally doing something wrong*, and **performance** is defined as *an action carried out to accomplish a task*. Great ball players sometimes strike out; great golfers can miss a key putt; great students can give the wrong answer on a test. While **perfection** can be defined as a *mistake-free consequence of performance*, no one is perfect all of the time.

Mistakes can be counted and used to assess the quality of a human performance. For example, on a 100-question, multiple-choice test, a test score of 85 percent means that eighty-five questions were answered correctly, and that 85 percent of the test performance was mistake-free. It also means that 15 percent of the test performance had mistakes. In a sense, mistakes are measures of performance quality that assess the level of inconsistency in human performance, when compared to a performance standard during a performance.

Mistakes are natural consequences of learning how to perform anything. For example, when babies learn how to walk, they fall down. When you first learned how to swim, you might have struggled to stay afloat. When you first learned how to ride a bike, you might have tipped over. When you learned how to write, you probably made grammatical, syntax, and citation mistakes. Mistakes are a natural and important consequence of learning and the educational process.

You can think of mistakes as being the doors through which ignorance enters and exits our bodies. We learn how to perform what to do and not to do by making mistakes. We learn to walk by falling down. Kids want to stay standing because falling hurts. The pain of making mistakes is the lesson.

How do you avoid making mistakes and improve your performances in life? The only way to reduce mistakes and improve human performance is time and practice. When babies learn how to walk, they practice. They fall down, get back up, and try again. Babies do not cheat when they learn how to walk. They keep making mistakes and keep falling down until they learn how to do it.

Time and practice are the only ways to reduce mistakes and improve performance in any endeavor. If you put in time and practice into reading,

---

Mistakes: Unintentional errors that are made during performances.

Errors: Unintentionally doing something wrong.

Performance: An action carried out to accomplish a task.

Perfection: Mistake-free consequence of performance.

mathematics, and writing, you will learn how to read, do math, and write. You will reduce academic mistakes and your academic performances will improve. The opposite is also true: If you do not put in time and practice into your coursework, you will increase mistakes and your academic performances will deteriorate. It is that simple.

What is the difference between mistakes and bad choices? Although there are many differences, the main difference is intention. MJ did not intend to miss when he would shoot the game-winning shot; infants do not intend to fall when they learn how to walk. Mistakes are unintentional errors during performances.

Bad choices, on the other hand, are *intentional decisions that can impact how well you perform.*

Bad Choices: Intentional decisions that can impact how well you perform.

For example, missing a foul shot during a basketball game is a mistake; not practicing your free throws is a bad choice. You can make mistakes on papers and tests, but not writing papers or studying for tests are bad choices.

Sometimes, people try to reclassify bad choices into mistakes to avoid taking responsibility for their own bad choices. For example:

- Two students missed an exam because they said that they got a flat tire. Their professor called them individually into the office and asked them one simple question: "Which tire was it?" The students gave different answers. When they got caught lying, they said that they "made a mistake."

- Two students had the exact same wrong answers on every question of a math exam. When they were caught cheating, they said that they "made a mistake."

- A drunk driver killed three people after a late evening at a bar. When he was sentenced to jail in the courtroom, he said that he "made a mistake."

- A tennis player did not practice for three months prior to entering a tournament. When she got beaten in straight sets, she said that she "made a mistake" by not practicing.

In each of these examples, people are attempting to deflect blame away from themselves by minimizing their own responsibility for their actions. They are reclassifying their bad choices as "mistakes." Mistakes are a natural consequence of performance and can be minimized by investing time and practice.

Think about It

For each of the following scenarios, indicate whether the person made a mistake or a bad choice and the reason for your selection. Remember there are no right or wrong answers.

Action	Mistake?	Bad Choice?	Why
Octavio overslept and was so tired that he ran his car into a tree.			
Lucy studied hard for her midterms but still got three answers wrong.			
After drinking heavily at a party, Adriana decided to go get a tattoo saying "Party on, dude" on her upper arm.			
Norm took a dance class but stepped on his partner's feet when he first tried to learn to waltz.			
Alonzo went ice skating when he knew it wasn't safe and fell through the ice, breaking his leg.			

Think about It

In what ways do students justify not attending class, walking in late, not doing their homework or studying, or cheating?

_____

_____

_____

_____

_____

_____

To see if your judgment and decision-making are consistently in your best interest, please take a few minutes to complete the self-assessment, Choice/Judgment Effectiveness: A Self-Assessment (table 6.2).

Using the behavioral observation scale (table 6.3) as a guide, for each statement write in the rating column the number corresponding to the degree to which you consistently exhibit the behavior described. Note, there are no right or wrong answers. All that is important is that you indicate how consistently you exhibit the behavior described in the action statement.

Now transfer your answers for each statement into the corresponding space in table 6.4.

Greater than 4: If your average is between 4 and 5, you are a good decision-maker, prioritize important matters ahead of unimportant matters, and require little guidance to use good judgment and make good decisions.

Between 3 and 4: If your average is greater than 3 but less than 4, with guidance, you are a good decision-maker.

Less than 3: If your average is less than 3, with guidance you might use good judgment. But occasionally, even with guidance, you fail to do the right thing.

Table 6.2. Choice/Judgment Effectiveness: A Self-Assessment

Below Expectations	Meets Expectations	Role Model
Even with guidance: • Fails to provide evidence (verbal, written, and behavioral) that their actions and words demonstrate good judgment and/or are aligned with audience expectations. • Fails to provide evidence of these behaviors and is unwilling to prioritize important matters ahead of unimportant matters.	With guidance: • Provides evidence (verbal, written, and behavioral) that their actions and words demonstrate good judgment and are aligned with audience expectations. • Provides evidence of these behaviors and is willing to prioritize important matters ahead of unimportant matters.	Independently: • Provides evidence (verbal, written, and behavioral) that their actions and words demonstrate good judgment and/or are aligned with audience expectations. • Willingly provides evidence of these behaviors and can be trusted to prioritize important matters ahead of unimportant matters.

Source: Author-created.

Table 6.3. Behavioral Observation Scale

5 =	Almost always performs as described by the Role Model standards.
4 =	Sometimes performs as described by the Role Model standards and sometimes performs as described by the Meets Expectations standards.
3 =	Almost always performs as described by the Meets Expectations standards.
2 =	Sometimes performs as described by the Meets Expectations standards and sometimes performs as described by the Below Expectations standards.
1 =	Almost always performs as described by the Below Expectations standards.

	Action Statement	Rating
1	I spend between ten and twenty hours, outside of class, on my schoolwork (e.g., doing homework, studying, or preparing for tests).	
2	I challenge myself to practice and understand subjects that I find difficult or do not understand well.	
3	I get all of my work done, no matter how long it takes.	
4	I go out only after my academic work is completed.	
5	I don't miss class, am always on time, and remain in class.	
6	I am ready to work and prepared for every class.	
7	I earn high grades (A's or B's) or marks in my classes.	
8	I am comfortable and like communicating with and meeting new people.	
9	When I do poorly or when I don't understand something, I try harder by spending more time on that subject.	
10	I can juggle large amounts of responsibility at school, work, and home and still produce high-quality work.	
11	I can figure out how to do almost any subject, if I put my mind and effort into it.	
12	I try to be polite, even when I don't need to be.	
13	I consider the other person and can find common ground when I am in a dispute.	
14	I am careful not to harm people with my words, even when I get frustrated.	
15	I challenge myself to help bring order to different situations, even when things do not go my way.	

16	I am interested in what others have to say, even when I disagree with them.	
17	I accurately assess potential future consequences of decisions on my life.	
18	I prioritize consequential matters before less consequential matters when I make decisions.	
19	I align my decision-making with the type of person I want to be.	
20	I accurately assess and understand my current reality before I make decisions.	

Source: Author-created.

Table 6.4. Choice/Judgment Behavior Mapping Table

Item	Variable	Behavior	Behavior Average	Behavior Rating
1	Commitment	Time		
2	Commitment	Deliberate Practice		
3	Commitment	Effort		
4	Commitment	Delayed Gratification		
5	Commitment	Reliability		
6	Commitment	Preparedness		
7	Commitment	Quality		
8	Coping	Change		
9	Coping	Adversity		
10	Coping	Capacity		
11	Coping	Capability		
12	Caring	Courteousness		
13	Caring	Negotiating		
14	Caring	Patience		
15	Caring	Helpfulness		
16	Caring	Listening		
17	Choice	Ethical		
18	Choice	Judgment		
19	Choice	Character		
20	Choice	Premeditated/Intentional		
Average				

Average = Σ of Behavior Rating/20: [ ] ←

Source: Author-created.

Take your behavior averages for this section, calculate the new average of averages, and input that information into the employability profile.

Think about It

You will define yourself by the decisions that you make, and those very same decisions will define you to others. The choice/judgment mapping table tells if you prioritize important matters ahead of less important matters. What is your average? How could you improve it?

How can you employ Fogg's Behavior Model tiny habits (see chapter 1) to improve the quality of your decision-making? Please take a few moments and try to come up with one tiny decision-making habit that you can use to help you make better decisions. As you think about changing your habits, think about framing the tiny habit in the following format suggested by Dr. Fogg: "After I (insert existing behavior), I will (insert new tiny behavior)."

After I _____ ,

I will _____ .

1	2	3	4	5
Below Expectations		**Meets Expectations**		**Role Model**
Even with guidance from others, fails to provide evidence of behavioral understanding of the 5C Elements and cannot be trusted with responsibility, and is unwilling to work on the responsibility of self-management.		With guidance, provides evidence of behavioral understanding of the 5C Elements and can be trusted with responsibility.		Independently and willingly provides evidence of behavioral understanding of the 5C Elements and can be trusted with responsibility.

Where:

5 =	Almost always performs as described by the "Role Model" standard.
4 =	Sometimes performs as described by the "Role Model" standard and sometimes performs as described by the "Meets Expectations" standard.
3 =	Almost always performs as described by the "Meets Expectations" standard.
2 =	Sometimes performs as described by the "Meets Expectations" standard and sometimes performs as described by the "Below Expectations" standard.
1 =	Almost always performs as described by the "Below Expectations" standard.

Communication
Trust a person to convey messages appropriately.

	Audience
	Involvement
	Message
	Evidence
	COMMUNICATION MEAN

	BEHAVIORAL COMPETENCY RATING (MEAN OF MEANS)

Choices
Trust a person to use good judgment.

	Communication
	Commitment
	Coping
	Caring
	Choice
	CHOICE MEAN

Commitment
Trust a person to be dutiful.

	Dependability Attendance
	Dependability Accountability
	Dependability Contribution
	Hard Work Time Deliberate Practice
	Hard Work Delayed Gratification
	Hard Work Effort Energy
	Hard Work Effort Determination
	Hard Work Effort Stamina
	Quality Measure of Excellence
	Quality Continuous Improvement
	COMMITMENT MEAN

Coping
Trust a person to demonstrate fortitude during difficult times.

	Coping Change Demonstration
	Coping Adversity Self-Awareness
	Coping Adversity Self-Restraint
	Coping Adversity Self-Improvement
	Coping Complexity Capacity
	Coping Complexity Capability
	Coping Complexity Activities
	COPING MEAN

Caring
Trust a person to show concern for others.

	Caring Civility Listening
	Caring Civility Courtesy
	Caring Civility Consideration
	Caring Helpfulness Concern
	Caring Helpfulness Cooperation
	Caring Helpfulness Compromise
	Caring Conscientious Thoughtfulness
	Caring Conscientious Carefulness
	Caring Conscientious Fairness
	Caring Common Good Respect
	Caring Common Good Equity
	Caring Common Good Goodwill
	CARING MEAN

Key Terms

If you learn to understand these words and phrases thoroughly—if you can explain each one and use them correctly—your ability to make sound choices will become much easier for you.

- Bad Choices
- Choosing
- Consequential Benefits
- Consequential Costs
- Contentment and Well-Being
- Cost-Benefit Analysis
- Errors
- Good Choices
- Good Judgment
- Key Performance Indicators
- Mistakes
- Opportunity
- Perfection
- Performance
- Premeditated and Intentional
- Pressure
- Principle of Causality
- Procrastination
- Rationalization
- Scarcity of Resources
- Self-Determination
- Total Long-Term Value
- Value Maximization

Discussion Questions

1. How do the principles of actuality and self-determination relate to choices and consequences?

2. Compare and contrast consequential costs and consequential benefits.

3. Describe the Consequence Prioritization Framework and use examples to explain each level.

4. Perform a cost-benefit analysis of going to college.

5. Is it possible to calculate the total long-term value of your choices and consequences? Explain why or why not.

6. Explain each of the variables that affect rule-breaking behavior. Please use examples in your answer.

7. What is a mistake and how does it relate to performance? Please use examples to illustrate your answer.

Choices Personal Policy Contract

To help you achieve your behavioral goals, you will be writing them down to create personal policy contracts like the one following. By signing and dating the personal policy contract, it becomes an obligation to yourself that cannot be broken.

Goals	Choice goal(s) that will guide my decision-making in college: _____ _____ _____ _____
Personal Policies	Personal policies I will follow when I make choices: _____ _____ _____
Public Commitments	Public commitments that I will make to regularly measure how I am doing regarding my choice goals and personal policies. I will send my goals, personal policies, and quick weekly progress reports to a supportive friend and the professor. _____ _____ _____ _____
	Signature: _____ Date: _____

To Sum Up

- There is a cause-effect relationship between your choices and consequences. Your choices are the cause of your consequences, and your consequences are the effect of your choices. This is the principle of causality.

- Self-determination involves the fact that:

  o You have power over your choice of consequences

  o You have more control than you think over your fate

  o You cannot not make choices that will have consequences, that will influence your fate

- Choices and consequences have long-term value that can be calculated.

- There are three prioritization levels in the Consequence Prioritization Framework:

  o Consequence to existence

  o Consequence to purpose

  o Consequence to lifestyle

- The three variables that affect the Rule-Breaking Behavior Model are:

  o Opportunity

  o Pressure

  o Rationalization

- Mistakes and bad choices are different. A mistake is a performance error that is made without intention; bad choices are personal choices made with intention.

Section IV

COMMITMENT

How to understand, communicate, and
assess activity-based trust relating to
dependability, hard work, and quality

7

UNDERSTANDING COMMITMENT AND DEPENDABILITY

After reading this chapter, you should be able to:

- Describe the three behavioral variables that demonstrate commitment and what commitment is, what it measures, and why it's important.

- Define dependability, why it is important, and the three variables that demonstrate dependability.

- Explain the Attendance, Contribution, and Accountability Models and the variables that make them up.

- Understand the impact of dependability on safety, cost, success, and teamwork.

The Commitment Model

Commitment is an act, not a word.

—Jean-Paul Sartre

In the first half of this text, we covered foundational content for self-management:

1. You cannot not communicate: everything you do communicates and therefore everything has message value.

2. You cannot not make choices: all of your daily choices communicate your values and ethics.

3. You cannot not experience the consequences of your choices: your consequences are inextricably linked to your choices.

These concepts are foundational because the remaining 5C Elements—commitment, coping, and caring—are all character traits that you choose to communicate and will have consequences on your ability to fulfill your unrealized potential. We will begin the second half of the text by uncovering what commitment is and is not, why it is important, and what you need to do to demonstrate this important character trait.

Your choices communicate traits about the way you function and those traits affect how others see you and how you see yourselves. **Character traits** can be defined as *distinguishing features about your nature*. Character traits create lasting impressions in the minds of people who experience your behavior. One of the most important character traits an individual can communicate is commitment. **Commitment** *communicates an individual's willingness to follow through and meet obligations*.

Commitment is an emotional and intellectual devotion to one activity over others. Individuals who are committed to an activity give it more attention and time compared to other activities. The activity is treated as a priority and is moved to the front burner to meet its requirements. As Jean-Paul Sartre explains, commitment is an act and as such is communicated nonverbally. Words cannot do homework, show up to clasDs, hammer a nail, build a bridge, play a guitar, or put a person on the moon: only activity (actions and deeds) can do these things.

We can think about commitment-related behavioral patterns as either strengthening or weakening trust, or as productive or unproductive, respectively. **Productive behavioral patterns**—such as showing up on time, working hard, and producing high-quality output—*strengthen trust connections with the audiences that experience the behavior*. **Unproductive behavioral patterns**—such as lack of effort, being unreliable, poor quality output, and lack of accountability—*weaken goodwill and cooperation and may require other people to step in to encourage more trustworthy performance*.

Suppose that you live in a house with your friends and the night before you all had a party. The next morning, you wake up and the house is a mess, and everybody pitches in to help get it cleaned up—except Hakeem. He was partying right alongside everyone else, but he stridently complains that it is not his responsibility to clean up the mess because he did not make it! Hakeem has done this exact same thing before, and he has a habit of transferring work onto others. His self-righteous com-

Character Traits: Distinguishing features about your nature.

Commitment: Communicates an individual's willingness to follow through and meet obligations.

Productive Behavioral Patterns: Behaviors that strengthen trust connections with the audiences that experience the behavior.

Unproductive Behavioral Patterns: Individual actions that weaken goodwill and cooperation and may require other people to step in to encourage more trustworthy performance.

plaining will not get the house clean or endear him to the other members of the house, and it will define him to his peers as someone that does not follow through and meet his obligations to others.

Three commitment behavioral variables can be measured and analyzed to determine an individual's level of commitment to an activity. Figure 7.1 shows the three variables that demonstrate commitment: dependability, hard work, and quality.[1]

Figure 7.1 demonstrates the overlapping relationship between the three commitment variables, which means that certain behaviors can affect all the variables simultaneously. For instance, undependable behavioral patterns, like not showing up to class, may reveal problems with a student's work ethic and, at the same time, may be the cause of poor academic performance (quality).

Committed behavior is a function of being dependable, working hard, and producing quality output. Skill, with very few exceptions, is learned and a direct result of these three variables. Playing the guitar, reading and writing, mathematics, nursing, accounting, plumbing, writing computer code, performing stand-up comedy, or playing basketball are all learned skills. And just as you can't expect to play lead guitar with a major rock group at a sold-out stadium without being dependable, working hard, and being a quality musician, you can't expect to have acquired skill in any academic, career, personal, or social activity without commitment. High levels of skill suggest high levels of commitment, while low levels of skill imply low levels of commitment.

Let's look at the three commitment variables in more detail. This chapter will only cover dependability, while chapter 8 will cover hard work and quality.

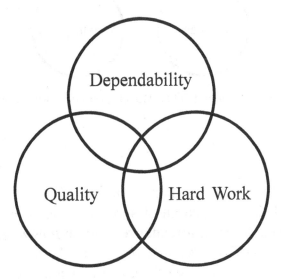

Figure 7.1. Commitment Model. *Source:* Author-created.

Understanding Dependability

Dependability: The degree to which individuals can be relied on by others.

The first and most essential component of committed behavior is dependability. **Dependability** measures *the degree to which individuals can be relied on by others*. Dependability is a necessary condition for involvement in working on organized activities with others, such as committees, teams, and other social groups. Regardless of the size of the group, dependable behavior communicates commitment to group goals. Undependable behavioral patterns (i.e., being regularly self-absorbed and insensitive to others) actually destroy group cohesion. For this reason, dependability is the behavioral minimum for committed behavior and must be a *group goal*. When other group members cannot count on undependable people, their presence in the group is counterproductive because it hinders the achievement of group goals. People do not want to work with people that they cannot depend on.

As shown in the Dependability Model (figure 7.2), dependability is a function of three behavioral variables: (1) attendance, (2) accountability, and (3) contribution.

Each of these behavioral variables is required to be dependable and is made up of different sub-variables. If *any* of the variables (or their accompanying sub-variables) is low, the resulting product or dependability rating will also be low. For example, if a student consistently shows up to class unprepared, he or she will not be perceived as being dependable.

Let's look at attendance, accountability, and contribution in more detail.

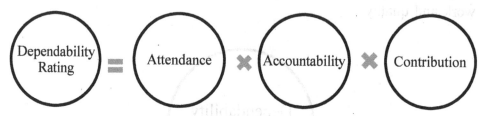

Figure 7.2. Dependability Model. *Source:* Author-created.

Attendance

Attendance: To be present (physically and mentally) at a specified place and time.

To be dependable, one must first be in attendance. Comedian Woody Allen once said that "80 percent of success in life is just showing up." He wasn't joking. To be in **attendance** is to be *present (physically and mentally) at a specified place and time*. Attendance involves three (3) variables: showing up, being on time, and remaining for the duration of the activity (figure 7.3).

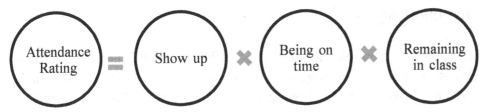

Figure 7.3. Attendance Model. *Source:* Author-created.

Although these three variables are all different attendance-related issues, they all relate to being present. Being present is a function of being in attendance. You cannot be present if you are absent, late, or leave early. Many students mistakenly believe that if they just show up to class they have attended the class. However, they cannot be considered present if they are not on time or leave early.

Attendance is dependability's behavioral minimum. Failure to willingly and reliably show up on time and remain for the duration of the activity reveals problematic dependability-related behavioral patterns. You cannot share responsibilities and support group goals if you are not dependably present.

Think about It

Our school's chess club meets every Wednesday night at 7 p.m. With just ten members, it's important that everyone show up on time so that the games can begin promptly; we only have use of the meeting room for one hour. But Julio always turns up at least fifteen minutes late. We've told him how much trouble this creates for us, but he doesn't seem to care. Now the other members are starting to drop out because they don't always have enough time to finish their games.

Lateness can be defined as *arriving after a planned or necessary time*. When people arrive late, other people wait. Lateness is selfish, insensitive, and in some instances dangerous behavior. Please explain why being late is selfish, insensitive, and sometimes even dangerous. Please use examples to illustrate your response.

_____

_____

_____

_____

_____

_____

Lateness: Arriving after a planned or necessary time.

Accountability:
Willingness to follow through and fulfill obligations.

Accountability

The second variable in the dependability model is accountability. **Accountability** is a *willingness to follow through and fulfill obligations*. Accountability involves three (3) variables: responsibility, preparation, and readiness to perform (figure 7.4).

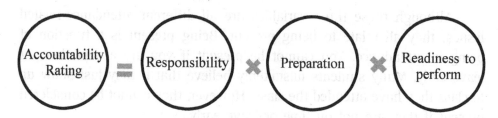

Figure 7.4. Accountability Model. *Source:* Author-created.

Responsibility

Accountability starts with being responsible. Responsibility is a palpable sense of duty about one's obligations to others. To explain responsibility, consider this scenario: After a hard day of work, three brothers are sitting on a couch with a big pile of laundry waiting to be folded. One of the brothers is responsible (Ned), one irresponsible (Fred), and the third's responsibility level is somewhere between the first two (Ed). How could we figure out who was who?

- Ned would step forward and fold the laundry without having to be asked.

- Ed would fold the laundry, but only after being asked.

- Fred wouldn't fold the laundry even after being asked.

Responsible people do what they are supposed to do without needing any guidance or prompting to do so. Irresponsible people don't do what they're supposed to do even after being asked.

Think about It

Do you fold your laundry without needing to be asked? If not, do you assume folding your clothes is somebody else's responsibility? Can you think of other things that you leave to other people to do that you should really do yourself?

_____

_____

_____

_____

_____

_____

_____

Preparation

Next, accountability involves becoming ready to meet your obligations, or being prepared. **Preparation** is *the process of becoming ready to perform*. In order to be ready to perform, you must prepare yourself. Only you can

Preparation: The process of becoming ready to perform.

Photos 7.1 and 7.2. A responsible person carefully folds their laundry and neatly puts it away; an irresponsible person leaves it in a messy pile. *Photo 7.1 Source:* U.S. Army Photo by Spc. Carlynn Knaak. *Photo 7.2 Source:* Yinan Chen; Creative Commons Public Domain.

prepare yourself so that you are ready to tackle the rigors of college. As such, preparation involves answering the who, what, when, where, and why questions of preparation (see figure 7.5).

Preparation is the mechanism that will enable you to become ready to perform and actualize your performance goals. It also will help you avoid feelings of regret, worry, and longing for something better than what you have achieved. Have you ever thought about how important preparation is to becoming ready to perform in college and university? Have you ever asked:

- Whom am I preparing for?

- What am I preparing?

- Where am I preparing?

- When am I preparing?

- Why am I preparing?

- How am I preparing?

We defined accountability as a willingness to follow through and fulfill obligations. And who is the person that you most accountable to? The answer is you. You cannot escape your responsibilities to yourself regarding your role in determining your destiny.

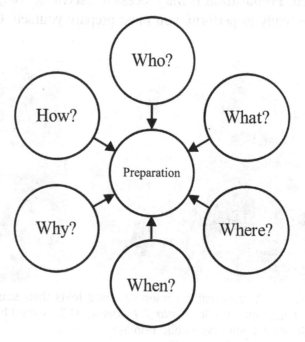

Figure 7.5. A Framework for Preparation. *Source:* Author-created.

Think about It

College is a type of preparation. Please answer the who, what, when, where, why, and how preparation questions regarding your decision to attend college. Note: The who question is simple to answer.

Who? _____

What? _____

When? _____

Where? _____

Why? _____

How? _____

You can also use the who, what, when, where, why, and how preparation question framework when you take tests, write papers, write posts, and everything else that you do. By using this preparation framework, you will be checking off all of the important boxes required to be ready to perform at whatever you choose to do or become.

Readiness to Perform

Dinner cannot be ready if you are still peeling the potatoes. Readiness to perform is a function of preparation. Following this same logic, students cannot be ready for class or a test if they have not adequately prepared. Preparation requires a willingness to independently complete the work necessary so you are ready to perform. To be ready to perform, students should willingly read all assigned materials, use the internet or tutors to supplement lecture and class materials, complete all homework and writing assignments, memorize key terms and formulas, and review notes. All of this requires a lot of time. Students who come to a test without preparing will not be ready to perform well on the test. In the words of Benjamin Franklin, "By failing to prepare, you are preparing to fail." Again, **readiness to perform** *is a function of preparation.*

Readiness to perform also requires having the proper tools to perform. Just as a carpenter cannot be ready to perform without having the proper tools (like a hammer), students cannot be ready to perform without books, calculators, paper, pencils, computers . . . the tools of all knowledge workers. Failure to willingly and independently prepare yourself to be ready to perform indicates a lack of accountability for your obligations. You cannot be viewed as dependable if you are not accountable.

Readiness to Perform: A measure of your level of preparedness.

Think about It

You are participating in a one-month group project for chemistry class. The group project is worth 50 percent of your final grade. Each group member is responsible for specific parts of the project. You've had five one-hour group meetings. Every team member showed up on time and stayed for the duration of each meeting. At the last meeting, the day before the project is due, everyone is supposed to hand in their work for inclusion in the final submission. However, one of the team members announces, "I just started working on my section a couple of hours ago and I'm not ready, but here's what I've done so far."

How would you react if the group's project was not ready to hand in? Does it matter that this team member had perfect attendance for every meeting? Why or why not? Please explain.

_____

_____

_____

_____

_____

_____

Contribution

Let's do a quick recap. The first two variables in the dependability model are attendance and accountability. The last dependability model variable is contribution. You cannot be viewed as being dependable if you do not reliably contribute. **Contribution** *measures the amount of value you bring to a group*. Although your willingness to add value to a group may be affected by many trust-related issues, contribution is simply a function of three (3) variables: availability, involvement, and participation (figure 7.6).

Contribution: Measures the amount of value you bring to a group.

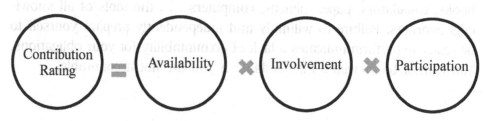

Figure 7.6. Contribution Model. *Source:* Author-created.

Availability

As discussed, rating your contribution to a group describes the amount of value you bring to it. To add value to any group you must first make yourself available to participate in group activities. Availability requires you to make time (scheduled or unscheduled) for group-related activities. **Availability** *is a measure of your willingness to make time to support group goals.*

Suppose that you are living in a house with Sasha, Lacresha, and Imani and a rain storm quickly dumps three inches of rain in just forty-five minutes into your neighborhood and causes a flash flood. There is so much water that is running down the street that it begins flowing into your neighbor's driveway and flowing downhill toward their house. You neighbor is frantically trying to stop the water. Sasha, Imani, and you rush out of your house into the rain and start moving landscaping blocks from a retaining wall on your property and laying them across your neighbor's driveway to create a makeshift dam. However, Lacresha refuses to help, saying, "That's not my responsibility." How would that make you feel about her? What do you think the neighbor would think about Lacresha's unwillingness to help out?

Making yourself unavailable to support group activities does not make the work go away; it simply transfers all of the work of the group to other more dependable people. Lacresha's refusal to help merely means that everyone else has to work harder to avoid a disaster. If Lacresha faced a similar emergency, do you think you, your roommates, or your neighbor would be willing to help her out?

Availability: A measure of your willingness to make time to support group goals.

Involvement

Because nobody can be in two places at the same time, you are either available to participate or not. It's a black and white variable. Continuing with this logic, you cannot be involved in group-related activities if you are not available for them. So, availability is a prerequisite for involvement and participation. **Involvement** *measures an individual's willingness to take on group responsibilities.*

Individuals who take on more responsibilities within a group are more involved than individuals who do not. Some people think that being available is all that is required to make a contribution to a group. Although they make themselves available, they are not actually involved in group activities. Returning to our previous example, suppose that Lacresha had put on her shoes and raincoat and gone outside, but just stood there and didn't move any of the landscaping blocks. Instead, she offered suggestions about what needed to be done while leaving the work to others. Although she made herself available, she did not contribute anything meaningful to what the others are doing.

Involvement: Measures an individual's willingness to take on group responsibilities.

Think about It

In college, you will be attending classes with other students. A classroom is a type of group setting. What are examples of negative and positive classroom involvement?

POSITIVE INVOLVEMENT

_____

_____

_____

_____

NEGATIVE INVOLVEMENT

_____

_____

_____

_____

Participation: A measure of the overall effect an individual's involvement has on groups.

Healthy Group Participation: Showing up on time, working hard, appreciating others, and adapting to difficult or changing situations that strengthens trust and group connections and creates goodwill among group members.

Unhealthy Group Participation: Individual actions that can cause others to feel upset, frustrated, scared, and angry, which can destroy goodwill and cooperation in groups.

If you are negatively involved in the work of a group and do not have a sense of duty about your obligations to it, you are nothing more than a warm body taking up space. You cannot meaningfully contribute to groups, teams, or departments if you are unwilling to be involved and do your fair share.

Participation

The last variable in the contribution model is participation. **Participation** is *a measure of the overall effect an individual's involvement has on groups.* We can think theoretically of the effect of our participation in groups as either strengthening or weakening group trust—or healthy or unhealthy, respectively. **Healthy group participation** *strengthens trust and group connections and creates goodwill among group members.* Examples of healthy participation are showing up on time, working hard, appreciating others, and adapting to difficult or changing situations. **Unhealthy group participation**—such as lack of effort and accountability, being unreliable, disrespecting others, using poor judgment, and making reckless decisions—*can cause others to feel upset, frustrated, scared, and angry, which can destroy goodwill and cooperation in groups.*

Participation is where all of the principles in this book are applied in the real world. Individuals who violate the principles of attendance, accountability, and contribution communicate an unwillingness to meet their obligations to others. In short, they deprioritize their obligations, and in doing so communicate that they cannot be trusted to perform their duties consistently. Undependable participation creates doubt in the minds of the people who experience it, which may cause them to act in a manner that safeguards their own interests.

Undependable behavior creates doubt that undermines trust. Undependable people prioritize their own desires ahead of the interests, needs, and wishes of others. Try to keep that in mind as you make choices during your day. Even the most casual decisions, like choosing to sleep in instead of consistently showing up, being on time, or being ready to perform, can weaken your credibility and possibly even sever the trust that binds you to other people.

Think about It

Ned showed up for every baseball team practice, but he didn't pay close attention to the team coach and held back during practice figuring it was just a waste of time. On the day of the big game, he fumbled a major play, letting the other team win the decisive point. His teammates were angered and asked the coach to drop him from the roster for the rest of the season. How did Ned's behavior affect his teammates' attitude toward him?

Please jot down some things that you can do that are healthy and strengthen group cohesion, and some behaviors that you consider particularly damaging to trust, goodwill, and group cohesion.

HEALTHY GROUP PARTICIPATION

_____

_____

_____

_____

UNHEALTHY GROUP PARTICIPATION

_____

_____

_____

_____

Safety, Success, Cost, and Teamwork

In addition to trust, goodwill, and group cohesion, there are other very practical reasons why dependability is critically important. Dependable people are safer, more successful, less costly, and better team members than undependable people. Let's look at each of these aspects of dependability.

Safety

The first and probably most serious reason that dependability matters is safety. In some occupations, not consistently being prepared, available, or ready to perform can actually endanger the health and welfare of others. Firefighters, police officers, and members of the armed forces must trust their coworkers to be dependable when they go to work. Being undependable is a major ethical breach in these professions. Undependable firefighters, police officers, or members of the armed forces could seriously compromise the safety of everyone on their team. You might imagine that other professionals—including doctors, lawyers, nurses, paramedics, security guards, air traffic controllers, and pilots, to name just a few—also must be dependable or they could compromise the safety of people that depend on them.

Think about It

A situation quickly can spiral out of control when an individual on a team is not dependable. Consider this personal account of what can happen when a coworker is not dependable:

When I was a patrol officer, there was another police officer who had recently been hired who had a reputation for not being dependable. I will refer to him as "Joe." On one occasion, I was dispatched to a bar fight. Serious injuries had already occurred. Joe was my backup officer. I arrived at the bar fight first. Unfortunately, the bar fight had spilled out into the parking lot, so I could not wait for my backup to arrive. As I got out of my car, I heard the dispatcher continuing to call Joe, but he did not respond. I continued anyway and in the process of breaking up the fight, I got hit a few times and stabbed.

Not until I got everything under control did Joe show up. As it turned out, Joe was busy away from his car socializing with a woman. The dispatcher finally got him on the radio and he "ran code red" all the way to the bar fight. But, it was too late. While I was stopping the fights, making the arrests, and heading to the emergency room, Joe was earning an undependable and untrustworthy reputation.[2]

What specific dependability variables or rules did Joe violate? How would you react to Joe in the future? Explain.

_____

_____

_____

_____

_____

_____

Success

The second reason why dependability is important is that it affects success. Being dependable influences your success as a student and an employee. To try to understand how student dependability impacts academic success, the Business Programs Department at SUNY Broome Community College performed a research study that gathered the attendance and grade data for the 206 students who completed financial accounting and human resources management courses over a seventeen-month period. The study only included students that received a final grade, and did not include students that withdrew before a final grade could be given. To gather the attendance data, students signed an attendance log at the beginning of every class. Table 7.1 summarizes the findings of the study.

Table 7.1. Student Attendance Records

Attendance	No. of Students	% of Total	GPA	Average Grade
0 classes missed	47	24%	3.3	B+
1–4 classes missed	96	46%	2.8	B–
5–8 classes missed	32	15%	2.2	C
More than 8 classes missed	32	15%	1.2	D
Totals	207	100%		

Source: Author-created.

As the numbers show, there is a substantial correlation between final GPA and class attendance. Students with fewer absences received higher grades, while students with lower grades had higher absenteeism. In fact, students who did not miss any classes had 15 percent and 33 percent higher grades than students that missed one to four classes or five to eight classes, respectively. On the other hand, 11 percent of the students in this study received failing grades, none of whom were among those with perfect attendance.

Attending class is one way that students acquire knowledge. In class, professors introduce subject material, answer questions, explain homework, review for tests, and discuss their expectations. Outside of class, students are expected to read their textbooks, complete assignments, and write papers. Students who consistently attended class were better prepared for tests.

Think about It

If you were to think about your attendance, how would you rate yourself on attendance on a scale of A to F? If you didn't give yourself an A rating, can you think of things that you can do to improve your attendance, such as setting alarms that can trigger your awareness of the obligation?

_____

_____

_____

_____

_____

_____

_____

Cost

In an employment setting, undependable people are expensive to keep around. Prior to teaching, I was as a member of a wireless start-up company that is now part of T-Mobile, USA. My last position at the company was in customer service senior management. My department was responsible for, among other things, scheduling a 1,000-plus-person workforce at two 24/7 customer contact centers.

One of the most important variables we tracked in the department was how well customer contact representatives kept to the schedules that we had given them. We tracked electronically when representatives were logged into the systems to take calls, how long they were logged into the systems, and how long they were logged out. Our goal was to achieve 90 percent schedule adherence. This meant that for an eight-hour shift, with thirty minutes for lunch and two fifteen-minute breaks, representatives should have been logged into the systems for 378 minutes each day. Our goal was to have all of our one thousand representatives logged into the systems, ready to take calls for a total of 1,000 representatives x 378 minutes = 378,000 minutes each day.

What we found was that our representatives were only keeping to their schedules 80 percent of the time, not the 90 percent we had budgeted for. This meant that all one thousand representatives were actually logged into our system ready to take calls for an average of only 336,000 minutes instead of the scheduled 378,000 minutes. The 42,000-minute difference in performance between scheduled to actual time meant that the company was paying for the equivalent of about one hundred full-time employees to show up and not work. If the average representative costs approximately $35,000 per year (in salary, benefits, and other costs), the cost to the company of operating at 80 percent schedule adherence is $3,500,000 per year ($35,000 x 100 representatives).

Think about It

Imagine that you are attending college under these conditions:

- Term length: fifteen weeks
- Number of courses: five courses
- Number of classes: forty-five classes
- Tuition: $2,000 per class
- Class length: sixty minutes per class

How much would failing to attend three classes for each course cost you?

How much would it cost you if you were consistently ten minutes late for every course?

_____

_____

_____

What is the total length of time you will spend in versus out of class?

_____

_____

_____

Teamwork

Being undependable creates a lot more work for everyone else on a team (see chapter 6). The work does not go away when people don't show up or are late, unprepared, or not ready to perform duties; it is moved or shifted to dependable group members.

Imagine the following scenario. It's a hot and humid summer afternoon and you are the owner of an ice cream shop. There is a continuous line throughout the day of about three hundred customers, but only two of three workers you had scheduled to work show up. The worker that did not come to work was a "no call, no show." Instead of servicing three hundred customers between a team of three workers, you must now service them with a team of only two. Without the third worker, customers wait longer for service, and some might get frustrated and leave the store, which would increase stress and frustration for the entire work team and hurt business.

Think about It

I once had an employee who would call in sick from time to time. When we pulled his attendance log, which shows what days he missed for an entire year on one sheet of paper, we noticed that every few weeks he got sick on either Monday or Friday.

What does the pattern tell you? Quick note: Many students also demonstrate this exact same dependability pattern in college.

How do you think his coworkers felt about having to cover for him when he was out?

How would you react to an undependable person who increased your workload?

_____

_____

_____

_____

_____

Dependability Effectiveness: A Self-Assessment

To see if you are dependable, please take a few minutes to complete the self-assessment in table 7.2.

Using the behavioral observation scale (table 7.3), write in the rating column the number corresponding to the degree to which you consis-

Table 7.2. Dependability Effectiveness: A Self-Assessment

Below Expectations	Meets Expectations	Role Model
Even with guidance:	With guidance:	Independently and willingly:
• Fails to provide evidence (verbal, written, and behavioral) that their actions and words are dependable and/or aligned with audience expectations.	• Provides evidence (verbal, written, and behavioral) that their actions and words are dependable and aligned with audience expectations.	• Provides evidence (verbal, written, and behavioral) that their actions and words are dependable and aligned with audience expectations.
• Fails to provide evidence that he or she can be relied on by others.	• Provides evidence of these behaviors and can be relied on by others.	• Provides evidence of these behaviors and can be trusted and relied on by others.

Source: Author-created.

tently exhibit the behavior described in the statement. Note, there are no right or wrong answers. All that is important is that you indicate how consistently you exhibit the behavior described in the action statement.

Now transfer your answers for each statement into the corresponding space in table 7.4.

Table 7.3. Behavioral Observation Scale

5 = Almost always performs as described by the Role Model standards.
4 = Sometimes performs as described by the Role Model standards and sometimes performs as described by the Meets Expectations standards.
3 = Almost always performs as described by the Meets Expectations standards.
2 = Sometimes performs as described by the Meets Expectations standards and sometimes performs as described by the Below Expectations standards.
1 = Almost always performs as described by the Below Expectations standards.

	Action Statement	**Rating**
1	I attend all of my classes.	
2	I arrive on time to class.	
3	I remain in class.	
4	I don't look at my cell phone in class.	
5	I pay attention in class.	
6	I complete assigned homework prior to class.	
7	I prepare in advance for exams.	
8	I bring required materials to class, including books, paper, computer, pencils, handouts, PowerPoints, completed/attempted homework, and so on.	
9	I ask questions that relate to the subject matter being discussed in class.	
10	I listen and try to make a positive contribution in class.	

Source: Author-created.

Table 7.4. Dependability Behavior Mapping Table

Item	5Cs	Variable	Behavior	Behavior Rating	Behavior Average
1	Commitment	Dependability	Attendance		
2	Commitment	Dependability	Attendance		
3	Commitment	Dependability	Attendance		
4	Commitment	Dependability	Attendance		
5	Commitment	Dependability	Attendance		
6	Commitment	Dependability	Accountability		
7	Commitment	Dependability	Accountability		
8	Coping	Dependability	Accountability		
9	Coping	Dependability	Contribution		
10	Coping	Dependability	Contribution		
Average					

Source: Author-created.

Greater than 4: If your average is between 4 and 5, you are dependable, can be relied on by others, and require little guidance regarding your attendance, accountability, and/or contribution.

Between 3 and 4: If your average is greater than 3 but less than 4, with guidance you are dependable, but you usually require guidance regarding your attendance, accountability, and/or contribution.

Less than 3: If your average is less than 3, you are sometimes dependable, but occasionally even with guidance you are not dependable.

Take your behavior averages for this section, calculate the new average of averages, and input that information into the employability profile.

Think about It

The dependability behavior mapping table shows you if others can rely on you. What is your average? Can you be relied on? If not, why not?

1	2	3	4	5
Below Expectations		**Meets Expectations**		**Role Model**
Even with guidance from others, fails to provide evidence of behavioral understanding of the 5C Elements and cannot be trusted with responsibility, and is unwilling to work on the responsibility of self-management.		With guidance, provides evidence of behavioral understanding of the 5C Elements and can be trusted with responsibility.		Independently and willingly provides evidence of behavioral understanding of the 5C Elements and can be trusted with responsibility.

Where:

5 =	Almost always performs as described by the "Role Model" standard.
4 =	Sometimes performs as described by the "Role Model" standard and sometimes performs as described by the "Meets Expectations" standard.
3 =	Almost always performs as described by the "Meets Expectations" standard.
2 =	Sometimes performs as described by the "Meets Expectations" standard and sometimes performs as described by the "Below Expectations" standard.
1 =	Almost always performs as described by the "Below Expectations" standard.

Communication
Trust a person to convey messages appropriately.

- Audience
- Involvement
- Message
- Evidence
- COMMUNICATION MEAN

- BEHAVIORAL COMPETENCY RATING (MEAN OF MEANS)

Choices
Trust a person to use good judgment.

- Communication
- Commitment
- Coping
- Caring
- Choice
- CHOICE MEAN

Commitment
Trust a person to be dutiful.

- Dependability Attendance
- Dependability Accountability
- Dependability Contribution
- Hard Work Time Deliberate Practice
- Hard Work Delayed Gratification
- Hard Work Effort Energy
- Hard Work Effort Determination
- Hard Work Effort Stamina
- Quality Measure of Excellence
- Quality Continuous Improvement
- COMMITMENT MEAN

Coping
Trust a person to demonstrate fortitude during difficult times.

- Coping Change Demonstration
- Coping Adversity Self-Awareness
- Coping Adversity Self-Restraint
- Coping Adversity Self-Improvement
- Coping Complexity Capacity
- Coping Complexity Capability
- Coping Complexity Activities
- COPING MEAN

Caring
Trust a person to show concern for others.

- Caring Civility Listening
- Caring Civility Courtesy
- Caring Civility Consideration
- Caring Helpfulness Concern
- Caring Helpfulness Cooperation
- Caring Helpfulness Compromise
- Caring Conscientious Thoughtfulness
- Caring Conscientious Carefulness
- Caring Conscientious Fairness
- Caring Common Good Respect
- Caring Common Good Equity
- Caring Common Good Goodwill
- CARING MEAN

Changing Habits

How can you employ Fogg's Behavior Model tiny habits (see chapter 1) to improve your level of dependability in college?

Please take a few moments and try to come up with one tiny communication habit that you can use to become more dependable. Remember to use the format "After I (insert existing behavior), I will (insert new tiny behavior)."

After I _____ ,

I will _____ .

Commitment Personal Policy Contract

To help you achieve your behavioral goals, write them down to create a personal policy contract. By signing and dating the personal policy contract, it becomes an obligation to yourself that cannot be broken.

Commitment Goals

Goals	Commitment goal(s) that will guide how I communicate in college: _____ _____ _____ _____
Personal Policies	Personal policies I will follow about my levels of commitment: _____ _____ _____
Public Commitments	Public commitments that I will make to regularly measure how I am doing regarding my commitment goals and personal policies. I will send my goals, personal policies, and quick weekly progress reports to a supportive friend and the professor. _____ _____ _____ _____
Signature: _____	**Date:** _____

Key Terms

Do you understand the definitions of the following terms and phrases? Can you use each one correctly to describe your own behavior?

- Accountability
- Attendance
- Availability
- Character Traits
- Commitment
- Contribution
- Dependability
- Healthy Group Participation

- Lateness
- Participation
- Preparation
- Productive Behavioral Patterns
- Readiness to Perform
- Unhealthy Group Participation
- Unproductive Behavioral

Discussion Questions

1. Explain the three behavioral variables that demonstrate commitment.

2. Describe what commitment is, what it measures, and why it's important.

3. What is commitment's behavioral minimum? Explain why this variable is commitment's behavioral minimum.

4. Define dependability and describe why it is important. Explain the three variables that demonstrate dependability.

5. Can people have good attendance but not be considered dependable? Why or why not?

6. The contribution model is an evaluation of the value that individuals bring to groups. Contribution is a function of what three variables? Explain each variable.

7. Accountability is defined as a willingness to follow through and fulfill obligations. The accountability model involves three variables. Explain each variable and provide examples.

8. What is the most serious consequence of undependable behavior? Explain your answer.

9. Dependability is described as a teamwork goal. Why?

10. Why is undependable behavior expensive for organizations?

To Sum Up

- Chapter 7 focuses on commitment.

  o Commitment is an act and as such is communicated non-verbally.

  o Commitment demonstrates your willingness to follow through and meet your obligations.

  o An overwhelming body of evidence indicates that talent and intelligence are developed through commitment.

- Commitment is a function of three variables: (1) dependability, (2) hard work, and (3) quality.

- Each of those variables was broken down further into sub-variables.

- Certain behaviors can affect all the variables simultaneously.

- Dependability is the degree to which you can be relied on by others. It is demonstrated by your attendance, accountability, and contribution to groups.

  o Dependable people are safer, more successful, less costly, and better team members than undependable people.

8

HARD WORK AND QUALITY

Commitment is what transforms a promise into a reality.

—Abraham Lincoln

After reading this chapter, you should be able to:

- Define hard work, why it is important, and how the three variables of hard work relate to commitment.

- Explain the distinction between practice and deliberate practice.

- Understand the roles that procrastination and delaying gratification play in academic success.

- Show how multitasking can reduce your ability to concentrate.

- Define quality, why it is important, and how quality is assessed in academia.

- Understand how grade point average (GPA) relates to academic quality and commitment.

In chapter 7 we learned that the 5C Element commitment communicates your *willingness to accept your obligations*. We also learned that:

1. Your level of commitment to any activity can be measured and analyzed using three elements: dependability, hard work, and quality.

2. There is an overlapping relationship between dependability, hard work, and quality, which means that certain behaviors impact all of the variables simultaneously (see figure 8.1).

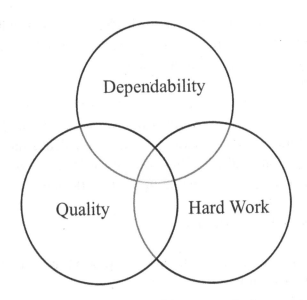

Figure 8.1. Commitment Model. *Source:* Author-created.

Chapter 7 focused on the first element, dependability, because it is the minimum behavior required to show commitment. Dependability includes your attendance, accountability, and contribution, which communicates that you are reliable to others.

Chapter 8 will cover the other two variables that communicate commitment: hard work and quality. Let us take a look at these two variables in more detail.

Understanding Hard Work

Nothing will work unless you do.

—Maya Angelou

The second variable in the commitment model is hard work. In tough economic times, it is easy to think that brains and talent alone create success. Although it may be true that innate talent and intelligence play roles in your success, these traits are only the first step to success and need to be developed. Decades of research provide an overwhelming body of evidence that talent and intelligence are developed through hard work over time. Hard work is necessary for your achievement and success.[1]

For a variety of political, technical, and economic reasons, many of the low- and medium-skill jobs that once paid good wages and helped countless workers enter the middle class have slowly been either automated or outsourced to countries with lower labor costs. In today's competitive global marketplace, employers in all fields are increasingly looking for employees who can use their knowledge, skills, and abilities (KSAs) to make organizations more efficient, effective, and competitive. They are searching domestically and internationally for people with highly developed KSAs that are a result of hard work.

So what is hard work? We can define **hard work** as *difficult mental or physical activity done to develop intelligence and talent*. Hard work has three defining characteristics: (1) time with deliberate practice, (2) delayed gratification, and (3) effort. As shown in figure 8.2, the product of these variables equals the value of your work output.

Hard Work: Difficult mental or physical activity done to develop intelligence and talent.

Time with Deliberate Practice

> Practice isn't the thing you do once you're good. It's the thing you do that makes you good.
>
> —Malcolm Gladwell

Time gives us the ability to see the effects of our choices on our lives. You cannot become a first-rate doctor, musician, lawyer, writer, salesperson, computer programmer, mechanical engineer, or artist without investing large amounts of time developing those skill sets. According to researchers, **time** is *a primary ingredient in developing skills*.[2]

Time: The primary ingredient in developing skills.

Research on exceptionally talented people estimates that it takes about ten years of practice (about 2.7 hours per day of practice every day) to develop world-class expertise in any field—or about "ten thousand hours."[3] These researchers also found that it did not matter how talented the individuals were when they started. The most talented people were not always naturally gifted when they started, or the smartest; they were the people who put in the most time and practice.

Research shows that attaining excellence in knowledge-based skills such as mathematics, reading, and writing also requires practice over time.[4] It takes a lot of time to learn how to read and write well or to become proficient in mathematics or a language. Although it helps to have great teachers, the research clearly shows that your own commitment to

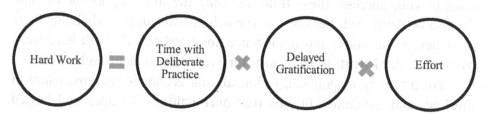

Figure 8.2. Hard Work Model. *Source:* Author-created.

succeed is far more important than any other factor. Genuine skill development requires a real sacrifice of time. The most exceptionally talented students put in a lot more time than less-talented students.

Investing time into developing yourself is particularly difficult when you think that you lack the requisite skills or ability for high levels of achievement. Practicing something that you are not proficient at requires much more concentration than practicing something that you excel at. In addition to practicing things that you do well, the researchers point out that **deliberate practice** involves *considerable, specific and sustained effort to practice thing you can't do well. It involves improving the skills you already have and extending the reach and range of your skills that you don't have.*[5]

For example, average basketball players may be better at shooting or dribbling with their right or left hands. However, the best basketball players in the world can shoot and dribble with both hands, consistently and equally. They can shoot the ball moving to the left and the right. They methodically and repeatedly practice every aspect of the game day after day, week after week, month after month, and year after year. They develop world-class basketball skills by systematically thinking through and practicing what they are good at as well as what they are not good at. They continually work to improve every aspect of their game for years.

Deliberate Practice: Considerable, specific, and sustained effort to practice something you can't do well. It involves improving the skills you already have and extending the reach and range of the skills that you don't have.

Photo 8.1. Great basketball players practice their three-point shot to ensure that they consistently score points. *Source:* Massimo Finizio; Creative Commons Attribution-Share Alike 2.0 Italy.

Because deliberate practice requires much more concentration, it is hard to do for long periods of time. One can only devote a couple hours a day to deliberate practice because it requires so much mental energy to maintain focus.[6] Nevertheless, people who are deliberate in their approach to skill development and hard work practice a couple of hours every day for years. It all adds up. For example, if you practice writing every day for a couple of hours, you will total almost three thousand hours in just four years. Three thousand hours is enough time to become a good writer.

College is all about learning new subject matter. Some subjects you may be good at and some you may not. Some classes are more demanding than others. Sitting and staring at material that you find difficult for hours on end is not productive. A better way is to concentrate for smaller amounts of time in a deliberate way. For some subjects involving problem solving—such as math, accounting, economics, or physics—the key is to know how to approach the problems. For students who are having difficulty with these types of classes, it may not be possible to do the work without a basic understanding of how the formulas work. To gain that understanding, deliberate practice might involve working with a tutor for a few hours every week to practice the formulas. After gaining a basic understanding of how to solve problems, deliberate practice might then involve doing problems repeatedly (a couple hours at a time) to reinforce the learning, going to a tutor to learn material that you do not understand, or even trying to review or teach the material to another person.

For courses that emphasize writing—whether essays, short stories, or research papers—basic writing skills will be required. A brilliant idea that is not written well will undermine the impact of your work. If you lack the basic writing skills required for these courses, deliberate practice might involve working at a writing lab for an hour or two each day to learn how to approach writing assignments and how to write. Deliberate practice is not just spending four hours after midnight the day an assignment is due to produce a poorly written paper.

Because deliberate practice involves doing things that you are not good at, you will be doing things that make you feel uncomfortable, frustrated, or even scared. These feelings are natural. Anytime you do something outside of your comfort zone, you might feel unsure of yourself. In order to develop the skills that you need to accomplish your goals, you must try as hard as you can to push yourself forward and cope with those feelings.

Think about It

Dede had a natural ability to play the saxophone; she could pick it up and make a pleasant sound on her first try. It was so easy for her that she rarely practiced, so she never became very good at playing and couldn't get a seat in the school band. On the other hand, the first time Mario picked up a saxophone, he could only make squeaking and squawking sounds. But he kept at it, because he was determined to become a better player. Eventually he earned first saxophone chair in his school's big band.

Do you think that you are a good student (Yes or No)? _____

Now, consider whether your answer was based on the amount of time and deliberate practice that you have historically dedicated to your course-work. Does the amount of time and deliberate practice that you have spent reading, writing, solving math problems, doing homework, preparing for exams, learning a foreign language, learning an instrument have anything to do with your response? Please explain.

_____

_____

_____

_____

_____

_____

Delayed Gratification

You cannot escape the responsibility of tomorrow by evading it today.

—Abraham Lincoln

The next hard work variable is **delayed gratification**, which can be defined as *resisting the temptation to take an immediate reward in the hope of gaining a more valuable one in the future*. An example might be that you could choose to get a dollar now if you complete one homework assignment or ten dollars if you wait until you've completed all of your assignments for the semester. According to researchers, people who are

Delayed Gratification: Resisting the temptation to take an immediate reward in the hope of gaining a more valuable one in the future.

unable to delay gratification (or postpone pleasure) "have more behavioral problems, in school and at home," than people who have developed this ability. Problems of "low-delaying adults" cited in the research include lower SAT scores, trouble paying attention, difficulty with friendships, higher body mass index, and problems with drugs and alcohol.[7]

High-delaying people *postpone fulfillment and handle work and problems immediately*. For example, high-delaying people do their homework before they go out with friends. **Low-delaying people** are more likely to procrastinate, which only magnifies tension and stress. By procrastinating, low-delaying people actually condense the amount of work that needs to be done into shorter time periods, which can create difficult problems in academia and learning. That is because new and conceptually difficult subject matter requires a great deal of time and concentration to process and learn, which limits the quantity of material one can learn each day. If it takes forty hours of deliberate practice to fully learn all of the material for a calculus exam, it is almost impossible to learn that amount of material in one or two nights. Yet we all have friends who pull "all-nighters" to cram for a test in hopes of making up for the lost time that was spent procrastinating.

Why is cramming not an effective strategy? The human brain functions in much the same way as the human stomach. You cannot starve yourself for three weeks and then eat three weeks' worth of meals in one or two nights. Your stomach would not be able to digest so much food that quickly. The same is true for your brain. No matter how hard you try, your brain cannot concentrate on conceptually difficult work like writing or complex math for more than two or three hours in a day before shutting down.[8] Also, it is doubly hard to focus when you are feeling stressed because you have to meet a deadline.

Multitasking, which can be defined as *trying to do more than one activity at a time*, is one of the ways students procrastinate. Because multitasking involves performing more than one activity at the same time, it distracts from the primary activity. This reduces your ability to concentrate, thus reducing comprehension. A 2009 study found that young people between the ages of eight to eighteen spent an average of seven hours and thirty-eight minutes each day multitasking with media.[9] By 2010, time spent multitasking with phones, computers, TV, music, video games, print, and movies increased by more than one hour and nineteen minutes, a 19 percent increase.

Texting while driving is a good example of why multitasking can be problematic. Driving requires that you have real-time knowledge of

High-Delaying People: Postpone fulfillment and handle work and problems immediately.

Low-Delaying People: People who procrastinate, which only magnifies tension and stress.

Multitasking: Trying to do more than one activity at a time.

what is happening on the road. Texting moves your attention away from controlling a motor vehicle to reading and typing words into a cell phone. Once attention is distracted, your ability to comprehend and react to what is happening on the road diminishes. The National Safety Council describes distracted driving as "when a driver undertakes any activity that diverts attention away from driving. Distractions can include using cell phones or other hand-held devices, talking with passengers, eating or drinking, reading, adjusting the radio, or using a navigation system while driving."[10] Multitasking, by definition, is distracted activity.

Distracted activity in learning reduces one's ability to concentrate, thus reducing comprehension. Any activity that takes your attention away from deliberately practicing a skill is a distraction. Let's say you're right-handed and are concentrating on how to learn to dribble a basketball with your left hand. However, your teammate keeps trying to steal the ball from you to distract you. Your teammate's defense takes your complete attention away from dribbling with your left hand, becoming something else that you need to deal with.

There are three main types of distractions that can impact your ability to perform deliberate practice to facilitate learning:[11]

1. **Visual**: taking your eyes off the learning material (reading, writing, lecturer).

2. **Manual**: taking your hands off the learning material (book, pencil, computer).

3. **Cognitive**: taking your mind off the learning material.

Any activity that takes your eyes, hands, and mind away from what you are deliberately trying to learn is a distraction and therefore a way that you can procrastinate. Suppose you are checking your emails or surfing the internet when you are trying to write a paper. When you are checking your email, you are not concentrating on writing the paper. Another example is texting a friend or your parents when you are in class or with a tutor. You are visually, manually, and cognitively distracted. When you are texting, you are not learning.

As you probably already know, distracted behavior and procrastination are hard habits to break. Delaying gratification is how hard-working people avoid procrastination. By postponing these activities until after their work is done, they can more fully enjoy their leisure time.

Photo 8.2. Texting while driving is a major cause of accidents on the road. You can't pay attention to the road if you're distracted by writing or reading a text message. *Source:* Intel Free Press; Creative Commons Attribution-Share Alike 2.0 Generic.

Think about It

Developing the ability to do something well requires a lot of time. As you have seen, time is one of the most important ingredients in developing skills of any kind. To help understand how you use your time, please fill out this worksheet. After calculating the time you spend on each activity, add the times together; they should come close to 168 hours, the total number of hours per week.

Item	Activity	Time
1.	Sleeping	
2.	School	
3.	Employment	
4.	Domestic (parenting, cooking, cleaning, shopping, dishes)	
5.	Leisure	
6.	Commuting	
7.	Exercising	
8.	Religious observance, volunteer work	
9.	Procrastination	
10.	Studying	
11.	Other, internet, TV, gaming, movies	
	Total hours per week	168

Do you feel that you have enough time to accomplish your academic goals? If not, what could you give up or spend less time doing to free up more time? Can you eliminate any obvious time-wasters to increase the amount of time you devote to your schoolwork? Remember that you should prioritize important matters before less important ones.

Effort

> Satisfaction lies in the effort, not in the attainment. Full effort is full victory.
>
> —Mohandas Gandhi

More than 2,400 years ago Sophocles said, "Success is dependent on effort." This is still true today. It is through effort that difficult tasks are accomplished. The more difficult the work, the more effort you must expend. For example, demanding mental activities, such as writing and math, may require much more concentration and focus than less demanding ones.[12] Effort is the outward, physical manifestation of hard work; it is what people see and hear. **Effort** can be defined as a *directed exertion of will*. We communicate our willingness to expend effort in many ways.

Effort: The directed exertion of will.

Effort has three defining characteristics: (1) energy, (2) determination, and (3) stamina. As shown in figure 8.3, the product of these variables equals effort.

In his "Last Lecture," the late Randy Pausch eloquently described life as "a series of brick walls" that are put in front of people to keep out those who don't want success badly enough.[13] The lesson is that your level of effort is visible to others. People who do not work hard may be considered by others to be lazy or undisciplined.

Figure 8.3. The Three Defining Characteristics of Effort. *Source:* Author-created.

Energy

> The world belongs to the energetic.
>
> —Ralph Waldo Emerson

Energy: The intensity of your resolve to accomplish work.

Energy relates to *the intensity of your resolve to accomplish work*. If your energy level is high, your resolve to work hard is high and vice versa. A consistently high energy level communicates a high tolerance for work or desire to work hard, while a consistently low energy level communicates a lack of concern or initiative to work hard. Although many things can affect your energy level in college (e.g., the difficulty of the work, interest in the subject matter), energy is simply a measure of the enthusiasm you bring to your schoolwork.

Determination

> Talent is nurtured in solitude. Character is formed in the stormy billows of the world.
>
> —Johann Wolfgang von Goethe

Determination: The firmness of your resolve to complete work, especially when conditions become uncertain or difficult.

Determination concerns *the firmness of your resolve to complete work, especially when conditions become uncertain or difficult*. Subjects that you find conceptually difficult or boring—perhaps including organic chemistry, calculus, literature, or corporate finance—may test your level of determination. Highly determined people will hang in there when the going gets tough. They persevere despite obstacles and setbacks. As the saying goes, "When the going gets tough, the tough get going." Less determined students might give up, withdraw, or even drop out of school when they face adversity. It takes a great deal of determination to hang in there when things don't go according to plan.

Stamina

> In the race for success, speed is less important than stamina.
>
> —B. C. Forbes

Stamina: How long a person can persevere under difficult or challenging circumstances.

Stamina relates to *how long a person can persevere under difficult or challenging circumstances*. Marathon runners are classic examples of people who possess stamina. They persevere through pain and exhaustion to finish long and grueling races. Similarly, graduating from college requires that students remain firm and continue moving forward when conditions become difficult.

You may feel bored, tired, confused, frustrated, and scared when studying for difficult exams or writing term papers. Students with stamina have the ability to work through these negative emotions over long stretches of time to reach their academic goals. Some majors may require you to have much more stamina and determination to overcome the negative emotions associated with certain areas of study than you may need with others, depending on how challenging you find the material. You may have difficulty and get stressed out with quantitative subjects such as math, physics, or economics, which will require more stamina to do well in.

The stamina required to overcome difficulty in academia is the exact same will to overcome fears in other walks of life. For example, there are many famous musicians that suffer from crippling stage fright, including Rihanna, Katy Perry, Adele, and Cher. Yet, even with this debilitating anxiety, these four women have become world-famous because of their consistent and sustained effort to overcome their fears. These four musicians have hung in there for years. They are a testament to how perseverance and determination over long periods of time can lead to world-class results.

Photo 8.3. Adele performing on stage in 2016. *Source:* marcen27 from Glasgow, UK; Creative Commons Attribution 2.0 Generic.

Likewise, you may have fears associated with a perceived lesser aptitude for courses involving large amounts of reading and writing, and you will need more stamina to achieve good results in those subjects.

Think about It

Astronaut Bruce McCandless II is famous for being the first person to fly untethered to the Space Shuttle, floating freely in space. He accomplished this amazing feat through long practice on earth in simulators and despite his fears and those of his wife and family that his mission might not be successful. While he was outside of the spacecraft, his wife was listening in on earth at NASA's mission control. As he later recalled, they were both feeling "quite a bit of apprehension. I wanted to say something similar to Neil [Armstrong] when he landed on the moon, so I said, 'It may have been a small step for Neil, but it's a heck of a big leap for me.' That loosened the tension a bit."

Can you think of a situation where you overcame personal fear or anxiety to achieve your goals? How did you ensure that you would be successful?

Understanding Quality

Without standards, there can be no improvement.

—Taiichi Ohno

What is a college student? To answer this question, it is first helpful to point out what college students are not. College students are not robots who come to college and university with predetermined sets of preprogrammed instructions for how to operate. They are trainees who come to college and university to acquire knowledge, experience, and judgment (aka, wisdom) so that they can work independently to fulfill their own unrealized potential. As a college student, you will have many opportunities to demonstrate that you have successfully acquired the wisdom to independently organize and assess the consequential effects of your choices on your life. For example, in college and university you will have opportunities to learn how to juggle many competing and complex priorities, such as dealing with large quantities of work (i.e., five full-time classes, possibly a job, demands of family and friends, planning a budget, and financial aid), and also conceptually difficult work (i.e., organic chemistry, calculus, and physics). These types of formative experiences are important because the wisdom required to independently create success in college and university is the exact same wisdom required for success in other aspects of life including career, family, and other relation-ships. The ability to successfully self-manage the complex and competitive nature of day-to-day circumstances is the hallmark of not only capable self-managed students but also capable self-managed employees, family members, and friends.

In college and university, you will be given opportunities to acquire knowledge, experience, and judgment in a number of ways, including: (1) reading, (2) studying, (3) attending lectures, (4) writing notes, (5) researching, and (6) performing lab experiments. But an often overlooked, and arguably the most important, wisdom acquired at college and univer-sity is the knowledge, experience, and judgment required to fulfill your unrealized potential in a world that is constantly changing, competitive, and imperfect. Not only are these skills valuable wisdom-creating oppor-tunities; they are also discrete academic products that can be assessed for their levels of quality.

Nobody throws open their dorm windows in the morning and shouts at passersby: "YAY, I get to write a paper about a subject that I care nothing about today"; or "HOORAY, I'm having a calculus test in two weeks that I get to study for today"; or "YIPPEE, I'm giving a speech next week in my philosophy class on the hazards of moral flexibility"; or "WOOPIE, I get to attend another jaw-droppingly boring and overly opinionated lecture from professor so and so." But, just because some activities are unpleasant does not mean that they are not beneficial. Most truly beneficial activities are objectionable in some way. Beneficial activi-ties can be boring, repetitive, intimidating, scary, nerve-wracking, and sometimes downright painful. For example, although studying inside for long periods of time during a perfect spring Saturday afternoon, speaking in front of a disinterested or hostile audience, writing research papers on boring topics, or attending uninspiring lectures are not particularly fun activities to do, it would be hard to argue that they are not good things to do. Nonetheless, you acquire wisdom when you push ahead to overcome and succeed despite this unpleasantness. The pain required to endure and overcome is the lesson. Potholes, rude drivers, detours, ice, and deer are not separate and distinct from the road, they are the road. Change, competitiveness, unfairness, and imperfection are not separate and distinct from life, they are life.

Your Grade Point Average (GPA) as a Measure of Success

Most employers will teach you the technical aspects of how to do a job. What is harder for employers to teach is the wisdom and good sense required to self-manage in order to overcome hardships, difficult deadlines, changing work priorities, and imperfect and annoying coworkers and bosses. A college and university degree is a credential that employers, transfer schools, and graduate schools use to validate that you possess the wisdom and good sense required to successfully complete complex, competitive, rigorous, and intellectually demanding endeavors. They do this because a college and university degree is not only recognized by society writ large as a noteworthy accomplishment; it is also a validated predictor of successful higher-level academic and labor market outcomes.[14]

Although earning a college and university degree is a notable accomplishment, employers, transfer schools, and graduate schools also will look at how well you did in your courses before they will swing their doors open for you. They will be looking closely at the quality of your academic accomplishments in college, which means that they will be reviewing your grade point average. Your **grade point average (GPA)** is *a key performance indicator of the overall quality of your academic accomplishments at college or university.* GPA is calculated by dividing the total number of grade points that you earned by the total number of credits awarded. For example:

Grade Point Average (GPA): A key performance indicator of the overall quality of your academic accomplishments at college or university.

Grade	Grade Points	Grade Range
A	4	90–100
B	3	80–89
C	2	70–79
D	1	65–69
F	0	< 65

Course	Credits	Total Numeric Average	Grade Awarded	Grade Points by Grade Awarded	Total Number of Grade Points Awarded
Self-Management	3	90	A	3	9
Marketing	3	80	B	3	9
College Writing	3	80	B	3	9
Business Law	3	70	C	2	6
College Algebra and Trigonometry	3	70	C	2	6
Total (s)	15	390	N/A	N/A	39

Grade Point Average: (Total Number of Grade Points Awarded) / (Credits Awarded) = 39/15 = <u>2.6 GPA</u>
Average: (Total Numeric Average) / (Number of Course) – 390/5 = <u>.78 or 78% Average</u>

Your GPA is an overall assessment of the quality of your academic work in college or university. A high GPA corresponds with a high level of academic quality, while a low GPA corresponds to a low level of academic quality. Although a 2.0 GPA may earn you a degree, it is the minimum GPA needed to receive financial aid and graduate from college. In our example, the student earned a GPA of 2.6, which equates to a numeric average of 78 percent. The 78 percent average represents two things: (1) the student's percentage of error-free academic work; and also (2) the student's percentage of error-prone work, or an error-rate of 22 percent (100% − 78% = 22%). So, a high GPA also represent low error rates, while a low GPA represents high error rates. In most colleges and universities and error rate of between 25 and 30 percent is an acceptable error rate and will earn you a degree.

Think about It

What would your opinion be of a new car that did not start 25 to 30 percent of the time, or a sanitation worker who only hauled away 70 to 75 percent of your trash, or a waiter who got 25 to 30 percent of your order wrong? In academia a 25 to 30 percent error rate is acceptable—but is a 25 to 30 percent average error rate in college or university acceptable to you? Explain your answer. What does a grade point average (GPA) communicate about student effort? For example, what do GPAs of 2.0 and 3.8 communicate? Explain your answer.

_____

_____

_____

_____

_____

_____

_____

In a sense, your GPA represents your ability to successfully organize and assess the consequential effects of your choices in college and university. Which means that your GPA represents the degree to which you possess the wisdom and good sense required to successfully complete complex, competitive, rigorous, and intellectual demands of college or university. And because transfer schools, graduate schools, and employers will use the average GPA as a predictor of successful academic and labor market outcomes, your GPA can either help or hurt you on your quest to fulfill your unrealized potential.

If your goal is to transfer to a highly regarded four-year college or university, or attend graduate school, a GPA of 3.5 or higher would be required for entry into the top transfer and graduate schools. That said, a GPA of between 3.0 and 3.5 would be adequate for admission to most transfer and graduate schools. Although many transfer schools will accept lower or below-average GPAs, a lower GPA may limit your transfer opportunities to more selective and highly regarded colleges and universities. You are investing a lot of your own money and time that you will never get back to earn a college or university degree, so your goal should be to maximize the value of that investment by increasing the opportunities for yourself, not limit opportunities.

As we've already mentioned, reading, studying, attending lectures, writing notes, researching, performing lab experiments, and even self-management wisdom are all discrete academic products that can be assessed for their levels of quality. Your grades and your GPA are outcomes of your commitment to your own education. As such, quality in academia is the outcome of committed behavior and therefore is the byproduct of all of these variables (see figure 8.4).

Figure 8.4. The Variables That Contribute to Quality. *Source:* Author-created.

Educators use a variety of tools to assess the quality of your academic work, including tests, quizzes, research papers, group projects, discussion posts, and oral presentations. As we've noted, your grades are measures of academic performance and are based on the percentage of error-free academic work that you produce. To reiterate, a grade of 75 percent means that the work had an error rate of 25 percent. High grades mean low error rates, while low grades mean high error rates. Grades are measures of academic quality. They are evidence of your commitment—or your willingness to expend time and energy, at the exclusion of other activities—to meet your obligations to your own education, goals, and life purpose.

Think about It

Steve Jobs and Steve Wozniak famously were working out of a garage when they first developed the Apple computer. To raise money for their venture, Jobs sold his car and Wozniak sold a fancy piece of electronic equipment, coming up with about $1,000; neither drew a salary, and both worked long hours perfecting their prototype. The level of commitment they invested in an untested idea—that individuals would want to purchase their own computer to use at home—showed how seriously they took this task. They knew that the quality of their product would determine its success. And, of course, the success of the Apple computer has become a legend in Silicon Valley and a measure for judging the work of many other entrepreneurs.

How committed are you to your own education? How did you do in high school? What is your grade point average goal for college? Explain your answer.

_____

_____

_____

_____

_____

Hard Work and Quality Effectiveness: A Self-Assessment

To see if you are working hard and producing quality work in college, please take a few minutes to complete the self-assessment (table 8.1).

Using the behavioral observation scale (table 8.2), write in the rating column the number corresponding to the degree to which you consistently exhibit the behavior described in the statement. Note, there are no right or wrong answers. All that is important is that you indicate how consistently you exhibit the behavior described in the action statement.

Table 8.1. Hard Work and Quality Effectiveness: A Self-Assessment

Below Expectations	Meets Expectations	Role Model
Even with guidance: • Fails to provide evidence (verbal, written, and behavioral) that their actions and words are appropriate and aligned with audience expectations. • Fails to provide evidence of these behaviors and is unwilling to follow through and meet obligations to others.	With guidance: • Provides evidence (verbal, written, and behavioral) that their actions and words are appropriate and aligned with audience expectations. • Provides evidence of these behaviors and is willing to follow through and meet obligations to others.	Independently and willingly: • Provides evidence (verbal, written, and behavioral) that their actions and words are appropriate and aligned with audience expectations. • Provides evidence of these behaviors and can be trusted to follow through and meet obligations to others.

Source: Author-created.

Table 8.2. Behavioral Observation Scale

5 =	Almost always performs as described by the Role Model standards.
4 =	Sometimes performs as described by the Role Model standards and sometimes performs as described by the Meets Expectations standards.
3 =	Almost always performs as described by the Meets Expectations standards.
2 =	Sometimes performs as described by the Meets Expectations standards and sometimes performs as described by the Below Expectations standards.
1 =	Almost always performs as described by the Below Expectations standards.

	Action Statement	Rating
1	I spend between two and three hours/night on homework, studying, or preparing for tests for every hour that I'm in class.	
2	I practice subjects more that I don't understand immediately.	
3	I seek out help from instructors, tutors, and study groups.	
4	I go out with friends only after my academic work is completed.	
5	I limit distractions or turn off phones, internet, TV, video games, print, movies while I am doing homework, studying, or preparing for tests.	
6	I have a level of energy to get my homework done, study, and prepare for tests.	
7	I have a "can do" attitude and seek help from tutors, teaching assistants, or professors immediately if I don't understand the material that I am learning.	
8	I hang in there and keep working hard for days, weeks, and months even when I don't understand something or when I don't get the grades I would like.	
9	I earn high grades (A's or B's) or marks in my classes.	
10	When I don't get the grades that I want, I work harder and my grades improve.	

Source: Author-created.

Now transfer your answers for each statement into the corresponding space into table 8.3.

Table 8.3. Hard Work and Quality Behavior Mapping Table

Item	5Cs	Variable	Behavior	Behavior Rating	Behavior Average
1	Commitment	Hard Work	Time and Deliberate Practice		
2	Commitment	Hard Work	Time and Deliberate Practice		
3	Commitment	Hard Work	Time and Deliberate Practice		
4	Commitment	Hard Work	Time and Deliberate Practice		
5	Commitment	Hard Work	Delayed Gratification		
6	Commitment	Hard Work	Energy		
7	Commitment	Hard Work	Determination		
8	Commitment	Hard Work	Stamina		
9	Commitment	Quality	Measure of Excellence		
10	Commitment	Quality	Continuous Improvement		
Average					

Average = $\sum$ of Behavior Rating/10: [   ] ←

Source: Author-created.

Greater than 4: If your average is between 4 and 5, with little guidance you perform difficult mental or physical activity done to develop your intelligence and talent.

Between 3 and 4: If your average is greater than 3 but less than 4, with guidance perform difficult mental or physical activity done to develop your intelligence and talent.

Less than 3: If your average is less than 3, with guidance you sometimes perform difficult mental or physical activity done to develop your intelligence and talent, but occasionally even with guidance, you do not.

Take your behavior averages for this section, calculate the new average of averages, and input that information into the employability profile.

1	2	3	4	5
Below Expectations		**Meets Expectations**		**Role Model**
Even with guidance from others, fails to provide evidence of behavioral understanding of the 5C Elements and cannot be trusted with responsibility, and is unwilling to work on the responsibility of self-management.		With guidance, provides evidence of behavioral understanding of the 5C Elements and can be trusted with responsibility.		Independently and willingly provides evidence of behavioral understanding of the 5C Elements and can be trusted with responsibility.

Where:

5 =   Almost always performs as described by the "Role Model" standard.
4 =   Sometimes performs as described by the "Role Model" standard and sometimes performs as described by the "Meets Expectations" standard.
3 =   Almost always performs as described by the "Meets Expectations" standard.
2 =   Sometimes performs as described by the "Meets Expectations" standard and sometimes performs as described by the "Below Expectations" standard.
1 =   Almost always performs as described by the "Below Expectations" standard.

Communication
Trust a person to convey messages appropriately.

	Audience
	Involvement
	Message
	Evidence
	COMMUNICATION MEAN

	BEHAVIORAL COMPETENCY RATING (MEAN OF MEANS)

Choices
Trust a person to use good judgment.

	Communication
	Commitment
	Coping
	Caring
	Choice CHOICE MEAN

Commitment
Trust a person to be dutiful.

	Dependability Attendance
	Dependability Accountability
	Dependability Contribution
	Hard Work Time Deliberate Practice
	Hard Work Delayed Gratification
	Hard Work Effort Energy
	Hard Work Effort Determination
	Hard Work Effort Stamina
	Quality Measure of Excellence
	Quality Continuous Improvement
	COMMITMENT MEAN

Coping
Trust a person to demonstrate fortitude during difficult times.

	Coping Change Demonstration
	Coping Adversity Self-Awareness
	Coping Adversity Self-Restraint
	Coping Adversity Self-Improvement
	Coping Complexity Capacity
	Coping Complexity Capability
	Coping Complexity Activities
	COPING MEAN

Caring
Trust a person to show concern for others.

	Caring Civility Listening
	Caring Civility Courtesy
	Caring Civility Consideration
	Caring Helpfulness Concern
	Caring Helpfulness Cooperation
	Caring Helpfulness Compromise
	Caring Conscientious Thoughtfulness
	Caring Conscientious Carefulness
	Caring Conscientious Fairness
	Caring Common Good Respect
	Caring Common Good Equity
	Caring Common Good Goodwill
	CARING MEAN

Think About It

The hard work and quality behavior mapping table reveals your willingness to follow through and meet obligations. What is your average? Do you communicate commitment to the activities that you're involved in? If not, why not?

_____

_____

_____

_____

_____

_____

Changing Habits

How can you employ Fogg's Behavior Model tiny habits to improve your level of commitment to college?

Please take a few moments and try to come up with one tiny commitment habit that you can use to help you improve your work ethic and academic quality. Remember to use the format, "After I (insert existing behavior), I will (insert new tiny behavior)."

After I _____ ,

I will _____ .

Hard Work and Quality Personal Policy Contract

To help you achieve your behavioral goals, write them down to create a personal policy contract. By signing and dating the personal policy contract, it becomes an obligation to yourself that cannot be broken.

Goals	Commitment goal(s) that will guide my commitment levels in college: _____ _____ _____
Personal Policies	Personal policies I will follow about my level of commitment: _____ _____ _____
Public Commitments	Public commitments that I will make to regularly measure how I am doing regarding my commitment goals and personal policies. I will send my goals, personal policies, and quick weekly progress reports to a supportive friend and the professor. _____ _____ _____
	Signature: _____ Date: _____

Key Terms

Do you understand the definitions of the following terms and phrases? Can you use each one correctly to describe your own behavior?

- Delayed Gratification
- Deliberate Practice
- Determination
- Effort
- Energy
- Grade Point Average (GPA)

- Hard Work
- High-Delaying People
- Low-Delaying People
- Multitasking
- Stamina
- Time

Discussion Questions

1. Explain the phrase "Quality is the outcome of commitment." In your answer explain what quality means.

2. What is the primary ingredient of skill development? What is the main point the book makes about skill development?

3. How does deliberate practice differ from practice?

4. Explain how delaying gratification impacts skill development.

5. Why is multitasking problematic for students?

6. What are the three variables associated with effort? Explain and provide examples of each.

7. How does multitasking impact deliberate practice?

To Sum Up

- Hard work in college involves doing difficult mental activities (i.e. studying, doing homework, writing) to develop understanding in a broad variety of subjects that you may not know anything about or have any interest in.

- Hard work in college is a function three variables.

  o Time/Deliberate Practice: spending long periods of studying, doing homework, solving problems, and writing about subjects that you may not be good at or have any interest in.

  o Delayed Gratification: the opposite of procrastination, it involves postponing pleasure until your academic work is completed.

  o Effort: the directed exertion of will, it involves three variables: (1) energy, (2) determination, and (3) stamina.

- Grades are measures of academic quality

- Grades are outcome of committed behavior and is improved through dependability and hard work.

- Grades represents two things (1) the student's percentage of error-free academic work, and also (2) the student's percentage of error-prone work.

- Your grade point average is a key performance indicator of academic of quality.

Section V

COPING

How to understand, communicate, and
assess situation-based trust regarding the quality
of decision-making during changing, difficult,
and complex times

9

COPING IN COLLEGE

Pain and suffering are always inevitable for a large intelligence and a deep heart.

—Fyodor Dostoyevsky

After reading this chapter, you should be able to:

- Define coping in the context of attending college and university.

- List the five challenges that are common to college, university, and career.

- Understand self-control and how it relates to attending college and university.

- List the three variables in the Self-Control Model.

- Explain what self-awareness is and how it relates to self-control.

- Understand the Complexity Model and the three variables that make up the model.

- Define activity complexity and explain how it impacts student success.

The job of being an effective college student has always been challenging. There have always been demanding professors, overly competitive students, financial pressures including high tuition and book costs, complex subjects, unreasonable deadlines, too much material to memorize, illness, and so on. Many students react negatively to the stress of college when things don't work out according to plan. They may stop going to class or doing their homework or even drop out rather than cope with the problems they encounter. These difficulties are one reason why only about 10.5 percent of the adult population in the United States over the age of twenty-five have associate degrees and 37.9 percent have bachelor's or higher degrees.[1]

Ultimately, coping with challenges in college and university requires an understanding of and belief in oneself. Because life is not all good, there must also be bad. There are ups and downs that you will experience. You will face painful hardships throughout your life that you alone must cope with. These hardships will create stress within you that you must overcome if you are to move forward and fulfill your unrealized potential.

Coping can be defined as *a process of consciously attempting to understand, manage, and/or tolerate the stresses experienced in college and university*. Coping involves trying to deal effectively with all the challenging situations that you will encounter in college and university. In college, and in life for that matter, you might cope well in some situations, but not others. For example, you might cope well in calculus class, but not so well in a public speaking class. So how well you cope depends on the situation. Unlike the other 5C Elements, coping is based on situation-based trust (see chapter 1, table 1.1).

The choices you make during challenging times will shape the kind of person that you become. It is through coping with challenges that your individuality and uniqueness become clear. Do you react before thinking? Do you let your emotions pull you in the wrong direction? Do you become critical of and blame others when you are stressed? Do you rationalize your behavior and poor decision-making?

Difficult times test your ability to cope and in doing so shape your character. Helen Keller said, "Character cannot be developed in ease and quiet. Only through experiences of trial and suffering can the soul be strengthened, vision cleared, ambition inspired and success achieved."[2]

Students that cope well grasp the deep, long-term moral significance of their decision-making in real time. They are guided by an inner conviction to do what is "right," even when doing so involves sacrificing something that is highly valued. They have an inner knowing that not doing the right thing is not an option because the alternative is an unending awareness of one's own moral shortcomings. Because we are at the center of everything that we do, we will know how we behaved and what we did forever. We cannot run away from our responsibilities to ourselves. You will define yourself and will be defined by the decisions you make in college and university, especially when the decisions are the most difficult to make.

> **Coping**: A process of consciously attempting to understand, manage, and/or tolerate the stresses experienced in college and university.

College and university have always been a difficult slog. Yelling, getting upset, holding your breath, burying your head in the sand, turning your back on others, dropping out, not going to class, being rude and disrespectful, and jumping up and down are not coping strategies. Coping effectively with these sorts of emotions and feelings involves real-time self-control at the exact time difficult situations occur. You cannot exercise self-control and cope with now after now has passed. Am I in control of my emotions in the present moment, or are my emotions in control of me?

Coping in college and university requires that you work outside of your zone of comfort. Physical, intellectual, and emotional growth happen most profoundly when you cope effectively with situations that are new, unfamiliar, or unpleasant, because you extend the reach and range of your understanding of the world in ways that dealing with more familiar and comfortable situations cannot. How can you grow if you only do that which you already know how to do?

Unless you are very dissatisfied with your current circumstances, when you do something outside of your comfort zone, you can expect to feel unsure of yourself because you are walking away from the people and activities that make you comfortable. To develop more fully though, you need to push forward despite those feelings.

Finally, the more situations people can cope with, the more value they bring to society. People with college and university degrees who can solve difficult and complex problems are in high demand in today's world. One reason that doctors, nurses, lawyers, engineers (civil, mechanical, electrical), computer scientists, and senior executives earn more than those without advanced degrees is because they can solve specific types of problems. According to US Department of Labor statistics, college graduates made nearly double the median weekly salary of those who had only completed high school, while those with advanced degrees earned at least double the median wages of college graduates.[3] College degrees are evidence of and a testament to one's ability to cope.

Coping with Challenges Common to College and Career

Life unfolds in stages. In each stage, you develop individually and socially. There is infancy (0–18 months), early childhood (1.5–3 years), preschool (3–5 years), school age (6–11 years), adolescence (12–18 years), young adulthood (18–40 years), middle adulthood (40–65 years), and maturity (65–death).[4] In each of these stages of life you cope with unique challenges. For example, when you are an infant, you learn to cope with the challenges of lifting your head up, sitting up, drinking from a bottle, crawling, and walking. When you are school age, you learn and cope with the challenges of sitting still, interacting with other students and teachers, reading, writing, solving mathematical problems, and even driving. When you are in the adult stages, you learn how to cope with all of the problems associated with being an adult, including the challenges associated with college and career.

The challenges that you will face in college and career are, for the most part, similar regardless of person or context. In fact, there is an overlapping relationship between the challenges faced in college and university, and the challenges associated with careers (see figure 9.1). Because the challenges that you will face in college and university are similar to the challenges that you will face during your career, the coping skills required for you to be successful in college and university are similar to the coping skills required to be successful in your career.

In college, university, and career many college students cope with similar categories of challenges including:

1. Financial (struggling with cost of food, housing, shelter, cell phone, internet access, transportation, computer, loan debt).

2. Interpersonal (experiencing difficult bosses, professors, co-workers, classmates, roommates, significant others, and even family members and friends).

3. Behavioral (addressing issues relating to work ethic, dependability, and quality, as well as inappropriateness, procrastination, poor judgment, and lack of concern for others).

4. Psychological (experiencing anxiety, stress, depression, perfectionism, and insecurity).

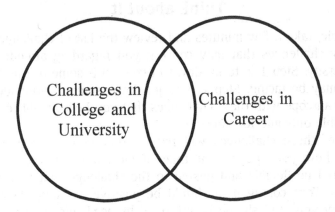

Figure 9.1. Relationship between Challenges Associated with College, University, and Career. *Source:* Author-created.

You too may be experiencing these types of challenges at college and university, and also in your career.

In addition to the four types of challenges previously mentioned, many high-paying career opportunities require that you also cope with a fifth challenge category, the academic challenges associated with attending college and university. There are three main types of academic challenges that college and university students cope with: (1) the volume of courses that you take per semester, (2) the level of conceptual difficulty of these courses, and (3) the additional costs and debt associated with attending college and university. None of these academic challenges is insurmountable, and all can be managed successfully with proper academic and financial planning. Although this fifth challenge may appear to be associated with attending college and university, in fact, it also pertains to many career fields because many industries require a college or university degree as a requirement for employment in these fields.

Yet, even though so many career opportunities are eliminated by not graduating from college and university, many students do not graduate. As of the date of the printing of this book, 39,040,099 adults in the United States of America have dropped out of college and university without graduating, which represents an astounding 11 percent of the entire population.[5]

If college dropouts must cope with the financial, relationship, behavioral, and psychological challenges outside of college anyway, regardless of whether they graduate from college or university, and coping with academic challenges does not seem like much of a heavy lift, why do so many students drop out when there are so many opportunities and benefits associated with earning a college and university degree?

Think about It

In this table, take a few minutes and review the list of challenges and try to identify challenges that may concern you regarding attending college and university. Step 1 is to jot down in column 3 some of the challenges that you may be facing. Step 2 is to jot down some of your ideas about how you can cope with these challenges that you believe will result in the best possible outcome for you.

Each of these challenges will require that you make good choices regarding how you spend your time, money, and energy. Your coping ideas should be flexible and geared to the challenge that you are trying to address. Your coping plan should be positive, seek the best possible outcome for you, and should be informed by academic advisors, financial aid counselors, professors, and other people that you trust.

Challenge Category	Challenge Examples	Step 1: Your Challenges	Step 2: Your Coping Ideas
1. Financial	Struggling with the cost of: food, housing, shelter, cell phone, internet access, transportation, computer, debt		
2. Relationships	Experiencing difficult or toxic: bosses, professors, coworkers, classmates, roommates, significant others, family members, and friends		
3. Behavioral	Grappling with issues relating to your own: work ethic, dependability, and quality, as well as inappropriateness, procrastination, poor judgment, and lack of concern for others		
4. Psychological	Experiencing feelings of: anxiety, stress, depression, perfectionism, and insecurity		
5. Academic	Worrying about academic work: volume, conceptual difficulty, cost of books, debt		

Coping and Self-Control

Self-control, which is sometimes thought of as self-discipline, is defined as *effortful regulation of the self by the self*.[6] To help us understand self-control more, let us look at a Self-Control Model (figure 9.2). This model's

Self-Control: Effortful regulation of the self by the self.

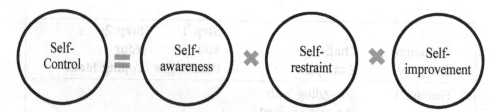

Figure 9.2. Self-Control Model. *Source:* Author-created.

components are: self-awareness, self-restraint, and self-improvement. This model helps guide thinking and behavior during challenging and stressful times, which can help put situations into perspective and ease the pain and stress associated with attending college or university.[7]

You are practicing self-control if you are:

1. Aware of your own desires, thoughts, emotions, and motives during stressful situations.

2. Managing your own behavioral reactions during stressful situations.

3. Transforming over time your personal coping skills by your own efforts during stressful situations.

If any of the variables on the right-hand side of figure 9.2 are low, self-control decreases. For example, if a father slaps his eight-year-old son hard across the face because he didn't clean his room, the level of self-restraint of the father would be zero, and the product for his self-control would be zero as well. (The product of anything multiplied by zero would, of course, be zero.)

Like all of the other behavioral competencies in this book, your ability to cope in college and university can be improved with practice and work. It requires a focused and concerted effort to practice self-control. The alternative to practicing self-control is to be a loose cannon. A loose cannon is a nautical term "for a cannon that breaks loose from its moorings on a ship during battle and has the potential to cause serious damage to the ship and its crew."[8] Not only can a loose cannon inflict heavy damage on its own ship and crew; it can also inflict heavy damage on friendly ships as well. A person thought of as a loose cannon is "someone who behaves in an uncontrolled or unexpected way and is likely to cause problems for himself or herself and other people."[9]

Think about It

Identify each of the following behaviors as examples either of exercising self-control or being a loose cannon. Give your reason why for your choice for each example.

	Self-Control	Loose Cannon	Why?

Self-Awareness

Adversity introduces a man to himself.

—Albert Einstein

We can define **self-awareness** as *an accurate understanding of yourself, including your own desires, thoughts, emotions, and motives during difficult situations*. None of us are as self-aware as we would like to be. We are all unique. Understanding our uniqueness, including our own

Self-Awareness: An accurate understanding of yourself, including your own desires, thoughts, emotions, and motives during difficult situations.

behavior during difficult times, is an important part of developing a strategy for how to cope with problems that we will face in the future. Are you usually good under pressure, or do you tend to get angry, upset, or disengage in some way that may undermine your own effectiveness? Do you blame others when things go wrong? Do you take responsibility for your own actions? Without an accurate understanding of your own predispositions (i.e., how you think and act during times of adversity), it is hard to effectively cope with difficult situations.

How can you make good decisions about how to react to a situation if you do not have a clear understanding of your own desires, thoughts, emotions, and motives? How would you know how to judge the appropriateness of your behavior if you did not have any standards for it? The ability to correctly prioritize matters during times of adversity requires self-awareness and behavioral understanding. It is at these times, at these decisive moments, when insightful self-awareness and appropriate behavioral action are most important. Without the understanding that accompanies self-awareness, clarity of judgment is very difficult.

Think about It

Take a few minutes and think about all of the possible stress-inducing problems that college students can encounter. In the space provided: (1) list all the problems that you can think of; (2) brainstorm as many possible reactions (good and bad) to each one; and (3) try to identify any insights into your own reactions to these stress-inducing situations. Break down the insights into things you did or do well (strengths) and things you can improve. (Please use an extra sheet of paper if the space provided is not enough.)

(1) List the stress-inducing problems that students face in college.

_____   _____
_____   _____
_____   _____

(2) List possible reactions (productive and unproductive) to each identified problem.

Productive   **Unproductive**
_____   _____
_____   _____
_____   _____

(3) List insights about your own reactions to stress-inducing situations in college.

Strengths   **Improvements**
_____   _____
_____   _____
_____   _____

In this exercise, you identified together stressful problems students face in college and university and a wide range of productive and unproductive reactions to these problems. You were also asked to list any insights into your own reactions to problems that you face in college. In the same way that you were able to see productive and unproductive reactions in others, they too can see your reactions. What will people see? Will they trust how you react to challenges that you face? Do you admire how you react to challenging situations?

Years from now, if your professors are asked about your reactions to the problems that you faced in college and university, what would they say? If you believe that they will say that your reactions to problems were trustworthy, what evidence can you provide to substantiate your belief?

Self-Restraint

> Forces beyond your control can take away everything you possess except one thing, your freedom to choose how you will respond to the situation.
>
> —Viktor E. Frankl

Self-restraint can be defined as *the ability to successfully manage one's reactions during stressful situations*. Coping effectively with difficult situations (i.e., solving problems without hurting oneself or others in the process) communicates a great deal about your ability to handle pressure. Self-restraint helps take the emotion out of solving difficult problems, which makes it easier to clarify the nature and meaning of situations, and thereby improve reasoning and judgment. People that cope well with challenging and stressful situations maintain their cool when the going gets tough. They do not throw a fit every time something goes wrong in their life and are able to maintain a calm and steady control over their emotions.

Self-restraint requires you to work consciously through anxious feelings without acting in an impulsive manner, or behaving in angry or unreasonable ways toward others. Self-restraint enables you to react in a manner that serves your best interests, but it is particularly hard when you are emotionally close to a situation. True self-restraint is keeping one's cool when immediately affected by a situation. Human beings are not machines. Each of us has lost our cool at one time or another and acted in incorrect, unwise, or unfortunate ways that we may regret. That is part of being human. However, when losing control of your emotions is a standard way of behaving, patterns may emerge that communicate a lack of proper regard for the needs, wishes, and feelings of others.

Self-Restraint: The ability to successfully manage one's reactions during stressful situations.

Self-restraint is good in almost every circumstance because it gives you time to make sure that you are acting in your own interest. It is a prerequisite for clarity of judgment when we are coping with important issues and making crucial decisions. Exercising self-restraint demonstrates that we have guiding principles or personal policies that inform our own behavioral decision-making during difficult times. Examples of personal policies for self-restraint might include: "I will try not to take things personally"; "I will always try to maintain my composure when facing adversity"; or "I will never punch another person with my fists or my words." There are many others. Without defined standards for self-restraint, any behavior may appear to be OK. Without predefined personal policies, human beings are capable of great harm.

Self-Restraint Personal Policy: Self-imposed rules that reduce ambiguity that could cloud your judgment and decision-making during stressful times.

Think about It

Ned and Alonzo were having a heated discussion about who was responsible for buying drinks and chips for a party that they were hosting in their dorm room. Alonzo got upset and began pointing at Ned, each time moving his finger closer to Ned's face. Meanwhile, Ned started to turn red and took on a defensive posture. Before long, they fell to blows, with Ned breaking Alonzo's glasses. Later that night, they both felt ashamed and embarrassed by their behavior.

Are you in control of your emotions or are your emotions in control of you? Please take a few minutes to think about and write down your own set of self-restraint personal policies or mantras, which will help guide your behavior during difficult times.

Establish a **self-restraint personal policy**, which can be defined as *self-imposed rules that reduce ambiguity that could cloud your judgment and decision-making during stressful times*.

For example, "It is never okay to pull the car over and attack another person" is a self-restraint policy that provides clarity for behavioral options in times of extreme stress while driving. Physical assault is not an option in any setting, except perhaps in the most extreme of unsafe circumstances. A less dramatic self-restraint policy might be "I will always maintain my cool and not damage others, even when I am under pressure and things do not go my way." These policies remove the behavioral guesswork when confronted with difficult emotional situations. What are the types of self-restraint personal policies one might adopt in an academic setting? List some of the ones that you have personally used in the past or think you might use in the future.

_____

_____

_____

_____

_____

One of the best self-restraint personal policies is to establish a **Count to Five and Think Policy**. This rule establishes a standard and a procedure that will give you time to step back and think and gain some perspective about what is in your best choice in a given situation. This is especially important because acting on impulse rarely serves your best interest.

Another good self-restraint policy is to establish a Stress-Reduction Policy so that you can gain control of your emotions and reduce stress during challenging and stressful times. For example, when you are stressed or angry, you could establish a personal policy that would trigger the following breathing technique. It works.

Step 1: With your head straight, look up and close your eyes while still looking up.

Step 2: Inhale as deeply as you can four times. (Breathe in through your nose slowly and out through your mouth, slowly.)

Step 3: On the fourth breath, hold your breath for five to ten seconds, and then slowly let your breath out.

Step 4: Sit still and then open your eyes after half a minute.

Self-Improvement

If there is no struggle, there is no progress.

—Frederick Douglass

No one is perfect. Everyone has shortcomings that can be improved in some way. This is particularly true for coping. Coping with adversity is a difficult skill to master, especially when the adversity immediately affects you. For our purposes, we can think about **self-improvement** as *a lifelong process of bettering your nature, abilities, and character by your own efforts during stressful situations*.

To improve coping skills, we must critically and honestly examine our own thoughts, emotions, behavior, and motivations after difficult events have passed. We need to continually evaluate our own behavioral performance against our personal policies and behavioral standards. This assumes that we have predefined standards against which our performance can be measured. Was my behavior in alignment with my predefined behavioral standards, or did I fall short in some way? Without an honest evaluation of our own behavior following difficult times, we might not know if our approach to coping was effective.

Improving your ability to cope can be difficult due to the painful emotions and feelings that accompany tough times. For that reason, you need to have the emotional and intellectual strength to endure hardship,

Count to Five and Think Policy: A rule that gives you time to step back and think and gain some perspective about what is in your best choice in a given situation.

Self-Improvement: A lifelong process of bettering your nature, abilities, and character by your own efforts during stressful situations.

accompanied by the desire to improve your own reactions to adversity. Without a willingness to cope with difficult emotions, improving your ability to cope is almost impossible. Life continually tests our ability to cope. As my mother used to say, "You gotta wanna."[10]

Stretch Goals: Long-term goals that you seek to attain.

Think about It

When Ramona faced a difficult situation, she'd hide in her dorm room and watch TV and gaze at social media for hours. After a while, however, she began to notice that her grades were suffering, while at the same time the problems that she was avoiding weren't going away. She decided to try to improve her approach by coming up with different and better strategies to cope with her fears. Instead of hiding in her room, she forced herself to go out and spend time with others. Rather than watch TV and looking at social media, she'd participate in sports or group activities that had more positive outcomes. She was able to exercise self-improvement in order to overcome her difficulties.

Establish a self-improvement stretch goal for yourself in all matters. **Stretch goals** are *long-term goals that you seek to attain*. They can help clarify the rightness or wrongness of your thinking and behavior during times of adversity and stress and serve as an example or rule to live by. They should be short and limited to one sentence (e.g., "I am committed to handling all matters with grace or dignity").

In addition to identifying your self-improvement stretch goal, please identify the steps you think that you need to improve your coping skills. What are things you can do to improve how well you cope?

Self-Improvement Stretch Goal

_____

Improvement(s) needed to improve your coping skills

_____
_____
_____
_____
_____
_____

Understanding Academic Complexity

Academic complexity can be defined as *the academic and nonacademic factors that complicate attending college and university*. A primary responsibility of students is to demonstrate that they can cope with the complexity of college and university. Can you handle the workload required for each course, as well as the combined workloads for all your courses? Do you have complete understanding of the course material, or has the course complexity hampered your comprehension in some way? Can you balance all the academic and nonacademic activities that you are participating in? Can you meet all of the deadlines? Can you manage all of the financial matters associated with attending college and university, and all of your other nonacademic responsibilities?

Professors assess student academic work to determine whether they understand and can cope with the level of academic complexity in their courses. Tests, quizzes, homework, oral and written reports, and class participation all measure a student's ability to cope with academic complexity. Most good professors will challenge their students to determine how much complexity they can handle before they fall behind. Specifically, college stretches students to find out their capability (what they know) and capacity (how much academic and nonacademic work they can handle) levels.[11] In addition, college will also be a time when you will need to manage financial matters closely to ensure that you have enough to cover your costs of living (food, clothing, and shelter) and the costs associated with attending college or university (tuition, books, student debt).

Academic complexity has three defining variables: academic capability, academic capacity, and academic activities. As shown in the Academic Complexity Model (figure 9.3), the product of these variables equals academic complexity.

Academic Complexity: The academic and nonacademic factors that complicate attending college and university.

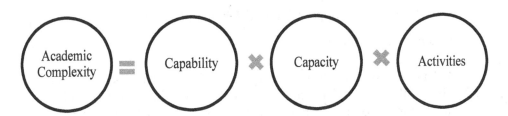

Figure 9.3. Academic Complexity Model. *Source:* Author-created.

Capability

Capability: An assessment of your ability to comprehend the academic and nonacademic world.

Capability is *an assessment of your ability to comprehend the academic and nonacademic world*. Is the level of comprehension complete or incomplete? Capability is not solely a function of your intellectual smarts. Good grades and academic understanding rely heavily on your behavioral choices. Student behaviors—that is, studying, showing up for class, putting in time to do homework, and delaying gratification—all influence student performance. Students who study and go to class learn more and perform better than students who do not.

Academic capability relies on behavioral performance, and grades represent student proficiency in both academic and behavioral areas. As discussed earlier, grades are measures of academic excellence, residual evidence of the percentage of error-free academic work submitted. In essence, grades are a measure of academic capability (see chapter 8). For example, a 75 percent grade means that the student capably handled 75 percent of the questions, with an error rate of 25 percent. High grades mean highly capability, while low grades translate to a lower level of capability within that subject area.

Think about It

One of the best ways to cope with courses that are difficult conceptually is to put together a workable plan to manage this complexity. A plan might include answers to the following questions:

- Can I space difficult classes out over several semesters so that I am not taking too many difficult courses at the same time?

- Can I take a course in the summer?

- When I do not understand something, how will I get answers to my questions?

- Is the professor approachable if I have questions?

- Can I use a tutor?

Are there any courses that worry you? If so, please jot them down and then talk to your academic department, advisor, a trusted professor, friend, or parent to get the help that you think you need so that you can worry less about these courses. Every student has academic strengths and weaknesses. Having an academic plan in place to help you address the courses that create concern for you is a great step that you can take to cope with this type of academic complexity.

_____

_____

_____

_____

_____

_____

_____

Capacity

Capacity is *a measure of the quantity of academic and nonacademic work a student can handle before their performance begins to erode.* When professors seem to be assigning too much work, they are trying to increase your capacity in their courses. Capacity, like capability, relies heavily on behavioral performance (i.e., putting in the time and effort required to get through large quantities of subject matter).

Textbooks are thick for a reason. Many textbooks and courses have content-rich vocabularies of technical terms. Every academic discipline has its own language. The languages may not be conceptually difficult to understand, but they may require learning many new terms. This means that you need to build your capacity to deal with this new information and language.

Capacity: A measure of the quantity of academic and nonacademic work a student can handle before their performance begins to erode.

Think about It

Actor Robert De Niro wanted to make a film about the life of the boxer Jake LaMotta. He had capacity issues—he was not built like a boxer, weighing just 145 pounds while LaMotta, a heavyweight champ, weighed considerably more—as well as capability issues (he had to learn to box, to speak with LaMotta's unique accent, and to mimic the way he moved). De Niro was ultimately successful but it took months of training and dedicated preparation to build both his capability (through training regimens, a trip to Italy to visit LaMotta's home town) and literally his capacity (by going on a binge diet to gain weight). The result was the classic film *Raging Bull*, leading to multiple Oscar wins including one for De Niro as best actor.

Coping with the complexity (capability and capacity) of college requires behavioral competency. Take a few minutes and jot down some of the capacity and capability issues that you deal with at college.

Capacity Issues

_____

_____

_____

_____

_____

Capability Issues

_____

_____

_____

_____

Have you been coping with the complex issues you face in college? Have you been putting in the time and effort required to cope with the complexity of college? If not, why not?

_____

_____

_____

_____

_____

_____

Activities

What are various roles that you play in life? How would you describe the way that you allocate your time and money to the different roles that you perform? **Activities** can be defined as *the normal actions that you spend time and money on when you are awake*. For example, in your role as a college or university student, you might spend time on attending class and completing assignments and money on buying supplies and paying your tuition. You might also spend time and money in your role in relationships with people outside of college or university (as a dad, mother, husband, brother, friend, coworker). Other pursuits that require spending time and money include:

Activities: The normal actions that you spend time and money on when you are awake.

- Leisure activities (going to parties, playing video games, learning the guitar)

- Jobs (professor, tile setter, landscaper, dental assistant, paralegal)

- Causes or beliefs (political activism, feminism, environmentalism, and spiritual beliefs)

- Health or being athletic (golfer, runner, swimmer, tennis player, club memberships, bike rider, rower)

The list is endless.

Activity complexity is a measure of how you prioritize all of these roles. Low activity complexity means that all activities are equally important to you, while high activity complexity means you prioritize activities differently.

For low–activity complexity people, there will be a great deal of ambiguity between where their priorities lie because none of these roles will take priority over others. For example, if you view social activities as equally important to you as being a student, you may be willing to prioritize your money and time to party and hang out with friends more than studying. If you view your friendships as equally important as your wife and kids, you may prioritize spending your time and money with friends over your family.

However, if you define yourself as being a husband and dad first above all other roles, and prioritize your time and money on your parental and marriage responsibilities above your other roles when you make choices, then you can be said to be a high–activity complexity person.

Another example: if you prioritize yourself as a prelaw student above your more social-related activities, then you will prioritize your time and money on academic-related pursuits, rather than on social pursuits.

Think about It

Do you have low activity complexity or high activity complexity? Rank the following list from highest to lowest priority.

Role/Activity	Examples	Your Roles	Priority
College or university student	business, biology, computer science, early childhood education		
Relationship	dad, mother, husband, brother, friend, coworker, student		
Leisure activities	partying, gaming, playing a sport, hunting, surfing, playing music, smoking, drinking, fishing, bird-watching		
Profession	professor, mechanic, tile setter, corporate manager, doctor, lawyer, landscaper, dental hygiene		
Behavioral traits	hard working, nice, polite, considerate, energetic, enthusiastic		
Causes or beliefs	spiritual, political activist, feminist, environmentalist, conservative, liberal		
Athlete or heath consciousness	runner, swimmer, footballer, tennis player, baseball player, weightlifter, bike rider, rower, moto crosser, skateboarder		
Other			

In chapter 8 you did a time assessment (page 176) in which you figured out how you are allocating your time. You can refer back to that exercise to help you determine if you are low- or high-activity complexity person.

- Do you prioritize your time and money based on the importance of each role?

- Can you do a better job allocating your time and money to activities that are aligned with your goals in college and life?

- Are you balancing your time and money appropriately?

- Please explain your answers.

_____

_____

_____

_____

_____

_____

Key Terms

As a student, you should understand thoroughly the following words and phrases. Can you explain them and use them correctly?

- Academic Complexity
- Activities
- Capability
- Capacity
- Coping
- Count to Five and Think Policy

- Self-Awareness
- Self-Control
- Self-Improvement
- Self-Restraint
- Self-Restraint Personal Policy
- Stretch Goals

Discussion Questions

1. At the very beginning of the chapter is the Fyodor Dostoyevsky quote "Pain and suffering are always inevitable for a large intelligence and a deep heart." What does this quote mean and why is it important?

2. Why is coping important? What is the basic idea of coping?

3. Coping is described in the book as a process of consciously attempting to understand, manage, and/or tolerate the stresses experienced in college and university. What types of stresses do college and university students cope with?

4. Many of the challenges that students face in college and university are the same types of challenges that they will face when they go out into the working world. Explain the five types of challenges that students cope with in college, university, and careers.

5. Explain the three variables in the Self-Control Model.

6. The book describes self-awareness as an accurate understanding of oneself, including one's own desires, thoughts, emotions, and motives during difficult situations. How can a lack of self-awareness affect our reactions to challenging situations?

7. There are three academic complexity variables that the book describes. Define the three complexity types and provide examples to help explain your answer.

To Sum Up

- Coping is the process of consciously attempting to understand, manage, and/or tolerate the stresses experienced in college and university.

- Coping communicates your ability to deal with challenging situations and, for that reason, is characterized as a situation-based trust trait.

- There are overlapping challenges associated with college, university, and career—financial, relationships, behavioral, psychological, and academic.

- Three important behavioral qualities enable us to communicate self-control: self-awareness, self-restraint, and self-improvement.

  o Self-awareness is an accurate understanding of yourself, including your own desires, thoughts, emotions, and motives during difficult situations.

  o Self-restraint is the ability to successfully manage one's reactions during stressful situations.

  o Self-improvement is a lifelong process of bettering your nature, abilities, and character by your own efforts during stressful situations.

- Academic complexity is defined as the academic and nonacademic factors that complicate attending college and university.

- There are three academic complexity variables that students must cope with in college and university: capability, capacity, and activity.

10

COPING WITH CHANGE

Every great dream begins with a dreamer. Always remember, you have within you the strength, the patience, and the passion to reach for the stars to change the world.

—Harriet Tubman

After reading this chapter, you should be able to:

- Define change and explain why change is so difficult for students.

- Explain why coping with change is a necessary behavioral competency.

- Understand what sense of loss and sense of mistrust mean and how these concepts relate to new routines and strangers.

- Describe the Beckhard and Harris Change Model, and the Student Readiness Change Model and the three variables within the model.

- Explain who Elisabeth Kübler-Ross was and how her research relates to student success.

- Explain the adapted version of the Scott and Jaffe Model called the Four Stages of Student Grief Model.

- Describe the three ways that students can react when they experience change.

Understanding Change

Like time, change happens.

According to the **Law of Change**,[1] *everything is continually in the process of becoming something else.* Like death and taxes, change is impossible to avoid. Think about how the United States has changed over the last century. According to the US Census Bureau, in 1910 the population of the United States was 92.4 million. In 2022, the population was around 332.4 million and growing.[2] In 1910 only 13.5 percent of the population completed high school. Today, about 85.3 percent completes high school. In 1910, average life expectancy for men was about 48.4 years and women 51.8 years. Today, average life expectancy is about 73.2 years for men and 81.1 years for women (see figure 10.1).[3] In 1910, Georgia, Missouri, Indiana, and Michigan had larger populations than California. Today, California's population is larger than all those states combined.

To begin to understand the pace and scale of change, it is helpful to think about the changes that have occurred just since the year 2000. At the change of the millennium, Tesla (started 2003), Meta aka Facebook (started 2004), YouTube (started 2005), Twitter (started 2006), and Instagram (started 2010) did not exist. As table 10.1 shows, only one of the top ten largest companies in the world in 2000 (Microsoft) still remains a top ten largest company. Moreover, in 1980, only twenty years before Microsoft was the largest company in the world, personal computers, cell phones, the internet, and CDs did not even exist.

Law of Change:
Everything is continually in the process of becoming something else.

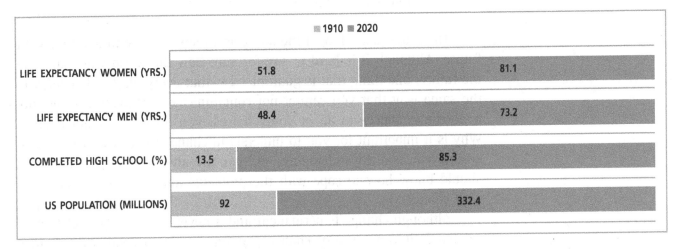

Figure 10.1. Changes in US Demographics, 1910–2022. *Source:* Author-created.

Table 10.1. Top Ten Companies Ranked by Total Revenue, 2000 and 2022

2000	Company	$ in Billions	2022	Company	$ in Trillions
#1	Microsoft	$606	#1	Saudi Aramco	$2.27
#2	General Electric	$508	#2	Apple	$2.25
#3	NTT Docomo	$367	#3	Microsoft	$1.94
#4	Cisco	$352	#4	Alphabet	$1.43
#5	Walmart	$302	#5	Amazon	$1.11
#6	Intel	$280	#6	Tesla	$707B
#7	Nippon Telegraph	$271	#7	Berkshire Hathaway	$612B
#8	Nokia	$219	#8	United Health Group	$485B
#9	Pfizer	$206	#9	Johnson & Johnson	$472B
#10	Deutsche Telekom	$197	#10	Tencent	$435B

Source: https://www.visualcapitalist.com/cp/largest-companies-from-2000-to-2022/.

What changes can you expect to see by 2040? It is hard to say, but here are some of the predicted changes for just the next twenty years:

- The world population is expected to grow from seven billion people to over nine billion people.[4]

- Fifty percent of global car sales will be autonomous self-driving vehicles.[5]

- Nuclear fusion, a form of clean and sustainable power generation, will almost be perfected.[6]

These are just a few of the amazing things that are in store for your future. Although it is hard to say for sure how the world will change in the future, one thing that is guaranteed is that everything will change. In the same way that you cannot not communicate, not make choices, not have consequences to all of your choices, you also cannot not change. Why is it important for you to understand change? Because, if the world around you is always changing, and you are always changing, then you should know how to cope with the problems and challenges associated with change.

Although change is permanent and a never-ending aspect of human existence, it can be very challenging for people to cope with change, because in order to change they must deal with new and unfamiliar people, places, and activities. This push toward the unfamiliar makes people feel uncomfortable; we are all more comfortable and confident in our ability to succeed in familiar circumstances. Think about it: You may have been comfortable in high school—where you were surrounded by familiar people, lived in the town where you grew up, and pursued your favorite activities—but experienced discomfort in your initial weeks in college, when the people were all new to you, the place was unfamiliar, and you had to find new activities to pursue. For some people, it may take some time before they can summon up the courage to deal with their fears and embrace change. They may resist change if they sense that it will force them out of their comfort zones. In psychology, the term for this is status quo bias. **Status quo bias** is evident *when people prefer things to stay the same by doing nothing or by sticking with a decision made previously.*[7]

To better understand what happens to new students psychologically and emotionally when they experience status quo bias, one of my colleagues asks new students a simple question, "What do you like better: variety or routine?" Many choose variety. Variety is fun and exciting. It is the spice of life. Routines, on the other hand, can be dull and mundane. However, when asked to look around and notice where everybody is sitting week after week, they observe that everyone usually sits in the same seat. Some students even get upset when someone is sitting in their usual chair. People may seek variety for some things—food, music, and entertainment—but often cling tightly to their basic routines.

Status Quo Bias: When people prefer things to stay the same by doing nothing or by sticking with a decision made previously.

New Routines and Strangers

Routines are *the familiar ways that you perform your daily rituals and chores.* They help you to process repetitive daily activities more efficiently. Like cruise control, routines make life easier by taking the thinking out of doing the recurring things that you do. However, like bad habits, bad routines can be very difficult to break.

Attending college or university will interrupt many of your comfortable routines, and as such forces you to turn off the cruise control and think about what you are doing. Because you are giving up the comfort and familiarity of your old routines when you attend college for the first time, you should expect that change involves a **sense of loss** because you are *giving up the routines that make you feel safe and secure.*[8] The unpleasant feelings that accompany the loss of something that has brought you comfort in the past is one of the aspects that makes change difficult for students. For example, students that go away to college will

Routines: The familiar ways that you perform your daily rituals and chores.

Sense of Loss: Grief because you are giving up the routines that make you feel safe and secure.

no longer be eating meals at their family home, or sleeping in their comfortable bed. Instead, they will be eating at an unfamiliar cafeteria and sleeping in a strange dorm room bed. It's important to realize that these feelings are mostly normal because you are grieving over the loss of something that you value: the comfort and familiarity of your old routines.

Stranger: Someone who is unfamiliar to you.

Sense of Mistrust: Being unable to confidently rely on others in situations where you are feeling vulnerable and at risk.

To complicate matters further, you may not know anyone at the college that you are attending, which means that you are forced to interact with strangers. A **stranger** is *someone who is unfamiliar to you*. Strangers in college include other students, professors, advisors, dormmates, teammates, coaches, and academic advisors. Because strangers are unfamiliar to you, you cannot know the strength of their character or trustworthiness. It is only after strangers become familiar to you that trust can develop. You should expect to feel a **sense of mistrust**[9] when you start college and university precisely because everyone you meet is a stranger. For students that go away to college or university, not only will they no longer be eating and sleeping in familiar surroundings; they will be doing these things with strangers. They will be eating with strange people and sleeping in a strange room with people who are new to them.

Photo 10.1. What has this student done to personalize her dorm room and make it feel more like home? *Source:* Benuski, Richmond, VA; Creative Commons Attribution-Share Alike 2.0 Generic license.

When you combine the sense of loss with the sense of mistrust, you may feel a bit overwhelmed and may even say to yourself, "This isn't for me." Even the best students can expect to feel this at some point in college, and it may take a bit of time for those feelings to go away. These uncomfortable feelings are for the most part a natural consequence of transitioning to college. Most students will be able to cope with these feelings as they make the transition to college, but some may not. They may not be emotionally or psychologically ready to make the transition to college.

The only thing that can fix the sense of loss and the sense of mistrust that accompany the changes associated with attending college is time. You need to give yourself time to make the transition to college so that your new routines become familiar routines, and the strangers become people whom you know and trust. When the unfamiliar becomes familiar, the unpleasantness can subside.

Think about It

Some students do not understand that many of their daily routines will need to change when they enter college. They bring their high school mentality into college and do the same things that they did in high school, because that's what they know. For example, some new college and university students may have been able to not study for tests and still earn passing grades in high school. In college, these same students may not do well because the volume of work and conceptual difficulty of the work may be too great to just "wing it."

For each of these new circumstances, please list the changes you'll have to make in your old routines and why these changes will be necessary.

New Circumstance	Changes Needed	Why
Moving to a new town to attend college		
Living in a dormitory		
Eating in a cafeteria		
Getting to class on time		
Trying out for a sports team		
Taking care of your own finances		
Taking care of your own health		

Student Readiness for Change

As discussed earlier, entering college brings students face to face with unfamiliar people and situations that they need to cope with. Some will embrace the change immediately, and some will accept it over time, but others may never fully adjust.

The US Department of Education estimates that 31.8 percent of college students leave school after the first year.[10] Many of these students do not return because they were unable or unwilling to cope with change. Although college costs, socioeconomic inequalities, childcare needs, and other factors can play a role, many students simply drop out because they do not cope well with the changes that college requires. They may not even realize that when making the transition to college it is normal to feel uncomfortable, confused, and, at times, overwhelmed.

We can refer to *the varying degrees of emotional and intellectual readiness that new students bring to college* as **student readiness for change**. Students who are fully emotionally and intellectually prepared for college will be able to cope with the new challenges that they encounter.

To help explain student readiness for college, let's look at an adapted version of the Beckhard and Harris Change Model (figure 10.2).[11] The **Beckhard and Harris** change formula is a simple and useful tool that helps organizations identify and analyze their employees' resistance to change. The model can also be used to evaluate the readiness risk of students entering college and university. In this model, the three variables on the left-hand side of the expression must outweigh the perceived cost of the change in order for the student to transition well into college. If the product is less than the perceived cost to the student, then a student may not be ready to change.

Students change most readily when the product of these three situational elements are greater than the perceived cost of the change to the student:

- Their dissatisfaction level with the current situation.

- How much they value their education.

- Their personal perceived probability of success.

Student Readiness for Change: The varying degrees of emotional and intellectual readiness that new students bring to college.

Beckhard and Harris Change Formula: A simple and useful tool that helps organizations identify and analyze their employees' resistance to change.

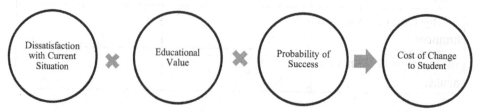

Figure 10.2. Student Readiness for Change Model. *Source:* Author-created.

If any of the variables are low, student readiness decreases. For example, if a student was completely satisfied with his or her current situation, then the level of dissatisfaction would be zero. Student costs may include physical and emotional tolls, financial expenses, disruption of current lifestyles, and opportunity costs. Finally, students need to believe that they will be successful in college and that earning a degree will help them achieve their life goals. If any of these three elements is not met, the student is less likely to make a good transition to college life.

Let's look at an example that involves a student who attends a local community college, Olivia Lopez. Olivia was an average student who graduated in the middle of her high school class. She never really applied herself much to academics and does not like math. She lives at home with her parents and eats with her family most nights of the week. Olivia works part-time at a local grocery store, with a friend doing lawn care in the warmer months, and shoveling snow during the winter months. She has a very active social life, including a boyfriend who is local, a car, and nightly still plays video games and parties with many of her friends from high school. She doesn't find community college too demanding but knows she will have to transfer to another college or university if she wants to pursue a higher degree.

Would Olivia be ready to change? Maybe not, for the following reasons. First, she is probably not dissatisfied with her current situation. She gets to continue to live in her comfort zone; she sleeps and eats at

Photo 10.2. Olivia works part-time at a grocery store while attending community college. *Source:* U.S. Department of Agriculture, PhotoJournalist/USDA/Lance Cheung.

her childhood home, surrounded by people whom she knows and loves. Second, she may not feel that she will benefit from attending college because all of her financial and emotional needs are already being met. She is making enough money working at the local grocery store, mowing lawns, and plowing driveways. She has a boyfriend and friends to socialize with. Third, because she never really applied herself in high school, she may not be confident about her ability to understand and do all of the work required to earn a college or university degree. That is especially true if going to college forced her to give up the grocery store, lawn care, and snow plowing work, pay out of pocket for her tuition and books, and spend a lot of time doing something that she does not particularly like doing (studying).

Think about It

Please answer the following questions (circle Yes or No).

1. Are you dissatisfied with your current situation outside of school (e.g., finances, work, friends, car)?

   Yes or No

2. Do you see a direct benefit to you in getting a college education (e.g., transfer or graduate schools, promotions, career)?

   Yes or No

3. Do you think that you can be successful at college balancing the demands of work and home obligations?

   Yes or No

According to the Beckhard and Harris Model, if you answered "No" to any of these questions, you may need some time to make the transition to college. Please explain your "No" answers. What might you do to change these "No" answers into "Yeses"?

_____

_____

_____

_____

_____

Phases of Change

People are like stained-glass windows. They sparkle and shine when the sun is out, but when the darkness sets in, their true beauty is revealed only if there is a light from within.

—Elisabeth Kübler-Ross

In 1969, Elisabeth Kübler-Ross first introduced the world to what happens when people receive news that they are fatally ill.[12] As you can imagine, this type of catastrophic news profoundly affects people and stirs up intense emotional reactions. What Kübler-Ross found was the way that people react to this type of news is actually predictable. She said that people typically experience five emotional stages that are referred to as the Five Stages of Grief Model: denial, anger, bargaining, depression, and acceptance.

Just try to image a doctor coming into your examination room. She closes the door behind her and says, "I'm sorry, but you have inoperable pancreatic cancer, and you only have six months to live." How would you react? What Kübler-Ross said was that you would react in very predictable ways. She discovered that you may first be in denial. You might say to yourself, "This isn't happening to me." After some time passed, you might then move out of the denial stage and into the anger or bargaining phases. In this phase, you might become very angry and lash out at the world, or become scared and/or try to negotiate or bargain with your God to save your life. After more time passed, and neither anger nor prayer worked to slow the progression of your illness, you might slip into the depression stage. Finally, toward the end, you might want to make peace with the world, so you might grow to accept your fate.

Kübler-Ross's insights can also help explain how people react to other, less traumatic changes or transitions that they experience. When new students enter college, many aspects of their lives can change. Their routines usually change, and they may not know anyone. In addition, they may be struggling financially and may not be confident academically. Having to cope with all of these changes, upheavals, and unknowns would make anyone feel anxious, confused, and even overwhelmed. It may be especially difficult for young people who are stepping out into the world by themselves for the first time.

We can use the Kübler-Ross model to help explain what happens to many students psychologically and emotionally when they enter college.[13] One of the most useful and compelling models that uses Kübler-Ross's work to explain what happens when people experience change was developed by Cynthia Scott and Dennis Jaffe, and called the "The Four Phases of Transition" grid. But instead of using the denial, anger, bargaining, depression, and acceptance terminology used in the original model, the Scott/Jaffe model simplifies the grief stages from five stages of grief down to four variables: denial, resistance, exploration, and commitment.[14]

With permission, we are simplifying the Scott/Jaffe model to help explain how change impacts students when they go to college. Rather than use the terms denial, resistance, exploration, and commitment, we are changing the terms to describe the typical ways that students react to college: denial, destruction, discovery, and demonstration. For our purposes, we can call this the Four Stages of Student Grief Model (see figure 10.3).

As figure 10.3 shows, the **Four Stages of Student Grief Model** is a four-quadrant model that can serve as a conceptual framework for

Four Stages of Student Grief Model: A four-quadrant model that can serve as a conceptual framework for understanding what happens to many students when they enter college.

5C Behaviors
Communications
Choice
Care
Commitment
Coping

	High	
	Stage 1 Denial	**Stage 4** Demonstration
Low	**Stage 2** Destruction	**Stage 3** Discovery
	Low	High

Time

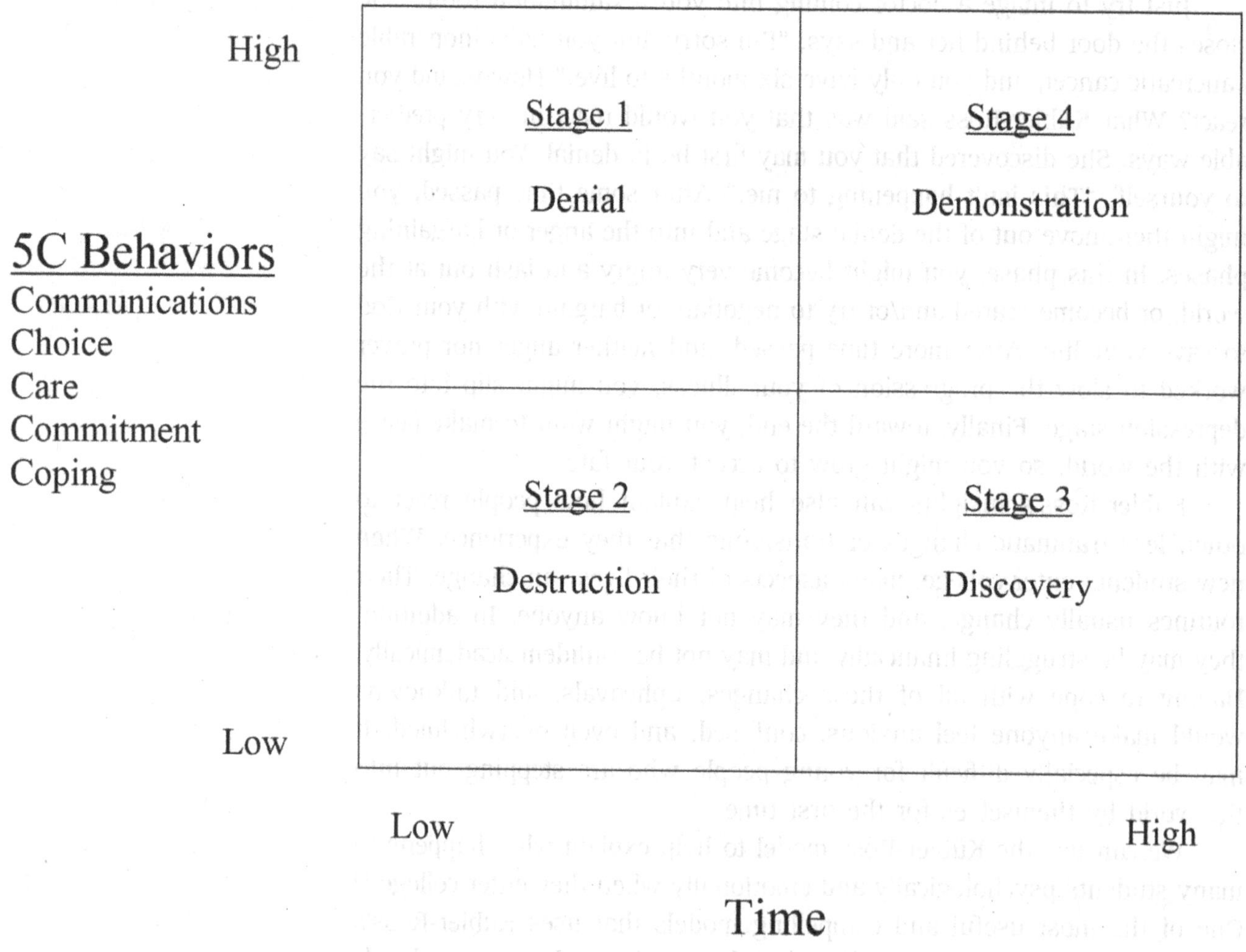

Figure 10.3. Four Stages of Student Grief Model. *Source:* adapted Scott/Jaffe model.[15]

understanding what happens to many students when they enter college. Each quadrant represents a particular way that students might react to this new situation. When students come into college, they can react in one of three predictable ways. They can either:

- Accept the change and immediately go to Stage 4 and demonstrate that they understand what is required of them in college. They walk the walk and talk the talk. They communicate appropriately, make good choices, commit to academic excellence, treat others with respect, and cope effectively with the rigors of college.

- Accept change over time, which means they might initially behave in ways that are antithetical to their own academic interests. They might take time to cycle through some or all four of the stages (denial, destruction, discovery, and demonstration). For a period of time, they might make poor choices and communicate inappropriately, appear less committed than they should be, seem indifferent or even antagonistic, and appear to be unable to cope effectively with what is required of college students. However, these students will make the behavioral adjustments necessary to end up in Stage 4.

- Reject college altogether and never adapt to the change.

Keep in mind that the stages can overlap, exist simultaneously, or be experienced out of order. With this model, we can actually predict how students will react to change, and see who is adjusting well and who is not. Let's look at each stage.

Stage 1: Denial

Students in the **denial stage** *do not demonstrate much, if any, interest in learning.* They typically act like none of the material being taught is important or applies to them. As they begin to realize that their old way of doing things doesn't work, they may begin to act in ways that are antithetical to the 5Cs. They might make poor choices about their levels of commitment and/or consideration, and may demonstrate signs that they aren't coping.

Denial Stage:
Demonstrating little, if any, interest in learning.

Think about It

What types of behaviors would you see that would identify students who are in the denial phase? What would you hear and/or see?

_____

_____

_____

_____

_____

Stage 2: Destruction

Destruction Stage:
Actively resisting the educational process.

Students in the **destruction stage** *actively resist the educational process.* They behave in ways that communicate that they are not coping with what is required of college students. They may make ill-advised choices; their level of commitment may decline; and they may not demonstrate a lack of concern for others. They may behave in antagonistic ways and in doing so fail to accept or comply with accepted behavioral norms. They seem unhappy. ☹

Think about It

What types of behaviors would you see that would identify students who are in the destruction phase? What would you hear and/or see?

_____

_____

_____

_____

_____

Discovery Stage:
Beginning to realize the ability to handle the class work.

Stage 3: Discovery

In the **discovery stage**, *students begin to realize that they can handle the work.* They might experience some success, which will give them feelings of hope, confidence, and courage. They begin to cope and start to take risks in class. It is as if a light bulb turns on and they begin to see what is in the darkness. They have a higher level of commitment, consideration, and energy in class. They start to smile. ☺

Think about It

What types of behaviors would you see that would identify students who are in the discovery phase? What would you hear and/or see?

_____

_____

_____

_____

_____

Stage 4: Demonstration

In the **demonstration stage**, *students know that they can cope with the rigors of college.* They know what they need to do, and they demonstrate student success. They may start to help their fellow students and may already be thinking about next semester or life after college. They are purposeful, confident, committed, and considerate.

Demonstration Stage: Showing the ability to cope with the rigors of college.

Think about It

What types of behaviors would you see that would identify students who are in the demonstration phase? What would you hear and/or see?

_____

_____

_____

_____

Think about It

What types of behaviors would you see that would identify students who are in the demonstration phase? What would you hear and/or see?

Student Behavior	Stage (Denial Destruction, Discovery, Demonstration)	Why?
Xavier shows up for class late and unprepared, refuses to participate in class discussions, and doesn't turn in his assignments.		
Annabelle shows up for class on time but refuses to participate in class and complains about the difficulty of the homework.		
Oscar shows up for class on time, is always well prepared, actively participates in discussions, and turns in all assignments completed and on time.		
Maria shows up for class on time and is prepared, turns in her assignments, but is still uncertain about participating in discussions and needs extra encouragement to do so.		

Coping Effectiveness: A Self-Assessment

To see if you are coping well as a student in college or university, please take a few minutes to complete the following self-assessment (table 10.2).

Using the behavioral observation scale (table 10.3) as a guide, rate each statement with the number corresponding to the degree to which you consistently exhibit the behavior described. Note, there are no right or wrong answers. All that is important is that you indicate how consistently you exhibit the behavior described in the action statement.

Table 10.2. Coping Effectiveness: A Self-Assessment

Below Expectations	Meets Expectations	Role Model
Even with guidance:	With guidance:	Independently and willingly:
• Fails to provide evidence (verbal, written, and behavioral) that their actions and words are appropriate and aligned with audience expectations. • Fails to provide evidence of these behaviors and is unwilling to do the right thing during trying situations.	• Provides evidence (verbal, written, and behavioral) that their actions and words are appropriate and aligned with audience expectations. • Provides evidence of these behaviors and is willing to do the right thing during trying situations.	• Provides evidence (verbal, written, and behavioral) that their actions and words are appropriate and aligned with audience expectations. • Provides evidence of these behaviors and can be trusted to do the right thing during trying situations.

Source: Author-created.

Table 10.3. Behavioral Observation Scale

5 = Almost always performs as described by the Role Model standards.
4 = Sometimes performs as described by the Role Model standards and sometimes performs as described by the Meets Expectations standards.
3 = Almost always performs as described by the Meets Expectations standards.
2 = Sometimes performs as described by the Meets Expectations standards and sometimes performs as described by the Below Expectations standards.
1 = Almost always performs as described by the Below Expectations standards.

	Action Statement	Rating
1	I am purposeful and committed to college.	
2	I get to class on time and stay put.	
3	I complete all of the work on time and am prepared for tests.	
4	I help other students when they are struggling with coursework.	
5	I am already planning for next semester and life after graduation.	
6	I notice my behavior and act in a manner consistent with my personal policies.	
7	I think before I react during difficult situations.	
8	I get proper perspective during difficult situations.	
9	I take the emotions out of difficult situations.	
10	I am patient with others and myself during difficult situations.	
11	I get my ego out of difficult situations.	
12	I value others and try not to judge during difficult situations.	
13	I don't take things personally during difficult situations.	
14	I am considerate to others during difficult situations.	
15	I am considerate even when I don't want to be during difficult situations.	
16	I don't blame others, especially when I may have been the cause of a problem.	
17	I accept responsibility for problems that I may have created.	
18	I apologize when necessary to those that I have harmed.	
19	I am honest with myself about my behavior.	
20	I understand and accept that difficult situations are a fact of life.	
21	I forgive others for their behavioral missteps when I can.	
22	I complete my coursework without missing deadlines or sacrificing quality.	
23	I complete my home responsibilities without mismanaging other responsibilities.	
24	I juggle all of my responsibilities without getting too stressed.	
25	I don't schedule too many difficult classes during one semester.	
26	I space out my classes throughout the week to avoid overloading.	
27	I take difficult courses in the summer to reduce complexity.	
28	I handle the conceptual difficulty of all of my classes.	
29	I talk to my professors when I struggle to understand subject matter.	
30	I prioritize my time and other resources on activities that are most important to my future.	

Source: Author-created.*Source:* Author-created.

Transfer your answers for each statement into table 10.4.

Table 10.4. Coping Behavior Mapping Table

Item	5Cs	Variable	Behavior	Behavior Rating	Behavior Average
1	Coping	Change	Demonstration		
2	Coping	Change	Demonstration		
3	Coping	Change	Demonstration		
4	Coping	Change	Demonstration		
5	Coping	Change	Demonstration		
6	Coping	Adversity	Continuous Self-Awareness		
7	Coping	Adversity	Continuous Self-Awareness		
8	Coping	Adversity	Continuous Self-Awareness		
9	Coping	Adversity	Continuous Self-Restraint		
10	Coping	Adversity	Continuous Self-Restraint		
11	Coping	Adversity	Continuous Self-Restraint		
12	Coping	Adversity	Continuous Self-Restraint		
13	Coping	Adversity	Continuous Self-Restraint		
14	Coping	Adversity	Continuous Self-Restraint		
15	Coping	Adversity	Continuous Self-Restraint		
16	Coping	Adversity	Continuous Self-Improvement		
17	Coping	Adversity	Continuous Self-Improvement		
18	Coping	Adversity	Continuous Self-Improvement		
19	Coping	Adversity	Continuous Self-Improvement		
20	Coping	Adversity	Continuous Self-Improvement		
21	Coping	Adversity	Continuous Self-Improvement		
22	Coping	Complexity	Capacity		
23	Coping	Complexity	Capacity		
24	Coping	Complexity	Capacity		
25	Coping	Complexity	Capacity		
26	Coping	Complexity	Capacity		
27	Coping	Complexity	Capability		
28	Coping	Complexity	Capability		
29	Coping	Complexity	Capability		
30	Coping	Complexity	Activities		
Average					

Average = Σ of Behavior Rating/30: [   ] ←

Source: Author-created.

Greater than 4: If your average is between 4 and 5, you cope well, and require little guidance to do the right thing during trying situations.

Between 3 and 4: If your average is greater than 3 but less than 4, it indicates that you cope well but sometimes require guidance from others to do the right thing during trying situations.

Less than 3: If your average is less than 3, it indicates that with guidance you sometimes do the right thing during trying situations but often fail to do the right thing even when advised to do otherwise by others.

Now take your behavior averages for this section, calculate the new average of averages, and input that information into the employability profile.

1	2	3	4	5
Below Expectations		**Meets Expectations**		**Role Model**
Even with guidance from others, fails to provide evidence of behavioral understanding of the 5C Elements and cannot be trusted with responsibility, and is unwilling to work on the responsibility of self-management.		With guidance, provides evidence of behavioral understanding of the 5C Elements and can be trusted with responsibility.		Independently and willingly provides evidence of behavioral understanding of the 5C Elements and can be trusted with responsibility.

Where:
5 = Almost always performs as described by the "Role Model" standard.
4 = Sometimes performs as described by the "Role Model" standard and sometimes performs as described by the "Meets Expectations" standard.
3 = Almost always performs as described by the "Meets Expectations" standard.
2 = Sometimes performs as described by the "Meets Expectations" standard and sometimes performs as described by the "Below Expectations" standard.
1 = Almost always performs as described by the "Below Expectations" standard.

Communication
Trust a person to convey messages appropriately.

- Audience
- Involvement
- Message
- Evidence
- COMMUNICATION MEAN

BEHAVIORAL COMPETENCY RATING (MEAN OF MEANS)

Choices
Trust a person to use good judgment.

- Communication
- Commitment
- Coping
- Caring
- Choice
- CHOICE MEAN

Commitment
Trust a person to be dutiful.

- Dependability Attendance
- Dependability Accountability
- Dependability Contribution
- Hard Work Time Deliberate Practice
- Hard Work Delayed Gratification
- Hard Work Effort Energy
- Hard Work Effort Determination
- Hard Work Effort Stamina
- Quality Measure of Excellence
- Quality Continuous Improvement
- COMMITMENT MEAN

Coping
Trust a person to demonstrate fortitude during difficult times.

- Coping Change Demonstration
- Coping Adversity Self-Awareness
- Coping Adversity Self-Restraint
- Coping Adversity Self-Improvement
- Coping Complexity Capacity
- Coping Complexity Capability
- Coping Complexity Activities
- COPING MEAN

Caring
Trust a person to show concern for others.

- Caring Civility Listening
- Caring Civility Courtesy
- Caring Civility Consideration
- Caring Helpfulness Concern
- Caring Helpfulness Cooperation
- Caring Helpfulness Compromise
- Caring Conscientious Thoughtfulness
- Caring Conscientious Carefulness
- Caring Conscientious Fairness
- Caring Common Good Respect
- Caring Common Good Equity
- Caring Common Good Goodwill
- CARING MEAN

The coping behavior mapping table (table 10.4) shows your willingness to do the right thing during trying situations. What is your average? Do you use good judgment during difficult situations? If not, why not?

Changing Habits

How can you employ Fogg's Behavior Model tiny habits to improve how you cope with being in college?

Please take a few moments and try to come up with one tiny coping habit that you can use to help you cope better with change, adversity, and complexity. As you think about changing your habits, think about framing the tiny habit in the following format suggested by Dr. Fogg: "After I (insert existing behavior), I will (insert new tiny behavior)."

After I _____ ,

I will _____ .

Coping Personal Policy Contract

To help you achieve your behavioral goals, you will be writing them down and creating a personal policy contract like the following one. By signing and dating the personal policy contract, it becomes an obligation to yourself that cannot be broken.

Goals	Coping goal(s) that will guide how I communicate in college. _____ _____ _____
Personal Policies	Personal policies I will follow when I cope with difficult situations. _____ _____ _____
Public Commitments	Public commitments that I will make to regularly measure how I am doing regarding my coping goals and personal policies. I will send my goals, personal policies, and quick weekly progress reports to a supportive friend and the professor. _____ _____ _____

Signature: _____   Date: _____

Key Terms

As a student, you should understand thoroughly the following words and phrases. Can you explain them and use them correctly?

- Student Readiness for Change Model
- Demonstration Stage
- Denial Stage
- Destruction Stage
- Discovery Stage
- Four Stages of Student Grief Model

- Laws of Change
- Routine
- Sense of Loss
- Sense of Mistrust
- Status Quo Bias
- Stranger
- Student Readiness for Change Model

Discussion Questions

1. Why is change so difficult for people? In your answer, explain how routines and status quo bias affect people's willingness to change.

2. Explain why being able to cope with change is such an important behavioral competency.

3. When students enter college, many aspects of their lives change. Using the Four Stages of Student Grief Model, briefly explain what might happen to students psychologically and emotionally when they come to college.

4. How does student dissatisfaction factor into a student's possible readiness for change?

5. According to the Student Readiness for Change Model, if a student does not value education, his or her willingness to complete college decreases. How can you tell if a student does not value education?

6. If students do not think that they can do college-level academic work, the probability that they will complete college decreases. What can students do to increase their academic confidence?

7. What are the three reactions to change that students can have when they attend college and university? Provide examples of each of these reactions.

To Sum Up

- Coping communicates your ability to deal with difficult situations and, for that reason, is characterized as a situation-based trust trait.

- It is hard for people to change their routines. Change forces people out of their comfort zones, which creates fear in people.

- When students attend college and university they should expect to feel a sense of loss because they give up all of their routines.

- When students attend college and university they should also expect to feel a sense of mistrust because everybody will be a stranger.

- The Student Readiness for Change Model is a simple and useful tool that helps organizations identify and analyze the change readiness risks associated with resistance to change within organizations.

- The Four Stages of Student Grief Model is a model that can help explain what happens to many students psychologically and emotionally when they enter college. The may cycle through the 4Ds: denial, destruction, discovery, and demonstration.

- When students experience change they can react one of three ways: (1) Accept change immediately and directly move to the demonstration phase. (2) Accept change over time and cycle through some combination of denial, destruction, and discovery prior to moving to demonstration. (3) Never accept the change.

Section VI

CARING

How to understand, communicate, and
assess relationship-based trust relating to
consideration, concern, and conscientiousness

11

CARING AND RELATIONSHIPS

After reading this chapter, you should be able to:

- Describe what caring behavior is, and the three variables in the Caring Model.

- Explain the main reason why caring behavior is so important to small- and large-scale human endeavors.

- Define civility and the three variables that make up the Civility Model.

- Explain what helpfulness is and the three variables that demonstrate helpful behavior.

- Describe the Conscientiousness Model and the three variables that make it up.

- Explain why civility is caring's behavioral minimum.

- Understand why you should be more careful when communicating via email or other electronic means.

- Explain Murray's Rule and how it is used in negotiating.

Understanding Caring Behavior and Relationships

Alone we can do so little; together we can do so much.

—Helen Keller

The last of the 5C Elements is Caring. **Caring** is defined as *a thoughtful concern that strengthens trust with others*. Caring measures the degree to which individuals are concerned about the well-being of other people. When you interact with other people, you form relationships. Relationships can be defined as types of interpersonal connections between yourself and others. You can have relationships with spouses, siblings, friends, coworkers, supervisors and employees, and others. The strength of your interpersonal connections with others will depend on the quality of caring in each relationship.

Although the psychology of behavior can be incredibly complex, at its most basic level, your behavior can either be caring or uncaring toward others. Relationships in which both people are equally concerned about the well-being of each other are caring relationships. Caring relationships are healthy because both parties have genuine feelings of concern for each other. For example, a parent and child can have a caring relationship. When a child is doing well, the parent experiences happiness and contentment, and vice versa. When a person in a caring relationship struggles, the other person experiences genuine feelings of concern about the well-being of the person experiencing the hardship. People in caring relationships experience the same kinds of emotional highs and lows because they both care about each other's well-being.

Caring: A thoughtful concern that strengthens trust with others.

Photo 11.1. A mother guides her young son as he learns to ride a bicycle, demonstrating their caring relationship. *Source:* Alextredz; Creative Commons Attribution-Share Alike 4.0 International license.

Caring relationships are created when both parties reciprocate relationship-affirming traits such as reliability, openness, honesty, fairness, understanding, loyalty, respect, and love. In caring relationships, both people willingly compromise to solve problems and honor commitments to each other. What makes caring relationships between people possible are not contracts and "lawyers, guns, and money,"[1] but rather trust and an implicit understanding of support between both people. Trust is the sum of traits like openness, honesty, fairness, understanding, loyalty, and mutual respect. These types of traits are the fertile soil in which healthy and caring relationships grow. Without these relationship-affirming traits, mutual caring relations between people are not possible.

Uncaring Relationships:
Types of relationships in which one person or both people do not care about the well-being of the other person.

At the other end of the relationship caring spectrum are **uncaring relationships.** Uncaring relationships are *types of relationships in which one person or both people do not care about the well-being of the other person.* You can have uncaring relationships between spouses, siblings, friends, coworkers, supervisors and employees, and others. Uncaring behavior can run the gamut from demonstrating disinterest to more serious forms of behavior such as emotional, verbal, and physical abuse. Uncaring behavior can include anger, control, drama, hostility, jealousy, narcissism, prejudice, and selfishness. These behaviors can take a toll

Photo 11.2. These people on the subway are ignoring each other and absorbed in their own activities, showing an uncaring relationship. *Source:* Marc Smith; Creative Commons Attribution 2.0 Generic license.

on others and make them feel abused, anxious, blamed, bullied, ignored, intimidated, isolated, lonely, ridiculed, and stressed. None of which is healthy for individual relationships or society at large.

Regardless of the form the uncaring behavior takes, people that engage in uncaring behavior toward others often attempt to explain or justify their behavior, even though it is plain to see, inappropriate, and unhealthy. These sorts of justifications are important to notice because conduct and attitudes that undermine another person's dignity, confidence, and self-worth will always weaken or possibly even sever the connections that bind people together. Interpersonal exchanges are what connects one person to another, and also what holds our society together. Caring exchanges strengthen connections, while uncaring exchanges weaken connections.

Why Is Caring Behavior Important?

Caring behavior is important because it is the primary binding agent that establishes firmly good relations with others. It is particularly important in situations that depend on willing cooperation between people. Alexander Graham Bell once noted, "Great discoveries and improvements invariably involve the cooperation of many minds." Bell's wisdom acknowledges that even geniuses cannot go it alone. One super-smart person working in a lab by themselves did not invent and manufacture the light bulb, land a person on the moon, or build an aircraft carrier. One person cannot possess all the knowledge, skills, and abilities or master all the competencies required to complete these types of large-scale and highly complex undertakings. However, thousands of willing and cooperative individuals working together over time brought these seemingly impossible accomplishments into reality. The key words are *willing and cooperative*. People do not willingly cooperate with other people who are uncaring. Of course, force is always an option to get people to capitulate, but capitulation is not willing cooperation.

One last point: caring is the glue that binds together all human interrelationships in our society. Uncaring behavior weakens social order because it destroys collective cooperation and goodwill among people. Individuals who are treated poorly will show little, if any, willingness to assist or engage with uncaring people. The road to a better world begins with caring.

Think about It

Label the following behaviors as caring or uncaring, and explain your choice.

Behavior	Caring	Uncaring	Why?
Joe listens carefully when Sarah speaks.			
Gary says that anyone who doesn't agree with him is a "real loser."			
Theodora throws a fit when someone compliments her older sister and ignores her.			
While working together on a project, Alejandro gladly considers others' suggestions.			
Eileen throws her food against the wall when she doesn't like how it tastes.			

How do you treat people that demonstrate that they do not care about your well-being? Would you willingly let them into your life? Would you marry them, hire them, or be friends with them? Explain why?

_____

_____

_____

_____

_____

_____

If caring behavior is the key to willing cooperation, and uncaring behavior destroys people's willingness to work together, then it is vitally important that you understand what caring behavior is and is not, so that you are not inadvertently behaving in a manner that is not in your best interest.

To help us understand what caring behavior is, let us look at the caring model (see figure 11.1). In order to be viewed as a caring person by others, you should always try to be (1) civil, (2) helpful, and (3) conscientious in your interactions with others. If you want people to willingly cooperate with you, you first need to show them that you care about them.

Figure 11.1. Caring Model. *Source:* Author-created.

Let's take a look at each of these variables in more detail.

The Civility Model

Civility does not . . . mean the mere outward gentleness of speech cultivated for the occasion, but an inborn gentleness and desire to do the opponent good.

—Mohandas Gandhi

Caring behavior starts with civility. We define **civility** as a *basic concern for the well-being of others*. At a bare minimum, to be viewed as a civil person you should be: (1) a good listener, (2) courteous, and (3) be considerate when you interact with others (see figure 11.2).

Civility: A basic concern for the well-being of others.

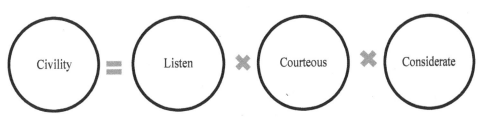

Figure 11.2. Civility Model. *Source:* Author-created.

Civility is the minimum behavior to show a basic regard for another person's feelings. To be civil toward another is to do what is minimally required in a civil society. Failure to listen, be polite, or be considerate toward another is to treat that person in a dishonorable and undignified manner. Uncivil people communicate loudly that what they think and feel is far more important than what others do. In fact, what uncivil people think and feel is so important that they will abuse, blame, bully, ignore, insult, intimidate, isolate, and ridicule others. Incivility is the sole recourse of emotionally out-of-control people who are motivated by anger, hostility, jealousy, narcissism, prejudice, and selfishness. Incivility is a behavioral trait employed by behaviorally untalented and uncaring people.

Let's move on to the elements of civility.

Listen

Listen or thy tongue will keep you deaf.

—Native American Proverb

Listening: A predisposition to take notice of the opinions and ideas of others.

Civil people pay attention and listen to what others are communicating. Their focus is outward leaning. **Listening** is *a predisposition to take notice of the opinions and ideas of others.* Civil people try to grasp the significance of alternate (or opposing) points of view because they understand how much they themselves may not know. Civil people understand that they cannot know all of the answers to every question, even if they are really smart, articulate, and well educated.

Uncivil people do not pay attention or listen to others, or make a real effort to understand what other people are saying. Their lack of interest stifles goodwill and cooperation because the other person knows that they are not even being heard. Uncivil people communicate loudly that what others have to say is not worthy of their time or attention. They close off the connections that bind them to others by disregarding the opinions and ideas of others as unimportant, irrelevant, or even untrue.

Listening is a skill that requires practice. In order to be a good listener, you should be careful not to dominate conversations and be mindful of the following listening tips.

LISTENING DOS AND DON'TS

	Listening Dos	Listening Don'ts
Be Attentive	Do focus your mind, ears, and eyes on the people with whom you are interacting.	Don't take phone calls or texts, check voicemail or emails, or play video games when someone is communicating with you.
Do Not Interrupt	Do be patient and let people finish talking before you start talking. Remember, "Are you listening or waiting to talk?"	Don't break the speaker's train of thought or interfere with continuity of what the speaker is talking about.
Ask Follow-Up Questions	Do ask questions to show interest, clarify understanding, find out more, or if you do not understand what is being communicated.	Don't ask questions on an unrelated subject. Also, do not make statements in the form of questions to counter what the speaker is communicating.
Stay on Topic	Do make sure any follow-up questions or responses are relevant to the subject or topic being discussed.	Don't change the subject; it implies a lack of interest in what is being communicated.
Be Patient	Do accept or tolerate delay. Think long-term instead of short-term. Healthy, trusting relationships with others may take a while.	Don't get angry or upset because the speaker is wasting your time by not getting to the point.
Reply Back	Do provide affirming verbal and nonverbal feedback to let the speaker know you understand and are interested in what is being said.	Don't not reply back. It shows a complete lack of interest in what is being communicated.

Courteous

Politeness is to human nature what warmth is to wax.

—Arthur Schopenhauer

Courteous behavior: Well-mannered and civil behavior that lifts up others.

You cannot be viewed as civil if you are not courteous. **Courteous behavior** is *well-mannered and civil behavior that lifts up others*. Courteous behavior avoids harm during interactions with others. Courteous people wait, hold the door for others, use turn signals when changing lanes, say "bless you" when someone sneezes or "thank you" when waitstaff brings their food. They take the time to respectfully acknowledge the presence of others. "Life be not so short but that there is always time for courtesy," Ralph Waldo Emerson reminds us.

Uncivil people, on the other hand, are distressingly impolite. They are rude and uncaring, and create enemies with their harsh and selfish indifference to others. Uncivil people don't wait to hold the door for others, or use turn signals, or say "gesundheit," or "thank you." They intentionally cause harm by ignoring, snubbing, denigrating, humiliating, or embarrassing people. They are deliberately hurtful and insensitive to the feelings of others and create situations where others feel upset, angry, or embarrassed, all of which is antithetical to social order. Discourteous people make others feel unworthy of their respect, which creates hatred.

Think about It

Erma always thinks she's right and isn't shy about telling others that they're wrong. As part of a group working on a new online mapping service, she constantly ignored the suggestions of the other team members, calling them "stupid" or "misguided." When Rosalita asked if the map should include callouts for local businesses like diners and gas stations, Erma replied, "Only a complete moron would think such a thing!" in front of all the other team members. Rosalita was humiliated and never made a suggestion again.

Would you be happy working with someone like Erma? Do you think she was an effective team leader? Why are people so reluctant to be polite when it costs nothing and can damage their own reputation?

_____

_____

_____

_____

_____

_____

_____

Considerate

> What is objectionable, what is dangerous about extremists is not that they are extreme, but that they are intolerant. The evil is not what they say about their cause, but what they say about their opponents.
>
> —Robert F. Kennedy

The last behavioral trait in the Civility Model is consideration. **Consideration** is *demonstrating a regard for the feelings, rights, or traditions of others*. Considerate people are approachable and empathetic and acknowledge others in a friendly and good-natured way. They are decent people and do not require anything in order to demonstrate decency toward others, even if they are the opposition. Consideration is what allows people to transcend differences and find common ground.

While civil people are considerate when they interact with others, uncivil people are inconsiderate, selfish, insensitive, and treat others harshly. They are mainly concerned with their own desires, interests, needs, and wishes, and tend to ignore the feelings of others. People who are treated in an inconsiderate way experience feelings of inadequacy, anger, hostility, resentment, and hatred. What can be gained by creating these feelings in others?

A former colleague of mine, who was an operations director at a major telecommunications company in California, once told me a story that illustrates how inconsiderate behavior poisons relationships:

> Two of my employees were arguing about a new corporate human resources policy. Although both of the employees reported to me, they were not on the same level. One of the employees was my assistant, and the other was an operations manager.
>
> I can't remember what exactly they were arguing about, but the exchange was very public and very heated. Before it got too ugly, my assistant stormed off to get a copy of the policy to figure out who was right and who was wrong. When he returned, he waved the policy paper in front of the manager and publicly scolded the manager in front of everyone in the office, yelling, "I just went to HR and they gave me the policy statement. It says exactly what I said. I'm right."
>
> At that point, the manager said, "OK, you're right," and went back to her office. After a few minutes, I called my assistant into my office and asked him what had happened, and he told me the details of the argument and repeated that "he was right." Then, I said, "You might have been right, but you're

Consideration:
Demonstrating a regard for the feelings, rights, or traditions of others.

dead right. You're now dead to Marianne. Was it worth it?" He didn't understand what I meant.

I explained that Marianne could be his next manager, evaluate his performance, be on a hiring committee for a job that he may be interested in, or on a promotion committee. Although he might never report directly to Marianne, she could have influence on his future career status; if she was asked about what it was like to work with him she might not give him a good recommendation. She might not say anything, she might just roll her eyes, but her point would be made. I explained that opportunities could be lost for him because of this event, and he'd never know why.

How do you think Marianne will react to you the next time you need to interact with her? I hope being right was really worth it.

The moral of this story is that other people don't really care if you are right or wrong, but they do care about how they are treated. If you are interested in establishing and maintaining healthy, trusting, long-term relations with others, you will be considerate. Relationships are more important than being right. As the axiom goes, "In terms of improving relations with others, it's better to be nice than right." The other important lesson in this story is to never publicly denigrate or openly treat another person like they are unworthy of your respect. Although they may forgive you, they will never forget. The communication rule to remember is: praise in public and criticize in private.

Think about It

Think of a recent interaction (whether or not you were involved in it) in which you observed inconsiderate behavior. What did you think of the person exhibiting the behavior? What reactions did you observe from others? What do you think of the way politicians publicly denigrate each other? Do you think the United States would be better off if politicians were more considerate toward each other?

_____

_____

_____

_____

_____

The Helpfulness Model

Look for the helpers. You will always find people who are helping.

—Mr. Rogers

The next variable in the Caring Model is helpfulness. **Helpfulness** is defined as *a willingness to provide useful assistance to those in need.* Helpfulness strengthens goodwill and trust because it communicates a willingness to adjust what you are doing to support other people. Helpfulness signals to others that you approve of what they are doing and are willing to be of service to others. It does not mean a blind allegiance to uncaring people or unworthy causes, but it does mean a willingness to cooperate and subordinate yourself in support of what others are doing.

For example, suppose you lived off campus in a house with five of your friends, and you had a party the night before and your house was a disaster the morning after. Now suppose that after a large pot of coffee and some aspirin, everyone gathers in the living room to divvy up chores to clean up the house, and one of your housemates proclaims, "I didn't make this mess, so I'm not cleaning it up." Her statement signals an unreasonable unwillingness to accommodate the equitable distribution of household chores. The unhelpfulness creates more work for everyone else, which will create rancor within the house.

While helpfulness creates goodwill, unhelpfulness creates ill will, because it demonstrates a failure to support others attempting to do something. It communicates a high degree of concern for oneself and a low degree of concern for others.

Helpfulness is caring behavior. To be viewed as a helpful person you should: (1) demonstrate concern for others, (2) cooperate with others, and (3) compromise with others (see figure 11.3).

Let's look at each of these variables in more detail.

Helpfulness: A willingness to provide useful assistance to those in need.

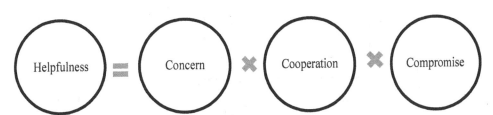

Figure 11.3. Helpfulness Model. *Source:* Author-created.

Concern

A fundamental concern for others in our individual and community lives would go a long way in making the world the better place we so passionately dreamt of.

—Nelson Mandela

Concern: The degree of interest that you have for another's well-being.

Concern is defined as *the degree of interest that you have for another's well-being.* Concern for others is a recognition that all people have common interests that should bind us together. Genuine trusting relationships with others are not possible without concern because a lack of concern creates the impression that others are unimportant, which signals an indifference to the plight of others. As said throughout this book, everything you say and do communicates information that influences how others see you. What and how you communicate helps others determine your underlying nature and whether they want to associate with you. Concern for others makes trusting, healthy, long-term relations with others possible.

We can understand concern by comparing the degree to which individuals show concern for others versus concern for themselves (figure 11.4).

If you show a high degree of concern for others, you communicate that you are interested in the well-being of others. As figure 11.4

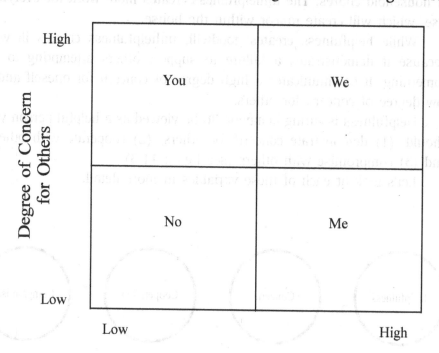

Figure 11.4. Concern Matrix. *Source:* Author-created.

shows, individuals who demonstrate a high level of concern for others have either a "you" or a "we" orientation. The distinction between "you" and "we" depends on the degree of concern they show for themselves. **We-oriented people** *demonstrate a high degree of concern for others and a high degree of concern for themselves*. They balance their own wants, needs, and desires with that of other people they interact with. In general, we-oriented individuals work hard at relationships and try to make sure that all parties feel like they are treated fairly when interacting. By contrast, **you-oriented people** have *high levels of concern for others, but low levels of concern for themselves*. You-oriented individuals subjugate their own needs to those of others.

Unconcerned behavior, which is at the other end of the concern for others spectrum, shows a low degree of concern for others and is labeled on the chart as having either a "no" or a "me" orientation. The distinction between a no and me orientation would depend on the degree to which the behavior reflects self-concern. We can define **no-oriented people** as *being indifferent or unconcerned about the outcomes of people's behaviors on themselves and on others*. In general, they would view the outcomes of their own behavior as being an unimportant consideration in their dealings with others.

Me-oriented people, on the other hand, have *a low level of concern for others, but a very high level of concern for themselves in their dealings with others*.

We-Oriented People:
People who demonstrate a high degree of concern for others and a high degree of concern for themselves.

You-Oriented People:
People who demonstrate high levels of concern for others, but low levels of concern for themselves.

No-Oriented People:
People who demonstrate indifference or are unconcerned about the outcomes of people's behaviors on themselves and on others.

Me-Oriented People:
People who demonstrate a low level of concern for others but a very high level of concern for themselves in their dealings with others.

What Do You Think?

In this table, identify each behavior as we-, you-, no-, or me-oriented and give your reason why for each.

Behavior	We-Oriented	You-Oriented	No-Oriented	Me-Oriented	Why?
Jose always makes sure that everyone has enough to eat even if he has to forgo eating himself.					
Marissa hogs the TV remote and won't let others choose their own shows to watch.					
Zelda couldn't be bothered to enter a contest to win free tickets for her and her friends or a rap performance.					
Ernesto is very happy when the entire soccer team does well, particularly when he's able to score a goal.					

What types of behaviors would people exhibit in the different quadrants of the Concern Matrix that follows? What quadrants do your associates, friends, and relatives fit into? What quadrant do you fit into?

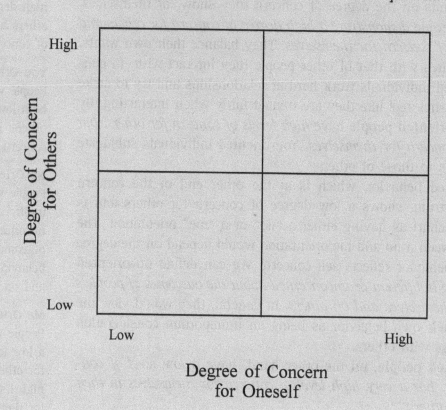

Cooperation

No man is an island.

—John Donne

Cooperation: Willingly working together with others for a common purpose.

When you cooperate you *willingly work together with others for a common purpose*. **Cooperation** is a requirement for social order and progress in a civilized world because it takes teamwork to do most large-scale things. It takes the combined action of groups of people, working cooperatively together, to accomplish great things because nobody can have all the necessary knowledge, skills, and abilities required to complete massive undertakings such as landing on the moon or creating organizations like Tesla, Amazon, and T-Mobile by themselves. But thousands of people cooperatively working together were able to achieve these goals. We all rely on each other to get the important work of progress and survival done.

The quality of our existence depends on the degree to which we can work with and find common ground with others. People that cooperate with each other willingly and openly interact and communicate with each other. They remain considerate when they reach impasses with others. It takes behavioral talent to build and maintain cooperation in others while interacting with others. As Martin Luther King reminds us, "We may have all come on different ships, but we're in the same boat now."

What Do You Think?

When people communicate that they are unwilling to work with others cooperatively for the common good, they damage goodwill between themselves, which can damage progress toward the achievement of goals. Why do you think that people have been unable to cooperate to make a more just, peaceful, and equitable world for everyone? What are the forces that are dividing us? What are the forces that bring us together?

_____

_____

_____

_____

_____

_____

Compromise

So let us begin anew—remembering on both sides that civility is not a sign of weakness, and sincerity is always subject to proof. Let us never negotiate out of fear. But let us never fear to negotiate.

—John F. Kennedy

There will always be disagreements between people. Like death and taxes, disagreements are part of not living alone on earth. To the Greek dramatist Sophocles there was "no greater evil than men's failure to consult and to

Compromise: Willingly making concessions to settle disputes.

consider" each other.[2] Cooperative people compromise to settle disputes. They are concerned about everyone, not just people that think, act, and look like themselves. When people **compromise** with each other they *willingly make concessions to settle disputes.*

Cooperative people openly and sincerely engage in discussions aimed at reaching agreements that break roadblocks with others. When we compromise with each other, we demonstrate that we care about each other. One way to demonstrate compromise is to "make sure everyone is happy" at the conclusion of negotiated settlements. "Making sure everyone is happy" was coined by my father in-law, Murray Sanders, when I asked him for his advice on a business matter; for this reason, I call this negotiating method Murray's Rule.[3] To follow **Murray's Rule**, *both negotiating parties do whatever they can to make sure that the opposing party is treated fairly during the negotiation.* It's logical: if you show me that you care about what's important to me, I'll be more likely to care about what's important to you. Murray's Rule is we- rather than me-focused and uses caring behavior as a tool in negotiating. We-oriented negotiating is win/win, while me-oriented negotiating is at best win/lose, and at worst, lose/lose.

Murray's Rule: Both negotiating parties do whatever they can to make sure that the opposing party is treated fairly during the negotiation.

Negotiating Dos and Don'ts

	Negotiating Dos	**Negotiating Don'ts**
Murray's Rule	Do remember Murray's Rule. Know what is most important to you and try to figure out what is most important to the other party.	Don't get hung up by unimportant details.
Considerate	Do remain considerate to the other party by actively listening, and being courteous and helpful.	Don't take negotiating personally. Remember that learning how to negotiate is part of life with others.
Negotiate	Do use disagreements with others as an opportunity to learn and practice how to negotiate better. Problems you face with others are actually opportunities to develop negotiating skills that you will use throughout your life.	Don't view negotiating with others as a sign of failure and weakness. You are not the only person on the planet and everyone has a right and duty to negotiate on their own behalf.

Remain Flexible	Do make statements or offer suggestions such as "How about if we . . . ," or "What if we try . . ." if you are at an impasse.	Do not box yourself in with too many absolutes.
Walk Away	Do walk away when other people are not negotiating or practicing Murray's Rule. You have a right to walk away feeling like you have been treated fairly.	Do not walk away when you are making progress. It may take time to negotiate an agreement that makes "everyone happy."

Photo 11.3. Jimmy Carter was able to negotiate a deal between Egypt and Israel in which both sides felt that they got something they wanted. Can you think of other moments in history when compromises were achieved? *Source:* US National Archives and Records Administration.

The Conscientious Model

Management is not being brilliant. Management is being conscientious.

—Peter Drucker

The last variable in the Caring Model is being conscientious. Conscientious people are thoughtful, careful, and fair in their dealings with others.

Figure 11.5. Conscientious Model. *Source:* Author-created.

They are guided by the dictates of their own thoughts and conscience (figure 11.5).

People that care about others are conscientious about what they do. **Conscientiousness** is defined as a *ceaseless awareness of what is right and wrong in every situation*. They purposely and methodically apply well-reasoned judgment to understand and evaluate the impact of their own behavior on each situation and follow the standards that they have set for themselves. They are mindful about all their interactions with other people. Conscientious people are:

- Thoughtful or mindful when interacting

- Careful not to demonstrate indifference to another person's well-being

- Fair when interacting

Thoughtfulness, carefulness, and fairness all relate to the seriousness of your intentions toward others and their work. Conscientious people pay attention to the well-being of other people. To do otherwise, to be mainly concerned with your own interests, at the exclusion of the interests of others, is to cause others to act in their own self-interest when dealing with you. How can this be good for you?

Thoughtfulness

When we are infants we do not think about how our behavior impacts ourselves and others, because we are all impulse. But as we mature we make connections in our brains to determine how our choices will impact ourselves and the world around us, before we make choices. People that care about others think about what they are doing before they make choices that impact themselves and their relationships with others.

Thoughtfulness is *the process of consciously gathering information to determine how to balance your own needs and the needs of others, before making choices that will impact yourself and your rela-*

Conscientiousness: Ceaseless awareness of what is right and wrong in every situation.

Thoughtfulness: The process of consciously gathering information to determine how to balance your own needs and the needs of others before making choices that will impact yourself and your relationships with others.

tionships with others. Thoughtful people care about the impact of their choices on themselves and on others. They are win/win and we-oriented decision-makers.

To do otherwise, to consciously make choices that do not balance your own needs and the needs of others is, by definition, not thoughtful. Choices that are not thoughtful do not balance the competing needs of all parties and therefore violate the 5C Element of caring in two basic ways: (1) they violate the caring principle of civility because they do not demonstrate a *basic concern for the well-being of others*, and (2) they violate the helpfulness model because they do not *provide any assistance to those in need*. In addition, they also violate all of the subvariables for both civility and helpfulness, including listening, courteousness, consideration, concern, cooperation, and compromise.

What Do You Think?

Can you think of a time when you were thoughtful in which you balanced your own needs with those of someone else? Describe the situation and how it made you feel to be part of a win/win relationship with someone else. Did you remain close to the person after the interaction?

_____

_____

_____

_____

_____

_____

_____

Carefulness

Every person has a legitimate right to pursue their own contentment and well-being. If you are a conscientious person, you are careful to avoid harming others when you are pursing your own contentment and well-being. **Carefulness** in this context is defined as a *genuine attempt to balance your own legitimate claims to contentment and well-being*

Carefulness: A genuine attempt to balance your own legitimate claims to contentment and well-being with those of other people when you make choices.

with those of other people when you make choices. Conscientious people ask questions and try to understand situational nuances that affect themselves and others, to avoid mistakes and maximize the chance that both parties will benefit.

The opposite of carefulness is, of course, carelessness. **Carelessness** is *negligent behavior that can be defined as making choices without giving sufficient thought to the consequences that inevitably follow.* Careless choices can impact you in college and university. For example, not doing homework, or studying for exams, or attending classes are all thoughtless ways that students neglect their academic responsibilities. Carelessness can also impact yourself and others, such as texting a friend while driving or driving while intoxicated, which can both have disastrous consequences. When you care about the well-being of others, you think about what you are doing before you make choices that can impact their well-being, and yours as well.

Carelessness: Negligent behavior that can be defined as making choices without giving sufficient thought to the consequences that inevitably follow.

What Do You Think?

Suppose that you live in a dorm room and your roommate is in your room studying for an exam. You had just completed your homework and also finished studying for the same exam. How can you balance your own legitimate needs to have fun with your roommate's legitimate need to study?

_____

_____

_____

_____

_____

_____

_____

Fairness

Fairness: Choices that are honest, just, and free from bias and prejudice.

The last variable in the Conscientious Model is **fairness**. When conscientious people interact with other people they make choices that are fair.

That is to say, they make *choices that are honest, just, and free from bias and prejudice.* They treat all people with dignity and decency, no matter their race, creed, color, religion, gender, identity, or sexual orientation. They do not distinguish between different types of people because they are guided by a sense of propriety about what is right and wrong in every situation.

People that treat people unfairly, have different standards for people. They apply the rules differently, which is another way of saying that they discriminate. Although we all discriminate in different ways, that is, our choice of partners, friends, and what kinds of food to eat, unfair discrimination is unjust and unequal treatment based on something that a person has no control over. Unfairness is the result of treating others in an unequal or unjust manner.

For example, before 1964 it was perfectly legal to discriminate against people because of the color of their skin and their gender. It was not illegal to say to someone, "I'm not hiring you because you are black." It was also not illegal to say, "I'm not hiring you because you are female." The Civil Rights Act of 1964 made it illegal to unfairly discriminate in employment-related matters on the basis of race, color, religion, sex, and national origin. Why do you suppose that the Civil Rights Act of 1964 was enacted?

Photo 11.4. President Lyndon B. Johnson signing the Civil Rights Act into law. *Source:* Cecil Stoughton, White House Press Office (WHPO).

What Do You Think?

Throughout the world, 160 million children—63 million girls and 97 million boys—are involved in child labor, accounting for almost 1 in 10 of all children worldwide. Nearly half of whom, 79 million children, are in hazardous work. In the United States there are laws against child labor. Why do you think that the United States has these laws? Why would other countries not choose to have similar laws?

_____

_____

_____

_____

Caring Personal Policy Contract

To help you achieve your behavioral goals, you will be writing them down to create personal policy contracts like the following one. By signing and dating the personal policy contract, it becomes an obligation to yourself that cannot be broken.

Goals	Caring goal(s) that will guide how I communicate in college:
Personal Policies	Personal policies I will follow when I am caring for others:
Public Commitments	Public commitments that I will make to regularly measure how I am doing regarding my caring goals and personal policies. I will send my goals, personal policies, and quick weekly progress reports to a supportive friend and the professor.

Signature: _____ Date: _____

Key Terms

As a student and citizen of the world, you should understand thoroughly the following words and phrases. Can you explain them and use them correctly?

- Caring
- Carefulness
- Carelessness
- Civility
- Compromise
- Concern
- Conscientiousness
- Consideration
- Cooperation
- Courteousness

- Fairness
- Helpfulness
- Listening
- Me-Oriented People
- No-Oriented People
- Thoughtfulness
- Uncaring Relationships
- We-Oriented People
- You-Oriented People

Discussion Questions

1. Why is caring about others important to success?

2. In light of what you have learned in this chapter, explain why caring behavior is crucial in situations that depend on cooperation between people?

3. What are the three behaviors that demonstrate civility? Explain each behavior.

4. Briefly describe the three behavioral variables that demonstrate that you care about others.

5. Explain and provide examples of each of the four quadrants in the Concern Matrix.

6. How can you tell if someone is cooperating?

7. Summarize the three behaviors that demonstrate helpfulness.

8. Conscientiousness is ceaseless awareness of what is right and wrong in every situation. Explain the three variables that demonstrate conscientiousness.

9. The opposite of conscientiousness is carelessness. What are some of the behaviors that would demonstrate that someone is careless when they interact with others?

To Sum Up

- Caring is defined by three variables: civility, helpfulness, and conscientiousness.

- Caring is the relationship-based trust trait; good relations with others may not be possible without it.

  o Caring behavior is particularly important for gaining cooperation from people.

- Civility is defined by three variables: listening, courteousness, and consideration.

- Helpfulness is made up of three variables: cooperation, compromise, and concern.

- We defined four types of concern:

  o We-oriented people care about both themselves and others.

  o You-oriented people care about others more than themselves.

  o Me-oriented people care about themselves over others.

  o No-oriented people are indifferent about the outcomes of people's behaviors on themselves or others.

- Murray's Rule is: "Do not stop negotiating until both parties are happy."

- Conscientiousness is defined by three variables: thoughtfulness, carefulness, and fairness.

12

CARING AND SOCIETY

After reading this chapter, you should be able to:

- Explain how caring relates to the common good.

- Define the term *common good* and the three variables that make up the Common Good Model.

- Understand what respect is and the three variables that demonstrate the Respect Model.

- Describe the Equity Model and the three variables that make it up.

- Explain what goodwill is and the three variables that make up the Goodwill Model.

Understanding Caring for the Common Good

What are the American ideals? They are the development of the individual for his own and the common good; the development of the individual through liberty; and the attainment of the common good through democracy and social justice.

—Justice Louis D. Brandeis

Although self-management is about becoming a more effective and autonomous thinker, this last chapter is a recognition that you are not alone; many of the problems we face are so large that neither you, nor any other person, nor any single country can tackle them alone. Just by reading the news headlines for a few minutes you will become aware of the problems that plague our world, including:

- Outsourcing of employment to inexpensive labor around the world

- Large-scale replacement of human labor with technology and artificial intelligence

- Child and slave labor

- Climate change catastrophes and population migration

- Sexual and child abuse

- Water, food, and energy insecurities

- Discrimination based on race, age, disability, sexual orientation, religion, national origin, color, and gender

- Political conflict, polarization, and extremism

- Social, economic, health, and educational inequity

The list of problems facing our world goes on and on and on. What do all of these problems have in common? They are all: (1) national and global in scope, (2) consequences of human choosing, and (3) only solvable by cooperation and collective action for the common good.

In this context, we can think about the goal of common good as working cooperatively and effectively with others to simultaneously fulfill both your own unrealized potential and support others in their quest. By adopting caring behaviors in support of the common good, you not only benefit yourself and others but you also do your part in helping to solve the issues that plague our national and global communities. Or as the Lorax says, "Unless someone like you cares a whole awful lot, nothing is going to get better. It's not."

Common Good: Working cooperatively together to determine by consensus how we should be conducting ourselves when we interact with each other.

The **common good** involves *working cooperatively together to determine by consensus how we should be conducting ourselves when we interact with each other*. By establishing behavioral standards for the common good, we can begin to see whether our behavior is beneficial or counter to the common good. For example, some people might think that it is perfectly OK for politicians, newsmakers, or social media posters to express scorn and contempt for others for having opposing points of view on matters that impact everyone. They might describe people who disagree with them as being radical, disloyal, un-American, unhinged, fanatical, stupid, or unethical. As we learned in chapter 11, this way of behaving is textbook incivility, and yet people still do it; and worse, people still listen, watch, and worse still, mimic the behavior. Free speech is one thing, but no one should stand alone when they are treated disrespectfully and bullied.

Why are standards for the common good more important today than in years past? The problems that we face today are simply too large for any one person or country to tackle alone. The planet has more than eight billion people that have the collective power to alter life as we know it. For example, the climate is warming because of human decision-making. Working alone, we cannot change the trajectory of our warming planet. But working cooperatively together, we can.

The common good might mean taking on additional responsibilities, or accepting that consensus building might involve going along with things that might not always perfectly align with your own way of thinking. But the tradeoffs of working cooperatively far outweigh these compromises because, without collective action, solving large-scale societal problems is impossible.

Also, with more than eight billion other people living together, we cannot behave as if they were living alone. For example, it is for the common good that people should not defecate in public, cough without covering their mouths, or not use turn signals on the highway. It may be time to create a list of behaviors that we can all agree are for the common good, and a list of things that are not.

The Caring for the Common Good Model

To help us understand what caring for the common good is, let us look at the Caring for Common Good Model (see figure 12.1).

In addition to being civil, helpful, and conscientious, people who are concerned about the common good demonstrate in their interactions:

1. Respect and graciousness

2. Equity and fairness

3. Goodwill and benevolence

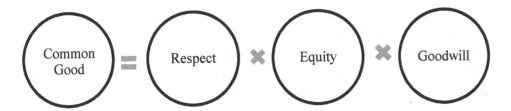

Figure 12.1. Caring for the Common Good Model. *Source:* Author-created.

It costs you nothing to come from a place of respect, equity, and goodwill toward others, and the reward in terms of improved human relations can be profound. Respect, equity, and goodwill all communicate that your motivations and intentions are well meaning and sincere. People that care about the common good pay attention to the well-being of other people, as well as their own. They try to balance the competing needs of the many with their own needs. They have a sense of propriety about their own behavior toward others and are also mindful about all of their interactions.

Like all of the other behavioral competencies covered in this book, these common good standards are reasonable and should not be too much of a stretch for any caring person to do.

Think about It

Choose one of the following topics and explain how it impacts the common good and what some potential group solutions might be to solve the problem. Can any one individual solve one of these issues on their own? What is the responsibility of each individual to address these problems?

1. Deforestation

2. War

3. Poverty

4. Pandemics

5. Racism

Respect

I'm not concerned with your liking or disliking me . . . All I ask is that you respect me as a human being.

—Jackie Robinson

Respectful people are deferential to the principles that underpin caring behavior and the common good. They accept people for who they are and are not contemptuous of differences between people. They interact with integrity and disapprove of people who flagrantly disregard or flout the rules that advance the common good. In order to be viewed as a someone that is respectful to others and the common good, you would respect: (1) people, (2) differences, and (3) decorum (see figure 12.2).

In addition to being civil, helpful, and conscientious, people who are concerned about the common good respect:

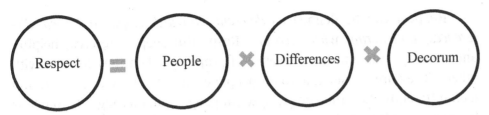

Figure 12.2. Respect Model. *Source:* Author-created.

1. **People**

   o Embrace people and choices that support the common good and caring people.

   o Question people and choices that are antithetical to the common good. That is to say, people who are not civil, courteous, or conscientious in their dealings with others.

2. **Differences**

   o Embrace people and choices that are honest, just, and free from bias and prejudice in pursuit of the common good.

   o Question people and choices that are biased against other people on the basis of gender, race, creed, color, religion, sexual orientation.

3. **Decorum**

   o Embrace people and choices that are benevolent, decent, and socially acceptable in pursuit of the common good.

   o Question people and choices that are uncivil, discourteous, and unprincipled.

Differences: Embracing people and choices that are honest, just, and free from bias and prejudice in pursuit of the common good.

Decorum: Embracing people and choices that are benevolent, decent, and socially acceptable in pursuit of the common good.

Photo 12.1. One example of decorum is that at the end of a tennis match, the winner and loser always shake hands at the net to show respect for the game. *Source:* Carine06; Creative Commons Attribution-Share Alike 2.0 Generic license.

Respect: Deference toward people and their differences, and acting with decorum.

Respect can be defined as *deference toward people and their differences, and acting with decorum*. Respectful people are civil, helpful, and conscientious and have a sense of propriety when they interact with others. They are considerate to all people even when they think, act, and look differently than they do. Respectful people build strong relationships because they honor the rights and feelings of others and ground their own conduct in integrity, trust, and goodwill.

One caveat: Respectful people do not submit to people who are disrespectful. Rather, they will take note of the uncaring behavior, and if circumstances compel them to do so, respectful people will reluctantly call attention to behavior that is contrary to the principles of caring and the common good.

Think about It

Are there things that you could do to be a more respectful person. If so, what would they be? List the things you could do to be more respectful to others. How might it benefit you in the long run to be a more respectful person?

_____

_____

_____

_____

_____

Equity

Neither love nor terror makes one blind. Indifference makes one blind.

—James Baldwin

People who care about the common good have a sense of propriety about how they interact with others. They treat others with respect and are concerned about other people's well-being, and they strive to treat all people fairly and impartially. To be viewed as someone that cares about equity and the common good of society, you should be (1) fair, (2) honest, and (3) impartial when interacting with all people, not just people who are similar to you (see figure 12.3).

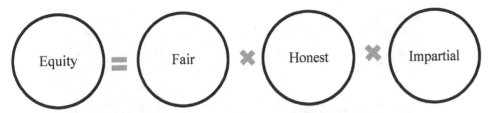

Figure 12.3. Equity Model. *Source:* Author-created.

In addition to being civil, helpful, and conscientious, people who are concerned about the common good embrace equity in their pursuit of the common good. They are:

1. **Fair**

   o Embrace people and choices that legitimately play by the rules and are just in pursuit of the common good.

   o Question people and choices that are antithetical to rules of fairness, honesty, and impartiality.

2. **Honesty**

   o Embrace people and choices that are sincere, and do not lie, cheat, or steal in pursuit of the common good. Tell the truth, the whole truth, and nothing but the truth.

   o Question people and choices that are morally flexible. That is to say, behave in a manner that is misleading, self-dealing, and unscrupulous.

3. **Impartial**

   o Embrace people and choices that are equal, fair, and just in support of the common good.

   o Question people and choices that are unequal, unfair, and antithetical to the common good.

Honesty: Embracing people and choices that are sincere and forgoing lying, cheating, or stealing in pursuit of the common good.

Impartial: Embracing people and choices that are equal, fair, and just in support of the common good.

It should come as no surprise that no two people are alike. It should also not be news that each of us was born with our own brain. It is reasonable to suppose that we were given our own brains so that we can think for ourselves. Why would we be given the gift of thought if life required that we think like everyone else? Is anything exactly like something else in nature? The point here is that wearisome uniformity is not a defining feature of reality. Sameness is the exception to the rule. Our differences are the norm, and not things to be ridiculed.

When equitable people interact with others, they make choices that are **fair** (see chapter 11). That is to say, they make *choices that are*

Photo 12.2. Judges are expected to be fair, honest, and impartial in making rulings in a trial. *Source:* maveric2003; Creative Commons Attribution 2.0 Generic license.

honest, just, and free from bias and prejudice. They treat all people with dignity and decency, no matter how they think, their race, creed, color, religion, gender, identity, or sexual orientation. They do not distinguish between different types of people because they are guided by a sense of propriety about what is right and wrong in every situation.

Another caveat: equitable people do not submit to people who are intentionally mean-spirited, insensitive, and biased. Rather, they will take note of the uncaring behavior, and if circumstances compel them to do so, equitable people will reluctantly call attention to intentionally malicious and unseemly behavior that is contrary to the principles of caring and the common good.

Think about It

If you were asked to write the rules of civility in public debates and discourse, what would your rules be? Would your rules include bullet points about respectful behavior, interrupting, patience, tolerance, listening, finding common ground, and embarrassing your debate opponent? Or would your rules allow for a free-for-all?

_____

_____

_____

_____

Goodwill

> Where people of goodwill get together and transcend their differences for the common good, peaceful and just solutions can be found even for those problems which seem most intractable.
>
> —Nelson Mandela

The last principle in the book is goodwill. To help you understand how goodwill relates to the common good, let's look at the Goodwill Model (see figure 12.4). In order to be viewed as someone that cares about goodwill and the common good of society, you would stand for (1) peace, (2) health, and (3) the well-being of others.

In addition to being civil, helpful, and conscientious, people who are concerned about the common good are people of goodwill. People that stand for goodwill value:

1. **Peace**

   o People of goodwill are nonviolent and avoid harming others with their words or actions when they have disputes. Peacemakers pay attention to their manner and try to avoid being aggressive.

   o They question people and choices that embrace aggressive, bullying, and violent means to solve problems.

   Peace: Nonviolence that avoids harming others with words and actions during disputes.

2. **Good Health**

   o People of goodwill protect the collective mental, social, and physical well-being of themselves and others.

   o They question people and choices that behave in harsh, unhealthy, misleading, unscrupulous, and destructive ways.

   Good health: People of goodwill protect the collective mental, social, and physical well-being of themselves and others.

3. **Well-being**

   o People of goodwill strive for contentment as a goal for all people, and as the end goal for the common good.

   o They question people and choices that are antithetical to individual and collective well-being.

   Well-being: Contentment or positive feelings.

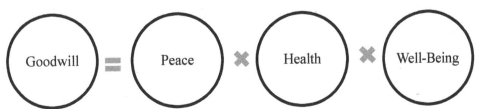

Figure 12.4. Goodwill Model. *Source:* Author-created.

Photo 12.3. Martin Luther King successfully used peaceful protest as a means of bringing social change. *Source:* U.S. News & World Report Magazine Photograph Collection (Library of Congress).

In your head and heart, always wish others peace, good health, and well-being. To be indifferent toward the plight of others is to act like a scoundrel. For the good of our collective well-being, care for the people that you know by wishing for them contentment and well-being.

Think about It

Make today a day that you will spread peace, goodwill, and well-being. How would you do that? If you could write the global rules of what peaceful and healthy behavior would be, what would your rules be? How would these rules improve our collective well-being?

_____

_____

_____

_____

_____

Quick Tips for the Caring Person

1. Use polite phrases such as please, and thank you, or would you mind if we tried this . . .

2. Ask meaningful questions.

3. Practice patience, tolerance, and forgiveness, especially with those with whom you disagree.

4. Limit your contact, if possible, with uncaring people. (We all come into contact with such people at work, school, and elsewhere, but you shouldn't seek out these personality types.)

5. Be aware of your demeanor and tone, and avoid aggressive and dismissive behavior, especially with those with whom you disagree. It takes time to create understanding between people.

6. Address people with a respectful tone, especially when you don't agree or feel upset.

7. Be silent if you do not think you can say anything positive.

8. Be constructive, nonconfrontational, and don't get personal.

9. Do not generalize or make assumptions about a person's character.

10. Make small goals for yourself. For example, if you get angry with another driver, imagine that the offending driver is rushing to the bedside of a dying loved one.

11. Remember that arguing about religion and politics is similar to getting into an argument with a New York City cab driver: you won't win.

12. Walk away when you're feeling like you are going to say something disrespectful or be disrespectful to another person.

13. Show people that they are worthy of respect until they prove otherwise by being uncaring toward you, and then distance yourself and limit contact if you can.

Caring Effectiveness: A Self-Assessment

To see if you are a caring person, please take a few minutes to complete the self-assessment in table 12.1.

Table 12.1. Caring Effectiveness: A Self-Assessment

Below Expectations	Meets Expectations	Role Model
Even with guidance: • Fails to provide evidence (verbal, written, and behavioral) that their actions and words are appropriate and aligned with audience expectations. • Fails to provide evidence of these behaviors and is unwilling to demonstrate thoughtful concern for others.	With guidance: • Provides evidence (verbal, written, and behavioral) that their actions and words are appropriate and aligned with audience expectations. • Provides evidence of these behaviors and is willing to demonstrate thoughtful concern for others.	Independently and willingly: • Provides evidence (verbal, written, and behavioral) that their actions and words are appropriate and aligned with audience expectations. • Provides evidence of these behaviors and can be trusted to demonstrate thoughtful concern for others.

Source: Author-created.

Using the behavioral observation scale (table 12.2) as a guide, rate each statement using the number corresponding to the degree to which you consistently exhibit each behavior. Note, there are no right or wrong answers. All that is important is that you indicate how consistently you exhibit the behavior described in the action statement.

Now transfer your answers for each statement into the corresponding space in table 12.3.

Table 12.2. Behavioral Observation Scale

5 =	Almost always performs as described by the Role Model standards.
4 =	Sometimes performs as described by the Role Model standards and sometimes performs as described by the Meets Expectations standards.
3 =	Almost always performs as described by the Meets Expectations standards.
2 =	Sometimes performs as described by the Meets Expectations standards and sometimes performs as described by the Below Expectations standards.
1 =	Almost always performs as described by the Below Expectations standards.

	Action Statement	Rating
1	I focus my mind, ears, and eyes on the people with whom I am interacting.	
2	I let people finish talking before I start talking.	
3	I ask questions to show interest or if I do not understand what is being communicated (verbally and nonverbally).	
4	I don't change the subject when someone is speaking.	
5	I am patient and tolerant with people when I interact with them.	
6	I provide verbal and nonverbal feedback to let the speaker know I understand and am interested in what is being said.	
7	I use polite phrases such as please, thank you, or would you mind if we tried this . . .	
8	I avoid doing harm when I interact with others.	
9	I take the time to respectfully acknowledge the presence of others.	
10	I ask people how they are doing.	
11	I inquire about what's going on in their life.	
12	I ask questions about things that others are interested in.	
13	I am available at times when people need assistance.	
14	I go out of my way to support others.	
15	I help create order when others need help.	
16	I use disagreements as opportunities to develop negotiating skills.	
17	I make suggestions such as "How about if we . . ." or "What if we try . . ." if I am at an impasse with another person.	
18	I know what is most important to me and try to figure out what is most important to the other party.	
19	I think about the impact of my choice of actions on others.	
20	I think about the impact of my choice of words on others.	
21	I think about the things that are important to others.	
22	I am careful not to offend others with my choice of actions.	
23	I choose my words wisely.	
24	I try to avoid potential problems with others.	
25	I am impartial in my dealings with others.	
26	I am reasonable when I interact with others.	
27	I am just when I make decisions about others.	
28	I always show people that they are worthy of respect.	
29	I treat everyone in an impartial and fair way.	
30	I wish all people peace, good health, and goodwill.	

Source: Author-created.

Table 12.3. Caring Behavior Mapping Table

Item	5Cs	Variable	Behavior	Behavior Rating	Behavior Average
1	Caring	Civility	Listening		
2	Caring	Civility	Listening		
3	Caring	Civility	Listening		
4	Caring	Civility	Courtesy		
5	Caring	Civility	Courtesy		
6	Caring	Civility	Courtesy		
7	Caring	Civility	Considerate		
8	Caring	Civility	Considerate		
9	Caring	Civility	Considerate		
10	Caring	Helpfulness	Concern		
11	Caring	Helpfulness	Concern		
12	Caring	Helpfulness	Concern		
13	Caring	Helpfulness	Cooperation		
14	Caring	Helpfulness	Cooperation		
15	Caring	Helpfulness	Cooperation		
16	Caring	Helpfulness	Compromise		
17	Caring	Helpfulness	Compromise		
18	Caring	Helpfulness	Compromise		
19	Caring	Conscientiousness	Thoughtfulness		
20	Caring	Conscientiousness	Thoughtfulness		
21	Caring	Conscientiousness	Thoughtfulness		
22	Caring	Conscientiousness	Carefulness		
23	Caring	Conscientiousness	Carefulness		
24	Caring	Conscientiousness	Carefulness		
25	Caring	Conscientiousness	Fairness		
26	Caring	Conscientiousness	Fairness		
27	Caring	Conscientiousness	Fairness		
28	Caring	Common Good	Respect		
29	Caring	Common Good	Equity		
30	Caring	Common Good	Goodwill		
Average					

Average = $\sum$ of Behavior Rating/30: ⟵

Source: Author-created.

Greater than 4: If your average is between 4 and 5, you are caring, show thoughtful concern for others, and require little guidance to do so.

Between 3 and 4: If your average is greater than 3 but less than 4, it indicates that you are caring but sometimes require guidance to show thoughtful concern for others.

Less than 3: If your average is less than 3, it indicates that you sometimes show thoughtful concern for others but occasionally fail to be caring even when advised to do otherwise by others.

Take your behavior averages for this section, calculate the new average of averages, and input that information into the employability profile.

1	2	3	4	5
Below Expectations		**Meets Expectations**		**Role Model**
Even with guidance from others, fails to provide evidence of behavioral understanding of the 5C Elements and cannot be trusted with responsibility, and is unwilling to work on the responsibility of self-management.		With guidance, provides evidence of behavioral understanding of the 5C Elements and can be trusted with responsibility.		Independently and willingly provides evidence of behavioral understanding of the 5C Elements and can be trusted with responsibility.

Where:

5 =	Almost always performs as described by the "Role Model" standard.
4 =	Sometimes performs as described by the "Role Model" standard and sometimes performs as described by the "Meets Expectations" standard.
3 =	Almost always performs as described by the "Meets Expectations" standard.
2 =	Sometimes performs as described by the "Meets Expectations" standard and sometimes performs as described by the "Below Expectations" standard.
1 =	Almost always performs as described by the "Below Expectations" standard.

Communication
Trust a person to convey messages appropriately.

- Audience
- Involvement
- Message
- Evidence
- COMMUNICATION MEAN

BEHAVIORAL COMPETENCY RATING (MEAN OF MEANS)

Choices
Trust a person to use good judgment.

- Communication
- Commitment
- Coping
- Caring
- Choice
- CHOICE MEAN

Commitment
Trust a person to be dutiful.

- Dependability Attendance
- Dependability Accountability
- Dependability Contribution
- Hard Work Time Deliberate Practice
- Hard Work Delayed Gratification
- Hard Work Effort Energy
- Hard Work Effort Determination
- Hard Work Effort Stamina
- Quality Measure of Excellence
- Quality Continuous Improvement
- COMMITMENT MEAN

Coping
Trust a person to demonstrate fortitude during difficult times.

- Coping Change Demonstration
- Coping Adversity Self-Awareness
- Coping Adversity Self-Restraint
- Coping Adversity Self-Improvement
- Coping Complexity Capacity
- Coping Complexity Capability
- Coping Complexity Activities
- COPING MEAN

Caring
Trust a person to show concern for others.

- Caring Civility Listening
- Caring Civility Courtesy
- Caring Civility Consideration
- Caring Helpfulness Concern
- Caring Helpfulness Cooperation
- Caring Helpfulness Compromise
- Caring Conscientious Thoughtfulness
- Caring Conscientious Carefulness
- Caring Conscientious Fairness
- Caring Common Good Respect
- Caring Common Good Equity
- Caring Common Good Goodwill
- CARING MEAN

Think about It

The caring behavior mapping table shows your willingness to demonstrate thoughtful concern that strengthens trust with others. What is your average? Do you communicate that you care about others? If not, why not?

_____

_____

_____

_____

_____

Changing Habits

How can you employ Fogg's Behavior Model tiny habits to demonstrate that you care about others?

Please take a few moments and try to come up with one tiny caring habit that you can use to show that you care about people that you meet. As you think about changing your habits, think about framing the tiny habit in the following format suggested by Dr. Fogg: "After I (insert existing behavior), I will (insert new tiny behavior)."

After I _____ ,

I will _____ .

Caring Personal Policy Contract

To help you achieve your behavioral goals, you will be writing them down to create a personal policy contract like the following one. By signing and dating the personal policy contract, it becomes an obligation to yourself that cannot be broken.

Goals	Caring goal(s) that will guide how I communicate in college: _____ _____ _____
Personal Policies	Personal policies I will follow when I am caring for others: _____ _____ _____
Public Commitments	Public commitments that I will make to regularly measure how I am doing regarding my caring goals and personal policies. I will send my goals, personal policies, and quick weekly progress reports to a supportive friend and the professor. _____ _____ _____

Signature: _____ Date: _____

Key Terms

As a student, you should understand thoroughly the following words and phrases. Can you explain them and use them correctly?

- Common Good
- Decorum
- Differences
- Good Health
- Honesty

- Impartial
- Peaceful
- Respect
- Well-being

Discussion Questions

1. What is the common good and why is it important?

2. Briefly describe the three behavioral variables that make up the Common Good Model.

3. Why is concern for others so important to building trusting relations with others?

4. Explain what equity is and the three variables that make up the Equity Model.

5. Summarize some of the behaviors that demonstrate good-will.

6. How would the world be different if people demonstrated that they cared about the common good?

To Sum Up

- Common good is working cooperatively together to determine by consensus how we should be conducting ourselves when we interact with each other.

- Common good is defined by three variables: respect, equity, and goodwill.

- Equity is a measure of a person's fairness, honesty, and impartiality.

- Goodwill is a sincere hope that others will experience peace, health, and well-being.

APPENDIX: EMPLOYABILITY PROFILE

1	2	3	4	5
Below Expectations		**Meets Expectations**		**Role Model**
Even with guidance from others, fails to provide evidence of behavioral understanding of the 5C Elements and cannot be trusted with responsibility, and is unwilling to work on the responsibility of self-management.		With guidance, provides evidence of behavioral understanding of the 5C Elements and can be trusted with responsibility.		Independently and willingly provides evidence of behavioral understanding of the 5C Elements and can be trusted with responsibility.

Where:

5 =	Almost always performs as described by the "Role Model" standard.
4 =	Sometimes performs as described by the "Role Model" standard and sometimes performs as described by the "Meets Expectations" standard.
3 =	Almost always performs as described by the "Meets Expectations" standard.
2 =	Sometimes performs as described by the "Meets Expectations" standard and sometimes performs as described by the "Below Expectations" standard.
1 =	Almost always performs as described by the "Below Expectations" standard.

Communication
Trust a person to convey messages appropriately.

- Audience
- Involvement
- Message
- Evidence
- COMMUNICATION MEAN

- BEHAVIORAL COMPETENCY RATING (MEAN OF MEANS)

Choices
Trust a person to use good judgment.

- Communication
- Commitment
- Coping
- Caring
- Choice
- CHOICE MEAN

Commitment
Trust a person to be dutiful.

- Dependability Attendance
- Dependability Accountability
- Dependability Contribution
- Hard Work Time Deliberate Practice
- Hard Work Delayed Gratification
- Hard Work Effort Energy
- Hard Work Effort Determination
- Hard Work Effort Stamina
- Quality Measure of Excellence
- Quality Continuous Improvement
- COMMITMENT MEAN

Coping
Trust a person to demonstrate fortitude during difficult times.

- Coping Change Demonstration
- Coping Adversity Self-Awareness
- Coping Adversity Self-Restraint
- Coping Adversity Self-Improvement
- Coping Complexity Capacity
- Coping Complexity Capability
- Coping Complexity Activities
- COPING MEAN

Caring
Trust a person to show concern for others.

- Caring Civility Listening
- Caring Civility Courtesy
- Caring Civility Consideration
- Caring Helpfulness Concern
- Caring Helpfulness Cooperation
- Caring Helpfulness Compromise
- Caring Conscientious Thoughtfulness
- Caring Conscientious Carefulness
- Caring Conscientious Fairness
- Caring Common Good Respect
- Caring Common Good Equity
- Caring Common Good Goodwill
- CARING MEAN

GLOSSARY OF TERMS

5Cs of Self-Management or SM: The five behavioral elements that every person must manage that cannot be delegated to others: communication, choice, caring, commitment, and coping.

7/93 rule: When interacting with others in person, only about 7 percent of the meaning of our feelings and attitudes is communicated through words.

Academic Complexity: The academic and nonacademic factors that complicate attending college and university.

Accountability: Willingness to follow through and fulfill obligations.

Activities: The normal actions that you spend time and money on when you are awake.

AIME (Audience, Involvement, Message, and Evidence) Model: A communication tool that can help you clarify, organize, and answer the five basic questions of communication.

Appropriateness: The extent to which all of your communications are perceived as suitable for a particular audience or situation.

Attendance: To be present (physically and mentally) at a specified place and time.

Audience: A person or group of people that are influenced by the content of your communication.

Audience Profile: A representation of the identifying qualities of each audience type.

Audience Types: An audience's unique combination of identifying characteristics, including different priorities and expectations of you.

Availability: A measure of your willingness to make time to support group goals.

Bad Choices: Intentional decisions that can impact how well you perform.

Beckhard and Harris Change Formula: A simple and useful tool that helps organizations identify and analyze their employees' resistance to change.

Behavior: How an individual or group acts or conducts themselves when interacting with another individual, group, or event.

Behavioral Adjustment Model: Behavioral approaches that focus on changing behaviors in behavioral decisions.

Behavioral Awareness: The degree to which you have knowledge of or are concerned about your own behavior relative to behavioral norms.

Behavioral Cause and Effect: Describes a process where "if A does this, B happens."

Behavioral Competency: A basic understanding and consistent practice of a set of skills that nurtures trust.

Behavioral Consequences: The result of our behavioral choices.

Behavioral Goals: The values and character traits that you aspire to achieve.

Behavioral Guidance: The degree to which you require others to help manage your own behavior.

Behavioral Norms: Generally accepted social qualities or characteristics that are deemed essential for successfully living together in society.

Behavioral Observation Scale: A measure of your behavioral performance of the 5C Elements.

Behavioral Occurrence: One-time event or a single behavioral incident that happens.

Behavioral Pattern: Conduct that is repeated, predictable, and self-created.

Behavioral Rules: Unambiguous personal policies that govern an individual's behavior within particular contexts involving others.

Behavioral Strengths and Weaknesses: Aspects of behavioral conduct that are either helpful or not in your relations with others.

Behavioral Talent: Achieving your goals without hurting others and yourself.

Behaviorally Impulsive: Behavioral actions that are done without forethought.

Capability: An assessment of your ability to comprehend the academic and nonacademic world.

Capacity: A measure of the quantity of academic and nonacademic work a student can handle before their performance begins to erode.

Carefulness: A genuine attempt to balance your own legitimate claims to contentment and well-being with those of other people when you make choices.

Carelessness: Negligent behavior that can be defined as making choices without giving sufficient thought to the consequences that inevitably follow.

Caring: A thoughtful concern that strengthens trust with others.

Character Traits: Distinguishing features about your nature.

Choosing: An organized and intentional approach to assessing its consequential effects on your purpose, values, and goals.

Civility: A basic concern for the well-being of others.

Commitment: Communicates an individual's willingness to follow through and meet obligations.

Common Good: Working cooperatively together to determine by consensus how we should be conducting ourselves when we interact with each other.

Communication: The process that creates a shared understanding of meaning between people.

Compromise: Willingly making concessions to settle disputes.

Concern: The degree of interest that you have for another's well-being.

Conscientiousness: Ceaseless awareness of what is right and wrong in every situation.

Consciousness: An awareness of and response to situations that we experience.

Consequential Benefits: The potential impact (good and bad) that is received when an opportunity is chosen. Consequential benefits are always associated with a choice that you have made.

Consequential Costs: The potential impact (good and bad) that is lost when a consequence is not chosen. Consequential costs are always associated with a choice that you have not selected.

Consideration: Demonstrating a regard for the feelings, rights, or traditions of others.

Contentment and Well-Being: Subjective measures of the state of mental satisfaction that results from being happy, satisfied, and at peace with the choices that you have made throughout your life. Contentedness and well-being are consequences of a life well lived.

Continuous Behavioral Improvement Process: A method for improving the 5Cs through incremental and informed thinking about one's own behavior.

Contribution: Measures the amount of value you bring to a group.

Cooperation: Willingly working together with others for a common purpose.

Coping: A process of consciously attempting to understand, manage, and/or tolerate the stresses experienced in college and university.

Cost-Benefit Analysis: An analytical process of determining which choices and consequences to make and forgo.

Count to Five and Think Policy: A rule that gives you time to step back and think and gain some perspective about what is in your best choice in a given situation.

Courteous: Well-mannered and civil behavior that lifts up others.

Credibility Gaps: The difference between what we say and what we do.

Critical Thinking: Analysis of available facts, evidence, observation, and arguments to form a judgment.

Decorum: Embracing people and choices that are benevolent, decent, and socially acceptable in pursuit of the common good.

Delayed Gratification: Resisting the temptation to take an immediate reward in the hope of gaining a more valuable one in the future.

Deliberate Practice: Considerable, specific, and sustained effort to practice something you can't do well. It involves improving the skills you already have and extending the reach and range of the skills that you don't have.

Demonstration Stage: Showing the ability to cope with the rigors of college.

Denial Stage: Demonstrating little, if any, interest in learning.

Dependability: The degree to which individuals can be relied on by others.

Destruction Stage: Actively resisting the educational process.

Determination: The firmness of your resolve to complete work, especially when conditions become uncertain or difficult.

Differences: Embracing people and choices that are honest, just, and free from bias and prejudice in pursuit of the common good.

Discovery Stage: Beginning to realize the ability to handle the class work.

Effective Communication: Produces an accurate understanding of your intentions.

Effort: The directed exertion of will.

Employability Profile: A log or scorecard of all the behavioral observation skills assessments.

Energy: The intensity of your resolve to accomplish work.

Errors: Unintentionally doing something wrong.

Ethics: The prioritization of values when you make a choice.

Evidence: Plainly visible criteria that audiences will react to and use in forming conclusions or judgments about you.

Fairness: Choices that are honest, just, and free from bias and prejudice.

Fogg's Behavior Model (FBM): Behavioral model that asserts that three variables must happen at the same time for any behavior to occur: motivation, ability, and trigger.

Four Stages of Student Grief Model: A four-quadrant model that can serve as a conceptual framework for understanding what happens to many students when they enter college.

Goals: Future-oriented ambitions that you would like to achieve, and that would bring you a sense of satisfaction with yourself and minimize regret.

Good Choices: Intentional prioritization and selection of more consequential matters ahead of less consequential ones.

Good Health: People of goodwill protect the collective mental, social, and physical well-being of themselves and others.

Good Judgment: Consistently prioritizes more consequential matters ahead of less consequential ones when making choices.

Grade Point Average (GPA): A key performance indicator of the overall quality of your academic accomplishments at college or university.

Guesswork: Knowingly making a choice with little or no information.

Hard Work: Difficult mental or physical activity done to develop intelligence and talent.

Healthy Behaviors: Behaviors that are responsible, strengthen trust connections, and create goodwill among people.

Healthy Group Participation: Showing up on time, working hard, appreciating others, and adapting to difficult or changing situations that strengthens trust and group connections and creates goodwill among group members.

Helpfulness: A willingness to provide useful assistance to those in need.

High-Delaying People: Postpone fulfillment and handle work and problems immediately.

Honesty: Embracing people and choices that are sincere and forgoing lying, cheating, or stealing in pursuit of the common good.

Impartial: Embracing people and choices that are equal, fair, and just in support of the common good.

Ineffective Communication: Creates an inaccurate understanding of your intentions, which can lead to communication problems.

Integrity: When our words and behaviors are in alignment.

Intentions: Choices that actualize your now-oriented ambitions in the present and are concerned only with your current state of being.

Involvement: Measure an individual's willingness to take on group responsibilities.

Key Performance Indicators (KPIs): Measures (indicators) of your performance over time toward a specific objective.

Lateness: Arriving after a planned or necessary time.

Law of Change: Everything is continually in the process of becoming something else.

Laws: Macroscale rules that societies develop and willingly follow for maintaining social order.

Listening: A predisposition to take notice of the opinions and ideas of others.

Long-Termism: Concentrating on your long-term objectives, such as maximizing well-being and minimizing long-term regret, at the expense of your short-term desires.

Low-Delaying People: People who procrastinate, which only magnifies tension and stress.

Me-Oriented People: People who demonstrate a low level of concern for others but a very high level of concern for themselves in their dealings with others.

Messages: The substance and meaning of communications to audiences.

Mistakes: Unintentional errors that are made during performances.

Multitasking: Trying to do more than one activity at a time.

Murray's Rule: Both negotiating parties do whatever they can to make sure that the opposing party is treated fairly during the negotiation.

Nonverbal Communication: Conveys understanding and meaning through your behavior and choices.

No-Oriented People: People who demonstrate indifference or are unconcerned about the outcomes of people's behaviors on themselves and on others.

Opportunity: An academic circumstance that gives students the possibility to break academic policies without any consequence.

Out-of-Character: Behavior that normally trustworthy individuals do that is thoughtless (intentionally or otherwise) and does not conform to their established or accepted pattern of behavior.

Participation: A measure of the overall effect an individual's involvement has on groups.

Peace: Nonviolence that avoids harming others with words and actions when during disputes.

Perfection: Mistake-free consequence of performance.

Performance: An action carried out to accomplish a task.

Personal Communication Strategy (PCS): A plan for how you will communicate.

Personal Policies: Self-created small-scale rules that govern your conduct.

Personal Policy Contracts: Commitments that you make to yourself about how you will apply your personal policies.

Premeditated and Intentional: Choices that are made that involve preplanning and thought before taking action.

Preparation: The process of becoming ready to perform.

Pressure: The reasons why students break rules.

Principle of Causality: Your consequences are always caused by your choices.

Procrastination: The act of delaying or postponing important matters until after you have done less important ones.

Productive Behavioral Patterns: Behaviors that strengthen trust connections with the audiences that experience the behavior.

Public Persona: Your public reputation.

Quality: The degree or grade of excellence associated with behavioral decision-making.

Rationalization: Using weak, but superficially believable, arguments to justify choices that are not aligned with your own values and ethics, goals, and personal policies.

Readiness to Perform: A measure of your level of preparedness.

Reason-Based Choices: Purposely and critically thinking and then making informed predictions about what will happen in the future by making choices.

Regret: Sadness associated with some wrong done or some disappointment.

Relationships: Types of interpersonal connections between yourself and others.

Respect: Deference toward people and their differences, and acting with decorum.

Responsibility: A palpable sense of duty about one's obligations to others.

Routines: The familiar ways that you perform your daily rituals and chores.

Rules of Conduct: Human-made social constructs or norms that help groups of people balance the competing desires of individuals so that everyone can interact without creating too much conflict.

Scarcity of Resources: Circumstances when the demand for your time and money is greater than your supply of time and money.

Self-Awareness: An accurate understanding of yourself, including your own desires, thoughts, emotions, and motives during difficult situations.

Self-Control: Effortful regulation of the self by the self.

Self-Determination: You (1) have absolute power over your choice of consequences; (2) have much more control over your destiny than you think; and (3) cannot not choose your consequences and your destiny.

Self-Improvement: A lifelong process of bettering your nature, abilities, and character by your own efforts during stressful situations.

Self-Management (SM): The ability to achieve one's own goals in a trustworthy manner.

Self-Reflection: Examination, contemplation, and analysis of your own thoughts, feelings, and behaviors.

Self-Restraint: The ability to successfully manage one's reactions during stressful situations.

Self-Restraint Personal Policy: Self-imposed rules that reduce ambiguity that could cloud your judgment and decision-making during stressful times.

Sense of Loss: Grief because you are giving up the routines that make you feel safe and secure.

Sense of Mistrust: Being unable to confidently rely on others in situations where you are feeling vulnerable and at risk.

Short-Termism: Choices that maximize your short-term objectives, at the expense of your long-term ambitions.

Situational Awareness: The ability to accurately comprehend the meaning of environmental factors at a given time and place and accurately predict the future consequences for ourselves and others.

Situational Blindness: Lacking the information required for understanding, discernment, and comprehension of meaning.

Social Order: Individuals and groups willingly abiding by rules that govern their public conduct to keep individuals and society safe, secure, and stable.

Stamina: How long a person can persevere under difficult or challenging circumstances.

Status Quo Bias: When people prefer things to stay the same by doing nothing or by sticking with a decision made previously.

Stranger: Someone who is unfamiliar to you.

Stretch Goals: Long-term goals that you seek to attain.

Student Readiness for Change: The varying degrees of emotional and intellectual readiness that new students bring to college.

Thoughtfulness: The process of consciously gathering information to determine how to balance your own needs and the needs of others before making choices that will impact yourself and your relationships with others.

Time: The primary ingredient in developing skills.

Tiny Habits: Repeated behaviors that are easy to do and require little motivation.

Total Long-Term Value: The sum of the value of all of your choices and consequences to you.

Trust: Confident reliance in others in situations involving vulnerability or risk.

Uncaring Relationships: Types of relationships in which one person or both people do not care about the well-being of the other person.

Unhealthy Behavior: Conduct that is harmful to you or others.

Unhealthy Group Participation: Individual actions that can cause others to feel upset, frustrated, scared, and angry, which can destroy goodwill and cooperation in groups.

Unproductive Behavioral Patterns: Individual actions that weaken goodwill and cooperation and may require other people to step in to encourage more trustworthy performance.

Value Maximization: Measured by the degree to which the choices and consequences align with your long-term purpose, values, and goals.

Values: Underlying set of principles (or rules) that govern your thinking, judgment, behavior, and, ultimately, every choice that you make.

Verbal Communication: Conveys understanding and meaning through your speaking and listening.

Well-being: Contentment or positive feelings.

We-Oriented People: People who demonstrate a high degree of concern for others and a high degree of concern for themselves.

Willingness: Behavior that is done by choice and without reluctance.

Written Communication: Conveys understanding and meaning through your reading and writing.

You-Oriented People: People who demonstrate high levels of concern for others, but low levels of concern for themselves.

NOTES

Introduction

1. Makenna Berry, "90 Percent of Us Have Big Regrets: Dealing with It Is a Crucial Skill for Healthy Living," *Unbound* (blog), https://www.saybrook.edu/unbound/90-percent-us-have-big-regrets-dealing-it-crucial-skill-healthy-living/.

2. Isabell Bauer and Carsten Wrosch, "Making Up for Lost Opportunities: The Protective Role of Downward Social Comparisons for Coping with Regrets across Adulthood," *Personality and Social Psychology Bulletin* 37, no. 2 (February 1, 2011): 215–228.

Chapter 1: Getting Started

1. Howard H. Stevenson and Mihnea Moldoveanu, *The Power of Predictability* (Boston: Harvard Business School, 1995), 8.

2. US Department of Health and Human Services, *The Health Consequences of Smoking—50 Years of Progress: A Report of the Surgeon General* (Atlanta, GA: US Department of Health and Human Services, Centers for Disease Control and Prevention, National Center for Chronic Disease Prevention and Health Promotion, Office on Smoking and Health, 2014), accessed February 21, 2017.

3. Kenton Bell, *Open Education Sociological Dictionary*, 2013 ed., s.v. "Behavior," https://sociologydictionary.org/behavior/, accessed January 6, 2023.

4. Robert F. Hurley, *The Decision to Trust: How Leaders Create High-Trust Organizations* (San Francisco, CA: Jossey-Bass, 2011), 25.

5. National Center for Education Statistics, Undergraduate Retention and Graduation Rates, in *Condition of Education* (Washington, DC: US Department of Education, Institute of Education Sciences`, 2022), https://nces.ed.gov/programs/coe/indicator/ctr, accessed January 6, 2023.

Chapter 2: Continuous Behavioral Improvement

1. Special note: In some professions (doctors, nurses, pharmacists, members of the military, public safety professionals, lifeguards) behavioral mistakes can cause injury or death. In these types of professions, even out-of-character occurrences may not be tolerated.

2. Christine Porath and Christine Pearson, "The Price of Incivility," *Harvard Business Review*, January–February 2013, 114.

3. Peter F. Drucker, "Managing Oneself," *Harvard Business Review*, On Point Article, Product 4444, January 2005, 1.

4. Said during South Eastern Kentucky Community College presentation at the 2015 National Institute for Staff and Organizational Development (NISOD) Conference in Austin, Texas.

5. Adapted from SHRM Effective Practice Guideline by Elaine D. Pulakos, *Performance Management: A Roadmap for Developing, Implementing and Evaluating Performance Management Systems* (Alexandria, VA: Society of Human Resources Management Foundation, 2004), 10–14.

6. Adapted from Pulakos, *Performance Management*.

7. Pulakos, *Performance Management*, 10.

8. Adapted from Pulakos, *Performance Management*.

9. BJ Fogg, Stanford University, http://www.tinyhabits.com.

10. Adapted from BJ Fogg, Fogg Behavior Model, www.behaviormodel.org.

11. BJ Fogg, Fogg Behavior Model.

12. Gail Matthews, Dominican University, https://www.dominican.edu/sites/default/files/2020-02/gailmatthews-harvard-goals-researchsummary.pdf.

Chapter 3: Communication Basics

1. Paul Watzlawick, Janet Beavin Bavelas, and Don D. Jackson, *Pragmatics of Human Communication: A Study of Interactional Patterns, Pathologies, and Paradoxes* (New York: W. W. Norton, 1967), 1.

2. Watzlawick, Bavelas, and Jackson, *Pragmatics of Human Communication*, 1.

3. Albert Mehrabian and Morton Wiener, "Decoding of Inconsistent Communications," *Journal of Personality and Social Psychology* 6 (1967): 109–114.

4. J. A. Hall, "Social Psychology of Nonverbal Communication," in *International Encyclopedia of the Social and Behavioral Sciences*, edited by James D. Wright (Boston: Elsevier, 2001), 10702–10706, https://www.science-direct.com/topics/social-sciences/nonverbal-communication#:~:text=Nonverbal%20communication%20refers%20to%20the,the%20use%20of%20verbal%20language.

5. Watzlawick, Bavelas, and Jackson, *Pragmatics of Human Communication*, 1.

6. Career Guide, "Top 11 Skills Employers Look for in Job Candidates," Indeed, https://www.indeed.com/career-advice/resumes-cover-letters/skills-employers-look-for.

7. Memorandum to Presidents: *Policy and Guidance: State University of New York General Education* (2021), https://system.suny.edu/media/suny/content-assets/documents/academic-affairs/general-education/suny-ge/MTP-SUNY-General-Education_Vol-21,-No.1.pdf.

Chapter 4: Developing a Personal Communication Strategy and Policy

1. Mehrabian and Wiener, "Decoding of Inconsistent Communications," 28.

2. Stephen R. Covey, *The 7 Habits of Highly Effective People: Restoring the Character Ethic*, rev. ed. (New York: Free Press, 2004).

Chapter 5: Understanding Judgment and Choices

1. Barbara Sahakian and Jamie Nicole LaBuzetta, *Bad Moves: How Decision Making Goes Wrong, and the Ethics of Smart Drugs* (Oxford: Oxford University Press, 2013).

2. "Breathing," Breathe: The Lung Association, https://www.lung.ca/lung-health/lung-info/breathing.

3. David Foster Wallace, "This Is Water," commencement speech delivered 2005 to the graduating students of Kenyon College. Listen to attribution starting 0:17 at https://www.youtube.com/watch?v=8CrOL-ydFMI.

4. Edward M. Glaser, "Defining Critical Thinking," International Center for the Assessment of Higher Order Thinking (ICAT, US)/Critical Thinking Community, retrieved March 22, 2017.

5. Melanie Hanson, "College Dropout Rates," EducationData.org, June 17, 2022, https://educationdata.org/college-dropout-rates.

6. World Health Organization (WHO), *Global Status Report on Road Safety 2018*, December 2018, accessed October 28, 2020. https://www.who.int/news-room/fact-sheets/detail/road-traffic-injuries.

7. Kim Mills (host), "Your Brain Is Not What You Think It Is, with Lisa Feldman Barrett, PhD," *Speaking of Psychology* (audio podcast), April 28, 2021, https://www.youtube.com/watch?v=e06ZanBKNcI.

8. Mills, "Your Brain Is Not What You Think It Is."

9. BJ Fogg, "How You Can Use the Power of Celebration to Make New Habits Stick," Ideas.TED.com, https://ideas.ted.com/how-you-can-use-the-power-of-celebration-to-make-new-habits-stick/.

10. Glaser, "Defining Critical Thinking."

Chapter 6: Choices and Consequences

1. Adapted from Donald Cressey and Edwin Sutherland's article "Why Do Trusted Persons Commit Fraud? A Social-Psychological Study of Defalcators," *Journal of Accountancy* (November 1951): 576–581.

2. Phillip Kelly, "Where Are the Children? Educational Neglect across the Fifty States," *The Researcher* 23, no. 1 (2010): 41–58.

Chapter 7: Understanding Commitment and Dependability

1. Adapted from Kathryn Jackson's writings from two articles: Kathryn Jackson, "How to Set Performance Standards to Ensure Excellent Service," Product No. 10038, Response Design Corporation, http://www.responsedesign.com/store/10038.pdf; Kathryn Jackson, "Adapting Schedule Adherence Measurement to Improve Performance," Product No. 10038, Response Design Corporation, http://www.responsedesign.com/store/10039.pdf.

2. Personal story of Greg Talley, former associate vice president, dean, and professor at SUNY Broome Community College and chief of police in Los Alamos, New Mexico.

Chapter 8: Hard Work and Quality

1. C. S. Dweck, *Mindset: The New Psychology of Success* (New York: Random House, 2006).

2. K. Anders Ericsson, Michael J. Prietula, and Edward T. Cokely, "The Making of an Expert," July–August 2007, https://hbr.org/2007/07/the-making-of-an-expert%20citation.

3. Ericsson, Prietula, and Cokely, "The Making of an Expert."

4. Dweck, *Mindset*.

5. Ericsson, Prietula, and Cokely, "The Making of an Expert."

6. Ericsson, Prietula, and Cokely, "The Making of an Expert."

7. Harriet Nerlove Mischel and Walter Mischel, *The Development of Children's Knowledge of Self-Control Strategies* (Stanford, CA: Society for Research in Child Development, 1983).

8. Ericsson, Prietula, and Cokely, "The Making of an Expert."

9. Victoria J. Rideout, Ulla G. Foehr, and Donald F. Roberts, "Generation M²: Media in the Lives of 8- to 18-Year-Olds," *A Kaiser Family Foundation Study* (January 2010): 2, https://www.kff.org/wp-content/uploads/2013/01/8010.pdf.

10. US Department of Transportation, "Distracted Driving Laws, Education and Enforcement," https://www.transportation.gov/mission/health/distracted-driving-laws-education-and-enforcement.

11. Center for Disease Control and Prevention, "Distracted Driving," https://www.cdc.gov/transportationsafety/distracted_driving/index.html.

12. Anders K. Ericsson, Ralf T. Krampe, and Clemens Tesch-Römer, "The Role of Deliberate Practice in the Acquisition of Expert Performance," *Psychological Review* 100, no. 3 (July 1993): 363–406.

13. Carnegie Mellon University, "Randy Pausch Last Lecture: Achieving Your Childhood Dreams," https://www.youtube.com/watch?v=ji5_MqicxSo.

14. Di Xu, Shanna Smith Jaggars, Jeffrey Fletcher, and John E. Fink, "Are Community College Transfer Students 'a Good Bet' for 4-Year Admissions? Comparing Academic and Labor-Market Outcomes between Transfer and Native

4-Year College Students," *Journal of Higher Education* 89, no. 4 (2018), DOI: 10.1080/00221546.2018.1434280, https://transferstudents.ucsd.edu/for-faculty-staff/Xu-et-al.pdf.

Chapter 9: Coping in College

1. United States Census Bureau, "Census Bureau Releases New Educational Attainment Data," https://www.census.gov/newsroom/press-releases/2022/educational-attainment.html.

2. Helen Keller (1880–1968), American blind/deaf author and lecturer.

3. US Department of Labor, "Usual Weekly Earnings of Wage and Salary Workers: Third Quarter 2022," press release, October 18, 2022, https://www.bls.gov/news.release/pdf/wkyeng.pdf.

4. Erik H. Erikson, *Dimensions of a New Identity: Jefferson Lectures in the Humanities* (New York: W. W. Norton, 1979).

5. Melanie Hanson, "College Dropout Rates," EducationData.org, June 17, 2022, https://educationdata.org/college-dropout-rates.

6. A. L. Duckworth, "The Significance of Self-Control," *Proceedings of the National Academy of Sciences of the United States of America* 108, no. 7 (2011): 2639–2640.

7. Stress is an ordinary and brief reaction to adversity. Stress usually doesn't lead to serious long-term problems. Although you may have great insight into your own ability to manage the stressors in your life, there may be times when you want to seek advice from professionals (counselors, therapists, etc.). If you suffer from long periods (weeks or months) of negative feelings (i.e., sadness, anger, irritability, fear, anxiety, helplessness, confusion, or embarrassment), it may be time to talk to a health care provider.

8. Wiktionary, s.v. "Loose Cannon," definition 1, last modified November 25, 2022, https://en.wiktionary.org/wiki/loose_cannon.

9. *Cambridge Dictionary*, s.v. "Loose Cannon," definition 1, http://dictionary.cambridge.org/us/dictionary/english/loose-cannon.

10. Kari Bonini-Roma (1937–1996), artist and devoted mother of four children.

11. Adapted from Charles M. Cadwell, *Leadership Skills for Managers*, 4th ed. (New York: American Management Association, 2004), 71.

Chapter 10: Coping with Change

1. Jack M. Balkin, *The Laws of Change: I Ching and the Philosophy of Life* (Branford, CT: Sybil Creek Press, 2009).

2. US Department of Commerce, "U.S. Population Estimated at 332,403,650 on Jan. 1, 2022," January 6, 2022, https://www.commerce.gov/news/blog/2022/01/us-population-estimated-332403650-jan-1-2022.

3. Elizabeth Arias, Batzaida Tejada-Vera, Kenneth Kochanek, and Farida Ahmad, "Provisional Life Expectancy Estimates for 2021," National Vital Statistics Report, United States Department of Health and Human Services, https://www.cdc.gov/nchs/data/vsrr/vsrr023.pdf.

4. Wikipedia, s.v. "Population Pyramid, https://en.wikipedia.org/wiki/Population_pyramid.

5. Todd Litman, "Autonomous Vehicle Implementation Predictions: Implementation for Transport Planning," Victoria Transport Policy Institute, October 12, 2022, https://www.vtpi.org/avip.pdf.

6. Robert Arnoux, "A 'True Engagement' to Bring about a Sustainable Future," *ITER Newsline* 286, 2013, https://www.iter.org/fr/newsline/286/1742, accessed October 31, 2022.

7. Richard J. Zeckhauser and William Samuelson, "Status Quo Bias in Decision-Making," *Journal of Risk and Uncertainty* 1, no. 1 (February 1988): 7–59.

8. Cynthia D. Scott and Dennis T. Jaffe, *Managing Change at Work: Leading People through Organizational Transitions* (Menlo Park, CA: Crisp, 1995), 30–31 (see also: https://changeworkslab.com/).

9. Scott and Jaffe, *Managing Change at Work*.

10. US Department of Education, National Center for Education Statistics, Integrated Postsecondary Education Data System (IPEDS), Spring 2008 through Spring 2021, Fall Enrollment component; and IPEDS Fall 2006 through Fall 2019, Institutional Characteristics component, https://nces.ed.gov/programs/digest/d21/tables/dt21_326.30.asp.

11. Richard Beckhard and Reuben T. Harris, *Organizational Transitions: Managing Complex Change* (Reading, MA: Addison-Wesley, 1987).

12. Elisabeth Kübler-Ross, *On Death and Dying* (New York: Scribner, 1969).

13. The Kübler-Ross model is widely used in business and change management and there are many variations and adaptations of the model that help predict and manage behavioral reactions to change.

14. Scott and Jaffe, *Managing Change at Work*, 35.

15. Adapted from Scott and Jaffe, "The Transition Curve," in *Managing Change at Work*, 36.

Chapter 11: Caring and Relationships

1. Warren Zevon, "Lawyers, Guns, and Money," in *Excitable Boy*, Asylum Records, 1978.

2. Greek dramatist (496–406 BC), author of seven extant tragedies: *Ajax*, *Antigone*, *Oedipus Rex*, *Trachiniae*, *Electra*, *Philoctetes*, and *Oedipus at Colonus*.

3. As stated in a conversation with the late Murray Sanders, spring 2004.

IMAGE CREDITS

TABLE, PAGE 47 (IN ORDER OF APPEARNCE)

Vastateparksstaff; Creative Commons Attribution 2.0 Generic.
OT Flow; Creative Commons Attribution-Share Alike 4.0 International.
Sharon Hahn Darlin; Creative Commons Attribution 2.0 Generic.
Umr Rehman; Creative Commons Attribution-Share Alike 4.0 International.

THINK ABOUT IT, PAGE 92 (IN ORDER OF APPEARANCE)

Dato (WMAM); Creative Commons Attribution-Share Alike 4.0 International.
Jirka Matousek; Creative Commons Attribution 2.0 Generic.

THINK ABOUT IT, PAGE 201 (SOURCES IN ORDER OF APPEARANCE)

Keith Allison, Creative Commons Attribution-Share Alike 2.0 Generic license.
OregonDOT; Creative Commons Attribution 2.0 Generic.
National Archives and Records Administration.
National Archives and Records Administration.

Index

Note: Italicized page numbers indicate illustrations.
Italicized page numbers with a *t* indicate tables.

caring: caring and uncaring relationships, 239–41, 242; caring model, 243; changing habits, 278; civility, 243–48, 257, 262, 264, 270; and the common good, 263–65, 280; conscientiousness, 243, 255–60, 262; definition and behaviors in, 239; helpfulness, 243, 249–55, 262; importance of, 241–43; personal policy contracts for, 260, 278–79; quick tips for caring people, 273; self-assessment for, 274–78; summary of competencies in, 238, 262, 263, 280. *See also* 5C Elements of Self-Management; Common Good Model

Carter, Jimmy, *255*

character: and activity complexity, 211–12; character traits, 28–29, 144; choices and, 8, 28, 29, 93, 94–96, 98–99, 110; communication and, 45, 60; development of, 195; out-of-character behavior, 21; and prioritization of choices, 122; and trustworthiness, 15, 21

Cher, 179

choice: communication through choices, 84, 97–99; consciousness and, 83–85, 110; cost-benefit analysis in, 116–18; frameworks for making choices, 88–96, 110; goals and intentions in making choices, *88*, 89–93; importance of choices, 82–83; learning and experience in making choices, 101–3; personal policies for, 92, 105–8; prioritization in, 118; reasoning in, *88*, 103–4; responsibility and, 85–88; self-assessment of behavior in choice-making, *135–37t*, 138; situational awareness and, *88*, 99–103; summary of basic competencies in, 81, 110; values and ethics in, 93–96. *See also* 5C Elements of Self-Management; consequences; decision-making

Civil Rights Act of 1964, 259

civility, 243–48, 257, 262, 264, 270

commitment: definition of, 144; dependability, hard work, and quality in, 145, 167, 168–69; nonverbal indicators of lack of, 64; personal policy contract for, 165, 190; summary of competencies in, 143, 167, 168, 191–92. *See also* 5C Elements of Self-Management

Common Good Model: elements of, 265–66; equity, 268–70, 280; goodwill, 271–72, 280; respect, 266–68, 280. *See also* caring

communication: audiences in, 54–55; definition of, 45; effective and ineffective, 48–49, 64, 72; importance of, 44–45, 143; law and ethics in, 65–66; nonverbal, 45–49, 52; risks in electronic means for, 51, 52; summaries of basic competencies in, 44, 53; verbal and written, 45, 49–51, 52. *See also* 5C Elements of Self-Management; personal communication strategies

concern for others, 250–52, 262

conscientiousness, 243, 255–60, 262

consequences: causality and, 111–12, 141; Consequence Prioritization Framework, 119–24, 141; cost-benefit analysis of choices and, 114–19; happiness and, 115–16; to health, safety, and freedom, 121–22; to lifestyle, 123–24; mistakes and, 131–34, 141, 293n1 (chap. 2); to purpose, 122–23; rules and, 125–31; self-assessment of effectiveness in choice-making, 135–37, 138; self-determination and, 113–14; summary of competencies in understanding choice and, 111, 141

consequential benefits and costs, 117

considerate behavior, 64, 247–48

Continuous Behavioral Improvement Process (CBIP), 23–29, 42